Taxifornia 2016: 14 Essays on the Future of California

Taxifornia 2016: 14 Essays on the Future of California

JAMES V. LACY
Author of the Politico.com best seller
Taxifornia, Liberals' Laboratory to Bankrupt America

Dedication

To Janice Lacy,
Attorney, Political Scientist, Musician,
And love of my life

Contents

Introduction

California is the nation's top tax collector, receiving $138.1 billion in the last fiscal year, comprising 16 percent of all state taxes collected in the nation and even more than New York and Texas combined.[1] As outlined in detail in my first book, *Taxifornia, Liberals' Laboratory to Bankrupt America*, it is the state with the highest income tax in the nation, the highest state sales tax in the nation, among the highest gasoline taxes in the nation, and the highest corporate tax west of the Mississippi.[2] The state controller's office reported that in April 2015, California's income tax collections alone grew by $8 billion over the prior year, bringing in extra revenues exceeding the governor's budget by $1.6 billion.[3]

In seeming disregard for all the staggering revenue the state already collects, its liberal politicians in control strive to tax even more, spend more, and then tax again. Case in point: the state's already sky-high sales taxes not only increased again in 2015,[4] but will likely do so once again in 2016, fueled by new legislation pending in the state legislature to empower local governments to raise sales taxes even more in the future.[5]

Yet liberal Democrats are poised to extend "temporary" income taxes and sales tax hikes even more, to raise real property taxes on businesses, to raise gas taxes, and to further regulate and put California business development at an even further competitive disadvantage, despite the state repeatedly earning the moniker from one respected national business publication as the "least business friendly state in the nation," now eleven years in a row.[6]

For all the money California collects from its citizens, the politicians in control in Sacramento are relentless in coming up with even more new taxes, more regulations, and the state remains awash in problems that more and more tax revenue and government regulation never seems able to fix. The never-ending avalanche of new taxes and regulations simply add to California's already high cost of living; they make owning or renting a home or an apartment more expensive, they drive up the cost of transportation and food, they hurt small businesses, depress new job growth, they degrade disposable income, and they make the poor in California even poorer.

Taxifornia 2016: 14 Essays on the Future of California is a blueprint to reform and fix California. It picks up where my first book ends. While my first book outlined the many problems of the state, and with over eight hundred footnotes rightly laid blame for most of them on the liberal policy makers in control, *Taxifornia 2016* brings California's issues current and gets much deeper "into the weeds" on specific public policy issues that will be of concern in the state in 2016. It includes important original research as in Katy Grime's chapter on criminal justice; and careful analysis as in veteran tax-fighter Joel Fox's chapter on taxes. Whether the issue is persistent high taxes; rising poverty; the drought; political corruption; "income inequality"; rising violent crime; out-of-control public employee union pay and pensions; California's changing demographics; the importance of our initiative system; public transportation spending; lack of transparency in government; or a failing educational system, all them are addressed in vivid detail in this book.

As will be revealed to you in this work, *Taxifornia 2016* represents an important and thoughtful collection of essays authored by a dozen prominent conservative and libertarian writers, both authors and analysts, who have opinions on the future of California. Understanding that liberal Democrats and their public employee union allies wield great control on state policy, these writers see California in crisis and in need of reform, and tackle the state's problems in 2016 with an eye toward new solutions that are faithful to the transformational value of limited government and personal freedom. This book exposes the truth about California's problems and offers commonsense solutions to fix them.

Of course, the opinions expressed by each author are uniquely his or her own and should not be inferred to also be the views of any of the other contributors to this book. Each writer offers his or her contribution independently of the others herein, and careful review of the entire book will reveal a few areas where a couple of the authors even disagree on a policy issue. But I have been delighted to select and work with each author in editing this book, and I take sole responsibility for *Taxifornia 2016*, which I hope will make an illuminating and useful contribution to the policy debate on and in California as we enter and experience the 2016 political season.

James V. Lacy
Dana Point, California
August 15, 2015

One

By Floyd Brown

Go west, young man, go west! was the clarion call for development of an expanding nation, first used by John Babsone Lane Soule in the *Terre Haute Express* in 1851. Soule's optimistic sentiment was later repeated by Horace Greeley, editor of the *New York Tribune*, who popularized the call to "grow up with the country" in an editorial in the *New York Tribune* on July 13, 1865.

This popular phrase was a passionate call for the adventurous to take a chance on themselves in a new state that rewarded initiative and ambition. It was the promise of a better future on our West Coast that caught fire in America. It was an invitation to a golden land of opportunity: California.

Indeed, California has always represented a land of greener pastures and adventure in a state blessed with natural beauty and abundant resources. California was the embodiment of the manifest destiny of an ambitious people and nation well suited to grow and prosper.

But 150 years after Horace Greeley made this pioneering sentiment popular, California's public officials have choked the life out of such passion. They have, through misguided enthusiasm for government control of every aspect of life and business development, unwittingly created a new message, "Go anywhere but here," because opportunity is the least important goal of

California's stifling government, which is busily squandering the state's wealth and erecting barriers to prosperity.

How to get more money from citizens for public employee unions is the real story of ever higher taxes, fees, and regulations and the enduring Democratic stranglehold on the California legislature. It is hard not to conclude that California's taxpayers are now considered, by those who work in and for government, as just the necessary sheep who may be ever more closely sheared so that government officials and public "servants" can impose their own distorted views of how life should work, all while they enjoy incomes and benefits that dwarf those of most of the citizens for whom they work.

As Victor Davis Hanson, a contributing editor of *City Journal* and a senior fellow at the Hoover Institution at Stanford University, wrote in 2014, the Democratic legislature, without either checks or balance, has been captured, heart and soul, by liberal interest groups—including powerful unions who found the past partnership between state government and business an ideological insult. Without restraint, the legislature has forgotten or simply ignored the cardinal rule of all economies: supply and demand. Hanson wrote:

Even as the state grew, energized by eager new immigrants, it shorted the very investments that had once made it great—a complex system of water storage and transference, a model freeway system, a blue-chip tripartite educational system, and encouragement of the oil, natural-gas, timber, and hydroelectric industries—and began to impose regulations and higher taxes on the private sector. The thinking was that wealth was now so assured that Californians needed no longer to create it. So a flurry of regulations and higher taxes followed, designed to consume and redistribute prior riches, while nurturing the dream of a return to a preindustrial paradise—as if nature alone, not California's visionaries, had made the state so livable and affluent.[7]

Today, the real growth industry in California is government itself. It is costly, consumed by ideological and self-serving zeal, and cares little for the reality of how government policies affect average people who are not blessed with millionaires' bank accounts or coastal liberals' sensibilities. It is not drought or wildfires or earthquakes that are the greatest danger to California's citizens. It is government itself. Policy makers on the West Coast have worked hard to bring their vision of "utopia" into law, and it has resulted in dropping California from the fifth largest economy in the world to the ninth.

According to a multitude of research studies, including the Los Angeles-based Milken Institute and the Tax Foundation of Washington, DC, California's taxes as well as regulatory costs to consumers and businesses are punitively higher than most states. The result is net outmigration as families and businesses seek business opportunities, jobs, and homes in states that offer lower tax costs and a less burdensome regulatory environment. Texas is the biggest winner in attracting relocating Californians because it has no state income tax and a business sector that is growing and seeking workers. Texas is also well known for a welcoming attitude toward business development and far lower housing costs.

Manhattan Institute researchers Tom Gray and Robert Scardamalia found in 2012 that "California's 2005 electricity-cost index was 168.0, on a scale in which 100 was the US average. Industrial rents were 36.8 percent above the national average, and office rents were 36.3 percent higher. The state's tax-burden index was not as outsized—111.1—but combined with the other factors, it helped push the state to an overall cost index of 124.2."[8]

Gray and Scadamalia found that "taxes, regulations, the high price of housing and commercial real estate, costly electricity, union power, and high labor costs" were the major drivers pushing Californians to seek a better life outside California. They found that the only two states with higher tax levels than California—New Jersey and New York—consistently pushed their citizens toward California.

Self-Defeating Relationship between Unions and Government

There is another reason, besides the obvious financial benefits to public employees, for the kind of largess that public officials have so generously bestowed on themselves and public employees—the naked self-interests of the political class. The more money taken from the pockets of citizens and businesses and pledged to public union employees, the more votes are guaranteed to the legislators and city officials who keep the unsustainable taxpayer-funded union gravy train growing. Thus, more and more generous policies toward public employee unions secure a more and more certain margin of votes for elected officials. It is a perverse and self-fulfilling arrangement that makes Tammany Hall politics of the past look tame.

The financial harm to taxpayers and California's businesses is then compounded by unchecked liberal legislators who have kowtowed to unions and liberal interest groups and California's liberal "coastal elites" to impose disastrous policies on the people of California.

The California legislature, once considered one of the best in the world, is now a destructive parody of self-interests and ill-considered "utopian" legislation that ignores the real needs of citizens, fails to plan for the future or rationally react to current crises such as the destructive drought, and delivers more and more services to those who don't work while punitively taxing the citizens and businesses who do produce wealth.

Liberal politicians and regulators in California now work tirelessly and without any brakes applied by conservative voices to impose their extreme views on California's citizens. They require heavy taxes to make their vision of a "utopian" state possible. In reality they are destroying the very things that in the past made California one of the most desirable destinations for young families looking to build their futures. It shows.

According to noted demographer Joel Kotkin, California has lost 4.4 million more residents over the last two decades than it has gained from in-migration.[9] This is a stunning reversal of fortunes for a state that once boasted 100,000 new residents every year. Net in-migration now is predominantly from Mexico and Central and South America. Nearly a third of all illegal immigrants in the United States now live in California. Liberal legislators have not only accommodated this massive influx of a low-income and largely uneducated, needy population, but have made California an even more desirable destination by allowing driver's licenses, in-state tuition costs, a cessation of immigration enforcement, and even recently by allowing illegal immigrants to practice law.

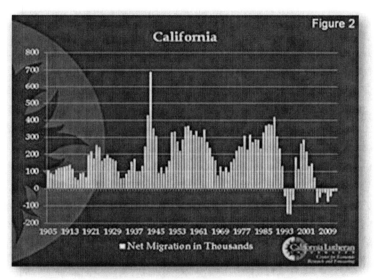

Kotkin, a Chapman University professor, writes that California residents' out-migration is the unsurprising result of government that increasingly strangles opportunity and new growth while taxing the life out of every citizen in order to create more liberal policies of redistribution of wealth, more power for bureaucrats, new red tape, and new restrictions on starting or growing businesses. He and other researchers have also focused on the stifling effects of "smart growth" that have artificially elevated housing prices to the point that a single-family home is simply unaffordable in many parts of the state.

In fact, California's tax structure disproportionately harms middle-class residents to satisfy the out-of-this-world salaries of public employees and the pie-in-the-sky dreams of limousine liberals who care a lot about reducing perceived environmental threats, as just one example, but give little thought to struggling families who can't afford far higher utility bills.

In city after city across the nation, the domination of the electoral process by liberal interest groups such as public employee unions that keep Republicans at bay and keep liberal Democrats in charge has resulted in unsustainable pension obligations, debt that cannot easily be repaid without punitive levels of taxation, and the erosion of both a vibrant business sector and an educational system that might offer hope for the future.

California now has the distinction of taking such union political dominance from the municipal level to a state level. Beyond joining the ranks of fiscally struggling states such as Illinois and Michigan, liberal California legislators seem intent to outdo them in environmental regulations, hostility to business development, and denial of the need for critical energy or water infrastructure improvements.

Government is now the primary reason that upward mobility is retarded in California, business growth is crippled, and citizens pay through the nose in taxes and fees. It is government of the politicians, by the politicians, and for the politicians. The historic drought that is desiccating the once green paradise state takes a back seat to overregulation, overtaxation, and overcriminalization of every aspect of citizens' lives. Not only does California claim a third of the nation's illegal immigrants, but in a state with 12 percent of the country's population, California has one third of the nation's welfare recipients.

Ideology Trumps Rational Development and Fiscal

The zeal of California's unchecked regulators and extreme interest groups has now prohibited development of huge natural gas and oil deposits near Bakersfield and Monterey, has created daunting regulatory roadblocks for development of highly efficient desalination plants to turn sea water into desperately needed fresh water, and has severely limited fresh water supplies to the San Joaquin Valley—where half of the nation's fruits, nuts, and vegetables are grown. Legislators have, with great enthusiasm, imposed the highest energy costs of any state in the nation on struggling young families.

The revenues from oil-rich shale deposits alone, for example, could go far in saving California from its vastly understated official debt of $27 billion. Instead, California legislators climb over each other to be first in "saving" the environment from development of California's natural resources. Hard-hit workers who once found employment in the Central Valley's agricultural industry find this zeal to put underground resources—and an estimated three million jobs—out of reach especially bitter. And every other California tax-payer helps carry the costs of such lost tax revenues and unemployed neighbors in their sales and income taxes.

A big chunk of newly hiked sales tax that has been wrongly credited with creating a fictional state surplus will be devoted to bigger payments to the huge unfunded public teachers' pension liability. The current state budget will send $4.5 billion in new tax dollars into this fund, but even this amount of taxpayer dollars will be insufficient to satisfy pension obligations now in the hole for more than $73 billion. Others estimate that unfunded pension obligations, taking both cities and the State of California into consideration, now top a half trillion dollars.

The reality is far from a "balanced budget" or "budget surplus," as recently claimed by Gov. Jerry Brown and others, but a much larger state debt that is kept "off the books." The California Public Policy Center estimates that the true California debt, taking into consideration municipal debt, now tops $1 trillion.[10] This debt represents about one half of the size of the state's economy. It also represents a huge citizen liability that is now and will in the foreseeable future drain and redistribute the wealth of families and California's business sector.

California Political Class: How Much Can We Take?

California started really borrowing in earnest against future taxes in 2009, and, even though it faces truly unsustainable debt, the Democratic-dominated legislature just can't stop spending or stop itself from blocking the use of natural resources that can produce revenues that could employ millions and produce billions of dollars of needed revenues.

Instead, the legislature and Governor Brown have begun a $100 billion "high-speed train" project that inexplicably links no major cities. To further deny the reality of their fiscal quicksand, legislators have liberalized immigration laws and rules beyond those of any other state in the nation. This has major consequences for public schools, hospitals, police forces, and nearly every other government-provided service. It also spells long-lasting pain for hard-hit California taxpayers—Go East, young man, go East!

Considered one of the most punitive business environments in the nation, California ranks forty-eighth worst for business taxes—eclipsed only by New York and New Jersey. California also captures the dubious honor of the highest taxes in the nation for "pass-through" taxes on small business (where the small-business owner is personally liable to the state for taxes on business income). The top marginal income tax rate on pass-through businesses in California is now a shocking 51.9 percent.

Californians pay higher taxes on income and for energy, the environment, and debt service than almost anywhere else in the nation. With the highest marginal state income tax rate of the fifty states at 13.3 percent of income, Californians pay a high price to live on the West Coast and pay the second highest state tax on gasoline (65.98 cents a gallon). California's "cap and trade" energy legislation was enthusiastically embraced by California's legislators after it was rejected in Congress by Democrats and Republicans. It not only dramatically raised the price of consumer energy but priced many new and existing businesses out of existence.

California's destructive policies are not just making it one of the hardest places for the young to start families and prosper, but are also chasing elderly retirees from the state. California is one of just five states with no breaks for pensions, no exclusions for retirement income, and zero tax credits for seniors. Some California cities also tax sales at 10 percent.

California is now both losing its children and getting older, and, by leaps and bounds, growing poorer. Los Angeles's population recently recorded the greatest decline of any US major metropolitan area in population under the age of fifteen—about double the US average of 7.4 percent.

According to the Census Bureau's *Research Supplemental Poverty Report*, California now has the nation's highest poverty rate.[11] Almost 24 percent of California's population is poor, compared to a national average of 15.8 percent. No other state exceeds 20 percent.

The combination of California's growing impoverished population, its crippling of new business development, and its migratory trends guarantee that the demand for additional government services in California will grow and the number of people paying for those services will shrink. It spells trouble for the state's finances and ability to responsibly provide services, and it means increasing pain for those who live there and actually produce tax revenues.

It isn't just the "wealthy" who pay so much to grow government in California, it is the middle-class worker earning over $48,000 a year who pays a top rate of 9.3 percent of his or her hard-earned dollars to the state—about the same rate that only millionaires pay in forty-seven other states. There is much hunger at city hall and in the state capitol for more of the citizens' wealth for "legacy" ideas such as the ludicrous high-speed train. But beyond any other spending, it is support of public employees' pensions, benefits, and salaries that drives the Golden State's finances.

As reported by citizen watchdog Transparent California,[12] the assaults on common sense and citizen pocketbooks are astounding. Citizens struggling to meet their own families' health care costs have a right, for example, to be outraged when they learn that one small water district in Los Angeles is providing one employee with health care insurance that costs a mind-numbing $42,942 a year! In fact, nearly half of the employees of the Water Replenishment District of Los Angeles have health care plans that cost more than $30,000 a year.

While these astronomical figures may seem like outliers, health care costs that far outstrip what any citizen could expect in the private sector are all too typical of the kind of largess that state officials have allowed both state and municipal employees to enjoy in both salary levels and benefits.

Take, as one of many examples, that California's Highway Patrol officers, on average, are entitled to a pension of $98,000 a year, beginning at age fifty and extending for the life of the officer or his or her spouse. Or consider that California's firefighters now enjoy pay and benefits that average $175,000 a year.

If that is not quite enough evidence of the truth that California's citizens now work and pay taxes that are increasingly for the benefit of "public servants," consider that the *Orange County Register* recently found that most of the lifeguards in Newport Beach were paid $120,000 a year—with the two highest paid lifeguards collecting $211,451 and $203,481 in salary and benefits.[13]

It is little wonder that the state's primary public employee retirement fund is estimated to face a shortfall of $329 billion (and, as we mentioned earlier, this figure is likely to be underestimated). Health care payments are estimated to be $64 billion in the red. Public employee health care costs are expected to rise by 59 percent in coming years. And while a favorable stock market can help California's pension funds, the fact that the state has the fourth highest unemployment rate in the nation and already owes more than $10 billion to the federal government for unemployment benefits (a consequence of government policies that cripple job creation) doesn't help.

The sad reality of the state that beckoned so many over the past 150 years is that California is now driving its productive residents out while also inviting those who count on government help in. It is a restructuring of the very idea of self-sufficiency and an opportunity to a kind of dysfunctional government "benevolence" that gets people elected but which will sooner or later destroy the very foundation of one of the most populated states in the nation.

California Public Employees Retirement System

The California Public Employees Retirement System (CalPERS) is the state's behemoth investment fund and the policeman and enforcer for all matters dealing with public employee pensions. Created in 1932, it was once the guardian of taxpayer dollars while providing public sector employees guaranteed retirement income.

A decent pension, its founders reasoned when creating CalPERS, would ensure that public employees did not simply stay on the job collecting a salary when they were too old to actually fulfill their duties. Pensions would enable workers to retire with dignity and security. When it began, CalPERS was very much the taxpayer's advocate and cautioned that the retirement age should not be so young that workers would retire when still able-bodied "in the middle life."

The retirement age was set at sixty-five, with pensions after years of work averaging less around 57 percent annually of the salary level for the last year of full-time work. A formula was set that added 1.42 percent of salary to the pension amount for every year worked. When CalPERS was created, of course, salary levels were modest and most pensions were funded from government contributions, employees' contributions, and investment income. Governmental entities would contribute greater amounts if fixed-level pensions could not be paid because of investment revenue shortfalls.

The treatment of California's public employee pensions and benefits has grown more and more generous over the years as the board of CalPERS has changed from taxpayer's advocates to union representatives always out for more wealth transferred from the taxpaying public they "serve." Here is a trust, financed by taxpayers, that has been captured by people who don't serve taxpayers, but themselves.

As Steven Malanga, the senior editor of *City Journal* and a senior fellow at the Manhattan Institute, has written about in a compelling and disheartening examination, CalPERS has abandoned its duty as a responsible taxpayer-funded protector of public employees' pension benefits to become an avowed advocate of rich, open-ended promises that have saddled California residents and following generations with hundreds of billions of dollars of debt.[14] And numerous board members have enriched themselves while doing it.[15]

Six of the board's thirteen members are chosen by public employees, and two more members, California's treasurer and controller, are beholden to the organized votes of union members, who dominate state politics. Another two are appointed by Governor Brown, an avowed friend of labor. The result has been an out-of-control regulating body that cares little, if at all, for the fortunes of California's taxpayers or institutions and that gives everything in its power to the government workers who control its deliberations.

As public employee worker unions gained clout on the CalPERS board and within the state legislature, the pension payout for California's public employees also started growing. By the 1960s, the formula for pension levels had grown to 2 percent of salary from 1.43 percent. Retirement age was also adjusted, with many allowed to retire at age sixty. Then in 1983, public safety workers got an even better formula: 2.5 percent of average final salary for every year worked, and the retirement age was dropped another five years to fifty-five. The terms kept getting better for public employees as unions' influence on CalPERS kept growing. Today most public safety officers can retire at age fifty with pensions that amount to 3 percent of their salaries per year worked. Thus, that Newport Beach lifeguard who earned an astounding $150,000 per year could retire at age fifty with a guaranteed pension for life of $135,000 per year.

By 1991, the pension obligations approved by CalPERS and the legislature had grown so large they threatened state, county, and city budgets. The day when every tax dollar would be devoted to overly generous public employee pensions could be foreseen. So new legislation was enacted that limited new pension agreements to 1.25 percent per year and withheld pension benefits until most workers reached age sixty-five. Workers would no longer be required to contribute to their own pensions, unlike private sector workers, but the new formula, called "Tier Two," was promised to bring relief to taxpayers and hard-pressed government budgets. The unions hated it and became determined to reverse this prudent legislation.

The virtual takeover of the CalPERS board by union advocates and those who owed their political fortunes to the union vote has produced disastrous results. In 1999 the fund's board reversed the 1991 decision for fiscal relief and not only recommended reinstatement of the previous financially ruinous benefits and lower age requirements, but, destructively and irresponsibly, wanted to do so retroactively. Then they went a step further and suggested lowering the retirement age for all state public employees to as early as age fifty-five and granting even richer benefits to public safety workers, allowing them to retire as early as age fifty with 90 percent of their salaries for life.

CalPERS wrote the legislation to turn these recommendations into law and, together with unions' formidable lobbying and political action arms, lobbied the now solidly Democratic legislature for passage. They got exactly what they wanted, and California's taxpayers became the victims of unbridled—and unchecked—union greed.

It gets even worse. Emboldened by the generous reversal of pension fortunes just won by state employees, local governments came under intense pressure to provide equally generous benefits to municipal employees. In 2001, legislators allowed municipal workers covered by the CalPERS system to bargain for the same level of benefits. Now cities and counties were faced with mounting political pressure to open the bank to public employees who felt they were owed the same generosity as state workers. No one spoke for taxpayers, and in city after city and county after county the foundation for fiscal disasters was laid.

At the same time that the state's pension obligations rocketed from $611.0 million in 2001 to $3.5 billion in 2010, cities began piling on huge and unsustainable pension obligations. Glendale's annual pension bill spiked from $1.3 million in 2003 to $13.7 million in 2007. San Jose's went from $73.0 million in 2001 to $245.0 million in 2010. San Bernardino's rose from $5.0 million in 2000 to about $26.0 in 2012. Because CalPERS alone sets the level of contribution from municipal employers and because the attitude of the CalPERS board always awards more funds to public union employees, California's cities began experiencing the same fiscal dangers as the state. Such debt requires higher taxes and fees of citizens and businesses, who responded, as we have seen, by increasingly moving elsewhere.

To add insult to injury, CalPERS also won new authority to invest a large percentage of its funds in stocks but shielded employees from any risk of loss when the investments didn't pay off or lost value. This is very bad news for taxpayers, because CalPERS's returns over the past five years are the worst of any large investment funds in the nation. The poor results by CalPERS are a reflection not just of changing market conditions and popped bubbles, but exceedingly bad investment decisions. CalPERS has, for example, adopted 111 different policy statements on the environment, social conditions, and corporate governance, all dictating or restricting how its funds could be invested. They essentially crippled investment where funds were growing in the name of liberal ideology. They did, however, like the finance sector and invested heavily in Fannie Mae and Freddie Mac—just before the housing collapse and bankruptcy of each. Investment decisions with a "social meaning" inspired CalPERS to invest billions on emerging third-world countries, in housing complexes that would later go bankrupt, and in risky "toxic mortgages." The losses amounted to almost half the value of CalPERS's real estate portfolio—and almost $100 billion lost from one bad investment after another. Those public workers who trusted CalPERS, however, never lost a dime.

Taxpayers are the guarantors of these bad investment decisions by CalPERS. And, once again, it is a destructive fact that California's public sector workers enjoy far more favorable treatment than just about anyone in the private sector. Most private sector workers would love retirement investment funds that have guaranteed pension payouts when IRAs lost money in the stock market, but that is exactly what California's public employees now enjoy…courtesy of CalPERS and the union-dominated California legislature.

The stock market has indeed lost great value several times since CalPERS convinced the state legislature that there was little downside risk to allowing them to invest heavily in the market to meet the newly generous benefits payout formulas. "The CalPERS staff assured us that even in the worst-case scenario, the state's general fund would take a $300 million hit," said state legislator Deborah Ortiz to the *San Jose Mercury* in 2003. When the market tanked, California's taxpayers were on the hook for ten times that amount. CalPERS had sold the legislators and taxpayers a bill of goods and then, with its power to order public employment contributions by city and county employers, made it all worse when the tech bubble burst and investment revenues lost billions of dollars.

CalPERS jealously guards rich payouts for public service retirees, including themselves. As much as any governmental body besides the state legislature, they are responsible for California's sad state of fiscal affairs. They always intercede to protect retirees' payouts, even when it means that cities may default or have to pay much, much more to satisfy debts.

Those who work at CalPERS have no problem paying themselves very well while enjoying every perk they can obtain. Despite the danger that unsustainable benefits and pensions have created for California's taxpayers, cities, and the state budget, when it comes to perks, few public servants feel more entitled than those who work at CalPERS.

Take, for example, the shareholder-enacted policy of CalPERS to insist that British Petroleum report on how their activities might affect climate risk. BP willingly agreed. BP's agreement, however, did not stop a CalPERS official from flying to London and staying in a pricey hotel so she could make a minute-long shareholder statement about the importance of such a report. The carbon emissions flying to London from California went without mention... as did the costs. Board member Priya Mathur later flew to Copenhagen, Paris, and Cambridge to attend climate change conferences.

Mathur has been found four times over the past nine years to have failed to submit reports on her campaign expenditure getting elected to the CalPERS Board of Directors, where she manages a fund worth about $300 million. To date she has paid a few modest fines that she says were for reports that were "overlooked."[16]

Over recent years Mathur's reporting lapses and expensive, if nonsensical, trips abroad pale in comparison to the charges of double-dealing and self-serving uses of CalPERS to financially and politically benefit one after another CalPERS board and staff member.

Another CalPERS scheme involved influence and business buying by a major political donor, who generously gave campaign funds to CalPERS's treasurer while he also employed another board member, former San Francisco mayor Willie Brown, on the side. He was nothing if not thorough, giving $600,000 to Gray Davis's gubernatorial campaign and appointing Davis's wife to the board of directors of one of his companies. The alleged payoff involved later decisions by CalPERS to invest $760 million in the donor's private equity funds from 2000 through 2002.

The record that emerges is one of an influential and powerful governmental body that serves many masters, including the profits of its union-dominated executives, but has little, if any, apparent duty to the taxpayers of California, who ultimately pay for such corruption. More than any other single California entity besides the one-sided state legislature, CalPERS is the architect of a failed state convincing its citizens to move elsewhere.

California's Historic Drought

The worst drought in California's history is now in its fourth year. Mandatory water savings have been ordered by Gov. Jerry Brown, and Central Valley farmers have let millions of acres turn into parched dust-bowls while drilling ever deeper to tap underground aquifers—which are quickly being depleted.

One half of America's fruits, nuts, and vegetables are grown in the Central Valley, but that is now changing because water from Northern California and the Sierra Nevada snowpack is not being made available in the first case and is not accumulating in snowpacks in the second.

Northern California still has water, but the "coastal elite" who dominate California's liberal politics have insisted that it be devoted to San Francisco and its wealthy suburbs—which still enjoy well-watered lawns. And these same coastal elites also call the shots for the environmentalist influence on California's political structure. They insist that scarce Northern California water be used to wash fresh water to the Pacific Ocean in a bid to both save endangered species such as the tiny baitfish the snail darter, and because they hope to forestall saltwater contamination of the watershed that might some-day, they hope, again see salmon migration and spawning.

Shortchanged are farmers and Southern California residents, who live or die according to whether water is available. The elaborate system of water redistribution from areas of abundance to growing population centers with not enough water to continue developing were key goals of past governors and legislators. Those infrastructure priorities have been long abandoned by liberal legislators and environmental interest groups, who often seem determined to see California return to a more nature-friendly preindustrial era.

The ancient Jewish proverb that "man plans and God laughs" is now playing out in California, because at the end of the day, rainfall and snowfall totals determine what resources can be readily used. Neither has provided California's farmers, businesses, or residents much hope in recent years, and government's reaction to the growing crisis has been ideological rather than practical—and punitive rather than helpful.

But another proverb dictates that "necessity is the mother of invention," and California's desperate need for fresh water has produced innovators who are ready to help. California's political class has, at the worst possible time, looked upon them with suspicion, and the environmental movement has treated them with hostility.

State Blocks Fresh Water from the Sea

Take the case of Carlos Riva, the CEO of Boston-based Poseidon Water, whose story was reported in detail by the *Wall Street Journal*'s Allysia Finley.[17] Mr. Riva wants to bring California fresh water from the Pacific Ocean with desalination technology that forces salt water through finely meshed "reverse osmosis" filters. It is expensive and energy driven, but Riva has studied advances in Israel and feels that less costly and energy-dependent solutions are available.

He has worked for ten years to get past shortsighted California regulators, who have put barrier after regulatory barrier in his path, and California's environmental groups, who unapologetically put fish that might be sucked into intake pipes in the ocean above the fates of the human citizens of California, who are growing increasingly desperate.

Riva's determination has resulted in the opening of a $1 billion desalination plant in Carlsbad, north of San Diego. When it opens it will be capable of producing fifty-four million gallons of water each day and will win the title of the largest such plant in America. To even begin construction, Riva's company, Poseidon, spent six years battling fourteen environmental lawsuits.

And then there was the maze of competing and overlapping regulatory agencies, which include the California Bureau of Reclamation, the State Water Resource Control Board, and the California Coastal Commission, as well as federal agencies. Between the lawsuit and regulatory agencies' foot dragging and sometimes obstruction, Riva will have to show similar determination to open a second plant, which has been on the drawing board for more than fifteen years.

His company has acceded to demands by environmental groups to restore separate inland wetlands at great cost, has battled in courtrooms for a decade at even greater cost, and now has agreed to modify the intake screen design to minimize the chances of sucking in anchovies and other nonendangered fish to satisfy the many voices that seem intent on stopping any development of his critically needed common sense solution.

The Coastal Commission has responded by recommending a complex system of underwater dams and filters a thousand feet offshore, which experts predict would take—if even approved—five to seven years to complete and which will cost many times the cost of the desalination plant itself.

Riva took his cue from Israel, which has faced its own severe drought that began in 2009. After researching and then building three huge plants, Israel now produces one hundred billion gallons of fresh water a year from seawater—nearly half of Israel's fresh water needs. Plans are now under way to build more than enough for Israel's population and future growth plans—enough to export water to a thirsty region.

The problem in California is that water produced from the sea is almost twice as expensive as what Israel achieved—because of California's high energy and regulatory costs and labor prices. Again, what has stopped California from prospering or even reacting responsibly to environmental conditions such as a historic drought is the State of California and its misplaced liberal policies.

Like so many residents who have "voted with their feet," Riva and his company are now reported to be looking more closely at Texas, where government welcomes business solutions that work and citizens appreciate a standard of living that Texas's government still encourages and tries to improve. Mr. Riva's struggle to bring badly needed help to California and make a profit while doing it is a case in point on the dysfunction of various levels of California's government. It would seem that in California, government has simply forgotten that its job is to protect citizens and help improve living conditions.

California's one-party system, dominated by public employee unions, coastal billionaires, and environmental interest groups, is hostile to business development—and, by extension, the upward mobility of its less-favored citizens and anyone in California's middle class. California is at the top or near the top of personal and business taxes and regulations that thwart business development and creation.

California's politicians are creating a high-tax, perpetually indebted welfare state where the middle class is increasingly being driven to find better places to live elsewhere in the nation. The perverse symbiotic political relationship between public employee unions and state government has benefitted both while harming the general population.

In recent years other states and cities have tackled the destructive circle of symbiosis between those who work for government and those who govern. Michigan's governor, Scott Walker, significantly took on the underlying basis of automatic dues checkoffs that fund the unions' outsize political power and influence, and other public officials have tackled the same policies and broken the stranglehold of pension and benefit promises that can only be satisfied by shifting public spending away from every other citizen need. Bankruptcy has been the solution for various cities such as Detroit, whose past political leaders have put off politically valuable but unsustainable pension contributions. Even Rahm Emanuel, Barack Obama's former chief of staff and now Chicago's mayor, has taken on, with mixed results, the unending hunger of public employee unions to take so much from the public treasury that there is little left for public needs.

But without the checks and balance of any other political viewpoint but that which is dominated by liberal Democrats, California citizens have few options for a less destructive future. Instead, California is on a path that has two classes of citizens—those who are so wealthy they can afford California's overpriced and overregulated housing markets and punitive tax burdens, and those who are so poor that they survive on the transfer payments from the productive segments of the population. The middle class in California is increasingly only those who profit from the union-dominated government salaries, pensions, and benefits.

California's decision makers, both inside and outside government, have created a system that is destined to collapse. That collapse is now under way both fiscally and in terms of out-migration to states where the possibility of an increasing standard of living, unharmed by government intervention, still exists.

Without the unlikely creation of a countervailing political force on the ill-considered and self-destructive policies of California Democrats, citizens living in California who want upward mobility really have but two choices—secure a protected job from the government or move to a better state. The first may prove a short-term solution, as it is dependent on a dwindling tax base, and the second requires citizens to vote—with their feet.

About the Author: Floyd Brown

Floyd Brown is chairman of Liftable Media Inc., a new media firm that built and manages several of America's largest social media news websites. Brown is also president of the Western Center for Journalism, a nonprofit dedicated to informing and equipping Americans who love freedom. The author of five books, Brown has written for publications as diverse as the *San Francisco Chronicle*, *National Review*, and WND.com.

Two

Taxes

By Joel Fox

California has more money in its state budget than at any time in its history. The general fund budget is over $115 billion; total spending with all funds and federal money is around $265 billion.[18] The Golden State also sits atop the Tax Foundation's rankings with the highest income tax rate of the fifty states, the second highest gasoline per-gallon tax, first in general state sales tax rate, and the eighth highest corporate tax rate. Overall, the Tax Foundation ranks California fourth highest of all the states in taxes per capita.[19]

Census Bureau statistics support the idea that Californians are heavily taxed. In a recent review of a Census Bureau report on state taxes, *Sacramento Bee* columnist Dan Walters wrote, "During the 2013–14 fiscal year that ended last June, California collected $138.1 billion in taxes of all kinds, 16 percent of all state taxes collected in the nation, and more than the next two states, New York and Texas, combined."[20] Walters noted these figures were just state taxes and did not include taxes levied by any local government or agency. The state budget is running a surplus. With money still coming in during April, it appears the budget surplus could be $2.5 billion or more.[21]

So, what's the buzz in Sacramento? How many *tax increase* measures will be on the 2016 general election ballot? There is now more talk of raising taxes using ballot initiatives than any time in recent memory.

An Avalanche of Tax Proposals

This strange combination of flush times and the desire for more tax revenue comes from a number of factors. To apply a police detective examination, for those who want more taxes they have means, motive, and opportunity.

Means comes from the ability of the pro-tax groups to qualify a tax increase for the ballot. Public employee unions in particular, which use a portion of member dues for political activities, have the resources to pay for the necessary signatures to get a measure on the ballot.

Motive is to get more money to pay salaries, cover retirement costs, and fund social and health programs—cover a slew of government requirements and requests. While government budgets and general services are particularly squeezed by pension and health care costs for current and former employees, the solution often being offered is to raise more money from the taxpayers to cover the cost of reduced services.

For example, in Los Angeles, pension costs have risen to nearly 20 percent of the city's budget from 3 percent in 2000, reducing available funds for other government services. According to Daniel DiSalvo, an assistant professor of political science in the Colin Powell School for Civic and Global Leadership at the City College of New York-CUNY and a senior fellow at the Manhattan Institute for Policy Research, "Statewide pension liabilities (in California) are increasing at a rate of $17 billion a year, which makes the state's current cash surplus a mirage."[22]

Opportunity is presented by the changing political demographics in a state that has become more liberal and that leans toward support for spending. More importantly, opportunity comes with the easier path to qualify measures for the ballot. California statutory initiatives are required to collect signatures from 5 percent of the number of people who voted for governor in the past election. A constitutional amendment needs 8 percent to qualify for the ballot.

The 2014 gubernatorial election set an embarrassing record for low voter turnout. Only about 42 percent of registered voters bothered to cast a ballot in the contest between incumbent Democratic governor Jerry Brown and his Republican challenger, Neel Kashkari.

Those who want to qualify a tax for the ballot need to collect 365,880 signatures to qualify a statute and 585,407 signatures for a constitutional amendment from a pool of nearly eighteen million registered voters in the state. Because of a bill that was signed into law by the governor last year, the proponents will even have more time to get those signatures—180 days instead of the previously mandated 150 days.

However, within this opportunity are also the seeds of potential failure. Seeing a number of tax increase initiatives on the ballot could shock the voters into shying away from all tax increases.

Continue Taxing the Rich: Extending Proposition 30

While a number of taxes are under consideration by advocates who want more revenue, the first focus is on extending or making permanent the Proposition 30 tax increases.

In 2012, Gov. Jerry Brown led a coalition of public unions and government program advocates with some business support to pass Proposition 30, a $7-billion-a-year tax increase. Prop 30 raised personal income taxes for seven years on taxpayers with incomes of $250,000 or more. It also increased sales taxes by a quarter-cent for four years.

Brown argued that the tax increase was needed to help the state recover from the Great Recession. Funding education was the key to the strategy employed by the Yes on 30 campaign. Brown emphasized that the tax increase would be temporary. In fact, the promise was written into the measure in the Findings Section of the initiative, which states unambiguously: "The new taxes in this measure are temporary."[23] The sales tax piece of the measure is due to expire at the end of 2016, the income tax in 2018. (The income tax piece was made retroactive for one year in a show of tax-writing chutzpa.)

However, as soon as January 2014, state officials started talking about extending Proposition 30 or making the temporary taxes permanent. State Superintendent of Public Instruction Tom Torlakson said flatly, "We need to extend Prop 30."[24] Legislators soon got into the act. In May of 2014, Sen. Mark Leno told a San Francisco rally that the governor's desire to create a budget rainy-day fund might undermine an effort to continue the tax increases. "If we have $10 billion in reserve, how do we go to the voters in two or three years and say we have to extend their (Prop 30) tax increase?" Leno asked.[25]

Governor Brown has steadfastly held to his campaign promise that the Proposition 30 taxes are temporary. Or is there some nuance in his language? Here is how I described in my *Fox and Hounds Daily* blog his response to a question about the temporary Prop 30 taxes at the press conference releasing his budget in January 2015:

> When Brown was asked about extending the Proposition 30 tax increases or making them permanent, he noticeably paused before answering, "I said that's a temporary tax and that's my position."
>
> It may be risky to see meaning in the pause but it suggested he was responding carefully. That prompts some parsing of the short answer. If the Prop 30 tax were extended a specific length of time, in the governor's mind would it still be considered a "temporary" tax with a new end date as opposed to making the tax permanent?
>
> Therefore, cloaked in the governor's answer is there now some wiggle room for discussing a tax extension?[26]

Brown's position on the tax is an important question because of his current popularity with the voters. In a January Public Policy Institute of California (PPIC) poll, 61 percent of all adults said Brown was doing a good job.[27]

According to PPIC president and pollster Mark Baldassare, "Of those who favor a Proposition 30 extension, 74 percent approve of Brown as governor, so the two poll responses are highly related. Given his record-high approval numbers at the start of an historic fourth term as governor, Brown's views on a wide range of fiscal and policy issues including a Proposition 30 tax extension will have an impact on voters' preferences."[28]

However, the supporters of extending the tax or making it permanent will probably charge ahead with or without the governor. Proposition 30 was the result of a compromise between the governor and the California Teachers

Federation.[29] The teachers' union had originally proposed a millionaire tax measure at the time that would collect more revenue than the compromise that became Prop 30. With the governor heading toward the end of his final term in office, there is less likelihood that the taxing interests would want to deal.

In an effort to continue the tax in one form or another, proponents will argue that the Proposition 30 tax is the reason for the state's fiscal recovery. Gabriel Petek, the lead California analyst for Standard & Poor's Ratings Services, challenged that theory.[30]

Examining the state's finances from the Legislative Analyst's report in 2010, Standard & Poor's concluded that the state eliminated its structural deficit by lowering expenditures. Proposition 30 played a role in reducing the state's debt. With the debt diminished and soon gone—and if the state holds the line on expenditures—the Standard and Poor's report concluded that there is no need to fear what some are calling a fiscal cliff—a big drop of revenue when the temporary taxes end.

At this time it is projected that the 2015 budget surplus could run well over $2 billion. Still, expect to hear a cry that ending the temporary taxes will devastate the state budget, especially education. An initiative effort to extend Proposition 30 is considered very likely. Changes might be made to convince the majority of the voters that they won't be paying the tax, for example, eliminating the sales tax piece in the extension, which is being discussed.

Whatever the formula, it appears an effort will be made to continue Proposition 30 in some form.

Touching the Third Rail: Changing Proposition 13

A campaign is building to take on California's iconic Proposition 13 property tax reform, often referred to as the third rail of California politics—"If you touch it you die"—by increasing taxes on commercial property. Proponents are suggesting that reassessing business property to market value will bring in up to $10 billion.

Passed overwhelmingly by the voters in 1978, Proposition 13 limited property taxes to 1 percent of the acquisition price of property with annual tax increases of up to 2 percent depending on inflation. The tax formula treated residential and business property the same, just as they had been treated before Prop 13 passed.

Advocates for more taxes see an opportunity to go after businesses to pay higher property taxes using the same game plan used successfully in the Prop 30 effort. In that case the argument was to tax the rich. Here it will be to tax the corporations. This ignores the fact that property tax increases hit all businesses, including small businesses, which are the greatest job creators in the state. Furthermore, as pointed out in a Pepperdine University study,[31] minorities and women own many small businesses. These groups would suffer with an increased business property tax.

Some defenders of Proposition 13 believe the move to increase business property taxes is the first step in undoing Proposition 13. The suspicion is that if the business property tax is increased, residential properties could be next.

That's the goal of some Proposition 13 opponents. In a seventeen-page documentary film proposal by a former SEIU official and Los Angeles City employee, one solution suggested to change Proposition 13 is: "Periodically reassess residential properties to bring their valuations up to current marketvalues."[32] He promises homeowner protections along with the tax increase, but such promises have rarely worked.

Different liberal groups are studying the possibility of attempting a split roll property tax, segregating business and residential property. One organization, Evolve, has secured one hundred resolutions at city councils and school boards to support a split roll.[33] There is usually no one at the meetings to oppose the nonbinding resolution.

A January 2015 PPIC poll found "[a] slim majority (54 percent) favor a split roll tax. Support is at its lowest point since PPIC began asking the question in January 2012."[34]

The poll asks if there is support for taxing businesses according to their market value, but no counterarguments are presented. If the poll respondents knew that a split roll would cost jobs, would they support such a measure? If they knew, as the California Taxpayers Association reports,[35] that business property and non-homeowner-occupied property pay the largest share of the property tax, would they support a split roll? Meanwhile, in numerous surveys Proposition 13 still enjoys two-to-one support from the voters.

A New Tax: Oil Severance Tax

California is the only top oil-producing state that doesn't tax oil when it comes out of the ground. Such an oil severance tax has been the goal of tax increase advocates for a long time. The reason for creating the tax has changed over the years from a desire for more revenue to support for the environment *and* a desire for more revenue.

In the 1990s a couple of oil severance tax proposals were put forth in the legislature (one by then assemblyman and future Los Angeles mayor Antonio Villaraigosa). When those measures failed, a ballot initiative, Proposition 87, made the ballot thanks in large part to the support of businessman, film producer, and real estate heir Stephen Bing. Over $155 million was spent on the campaign by both sides ($61 million by the yes side) and the measure was defeated 55 percent to 45 percent.

Additional bills were introduced over the years but did not become law. Now hedge fund billionaire and environmentalist Tom Steyer has said he might be interested in funding a ballot measure to create an oil severance tax if the legislature doesn't act. One proposal he pushed would levy a 9.9 percent per barrel tax and raise up to $2 billion.[36]

While supporters of an oil severance tax continually point out that California is the only major oil state that does not tax oil as it is extracted from the ground, the oil industry says that is not the whole story. In fact, California oil producers pay plenty of taxes on their businesses that are on par with other oil-producing states—it's just that the taxes are levied in a different way in California.

Catherine-Reheis-Boyd, president of the Western States Petroleum Association, notes that California has the highest income tax and highest sales tax in the nation, both of which affect the oil business. Oil producing Texas has no income tax; oil producing Alaska has no sales tax. That's just for starters.

"California also assesses oil-producing property based on the current value of the oil in the ground, meaning California oil is taxed whether or not it's produced," Reheis-Boyd writes.[37] "As the oil is produced, refined, and sold, companies are subject to a host of other taxes that generate an estimated $6 billion in revenue for state and local governments."

In 2009, the Milken Institute issued an economic report that lead with this fact:

The oil and gas sector as a whole directly employs approximately 65,000 people in California, with a ripple impact, as the company and its employees consume goods and services, of 304,500 jobs, $16.3 billion in workers', earnings, and $46.3 billion in economic output.[38]

If the oil severance tax becomes a reality, many of those jobs would be threatened. Yet the push for an oil severance tax has been going on for years, and, with a rich benefactor behind the latest effort, voters in the state may once again be asked to decide whether to levy such a tax—economic consequences be damned.

An Old Tax Again: Cigarette Tax

Another tax with a long history in California, the cigarette tax, may also be headed for the 2016 ballot. It's a familiar place for the cigarette tax to appear. Four initiatives have been before California voters to raise the cigarette tax over the past three decades, with mixed results. Proposition 99 of 1988 and Proposition 10 of 1998 passed. Proposition 86 of 2006 and Proposition 29 of 2010 failed.

Presently, the effort to raise a cigarette tax an additional $2.00 a pack, up from the current $0.87, is in the legislature. If the proposal fails there, proponents said they expect to go back to the voters via the initiative process.

An interesting aspect in the debate over cigarette taxes is that the revenues diminish as the use of the product is reduced. Often proponents of the tax tie the revenue source to some goal, such as health research, as was proposed in the last unsuccessful ballot measure. There are consequences when a new program is set up reliant on an earmarked revenue source and the revenue starts to disappear.

If the cigarette taxes are increased, some smokers will abandon the product, one of the goals of the tax increase proponents. But what happens to the revenue needs of the newly established program? Will program advocates demand a draw against the state general Fund? Probably. Once a government program is established, it is very difficult to close down.

There is another real possibility if cigarette taxes are increased dramatically: smokers would turn to the black market to secure the cigarettes and escape the tax. In a recent *Wall Street Journal* opinion article, Patrick Gleason, director of state affairs at Americans for Tax Reform, pointed out that the higher the tax on cigarettes, the more smuggling of cigarettes takes place.[39] In New York, where the cigarette tax is the highest, 58 percent of the cigarettes are smuggled in. Illegal cigarettes explain why some of the initial tax revenue goals established by legislatures when they raise the taxes are not met, according to Gleason.

But here's the rub for California. Despite being one of the states with lower taxes per pack, according to the Tax Foundation, the Golden State already ranks sixth on a cigarette smuggling chart.[40] A tax increase would likely place California higher on the chart, increasing the illegal activity.

Taxpayers to Be Buried in an Avalanche of Taxes?

Whether all the above taxes—and more—make it to the ballot will be determined by political expedience. Proponents of the above-mentioned taxes want to see them all on the ballot and passed. However, the tax advocates are concerned how the voters would react if so many tax increases appear on one ballot.

While there may be conversations among the groups to find a solution and prevent a multitax initiative avalanche, there are still differences that could see various promoters move ahead with their plans.

For example, city and county workers don't get a direct benefit from a Proposition 30 extension, especially if the only piece extended is the income tax. Proposition 30 mostly goes to education, which means other public sector workers are on the outside looking in.

On the other hand, a multitax ballot could run into opposition from the voters. PPIC president and pollster Mark Baldassare dissected his organization's recent poll to discover that seven of ten likely voters believe California is near the top (45 percent) or above average (26 percent) in state and local tax burden. Voters in the poll were closely divided over extending Prop 30 (48 percent favor, 45 percent oppose). Baldassare cautioned,

There are many reasons why tax proposals are a tough sell even in Blue California. They include high government distrust and little fiscal knowledge. We have identified a major force to be reckoned with as tax initiatives take shape for the 2016 ballot: a widely held perception that Californians are among the most burdened with state and local taxes in the nation.[41]

One other way California residents may see more taxes paid to government is if certain tax restructuring reforms move forward and end up on the ballot.

Bring the Tools for a Remodel: Tax Restructuring

David Doerr has been around the California tax world since before Ronald Reagan was governor. He spent twenty-four years as chief consultant to the Assembly Revenue and Taxation Committee before becoming chief tax consultant to the California Taxpayers Association in 1987. Doerr wrote the book *California's Tax Machine*, considered the bible on California taxation, which traces California's tax history from the Spanish colonial period to present day. Doerr says there have been seven major tax-restructuring efforts in the state's 165-year history. Of the seven, he says only two were successful and accomplished what they set out to do: the tax overhaul that reduced the state income and sales tax under Gov. Earl Warren in the 1940s and the Proposition 13 property tax reform of 1978.[42]

Doerr's warning: most of the unsuccessful reforms ended up increasing taxes. There is much talk in Sacramento today about the need to restructure the state's tax system. One obvious reason is that California relies heavily on high-end taxpayers for revenue. These taxpayers' investments are sensitive to changes in the economy. California's budget has been on a roller-coaster ride for a couple of decades because of this reliance on the income tax.

In 1950 the income tax accounted for 10 percent of the state's revenue. The sales tax generated 60 percent. Now the income tax accounts for 60 percent while the sales tax generates 25 percent.[43] The economy has changed in California from an agricultural and manufacturing economy to one that is driven by services and information. This circumstance has led to calls to change the tax system to more closely mirror the economic activity of the state.

Two recent governors, Gray Davis and Arnold Schwarzenegger, appointed commissions to consider major changes to the tax system. Even the names of the commissions indicated they were designed to deal with a changed economy. Davis's committee was titled the California Commission on Tax Policy in the New Economy.[44] Schwarzenegger's group, chaired by financier Gerald Parsky and informally called the Parsky Commission, went by the formal title Commission on the 21st Century Economy.[45] The commissions both produced detailed plans that went nowhere.

Proposals for tax reform have also come from the private sector. Renowned economist Arthur Laffer, a former California resident, has offered up a major tax reform for the state that would rely on a flat tax and a value-added tax while eliminating all other taxes except "sin" taxes.

The Think Long Committee for California, sponsored by billionaire Nicholas Berggruen's Institute, has put together an all-star cast of noted Californians, including former US secretaries of state George Schultz and Condoleezza Rice, former governor Gray Davis, and former Clinton administration chief economist Laura Tyson, among others, and worked up a tax reform plan.

Yet the calls for tax restructuring have only gotten louder. Top Democratic consultant Garry South recommended "tearing up the tax code" and "tearing the tax structure down" at a recent conference, the *Wall Street Journal* reported.[46] In his daily video clip on the *Sacramento Bee* website, columnist Dan Walters argued that "Jerry Brown Should Push for Tax Reform."[47] The *Sacramento Bee* editorial board said of tax reform, "[T]here's no better time than now for policy makers to show the courage to tackle one of the state's most vexing problems."[48]

To put it simply, there has been a lot of discussion about tax restructuring. The current focus is on a plan proposed by state Sen. Bob Hertzberg, which is modeled on the Think Long Committee plan. Hertzberg is a veteran legislator, chairman of the Senate Governance and Finance Committee, and the deep resources of the Think Long Committee back him, so his proposal will be taken seriously.

To achieve his goal, Hertzberg would raise taxes on services while "restructuring and modernizing" the personal income tax and consider changes to the corporate tax to make California more competitive.

Unlike many tax reform proposals of the past, Hertzberg makes no pretense that the end result of his tax reform will be revenue neutral. Hertzberg calls for a $10 billion revenue increase. Hertzberg wants to use the money for K-14 education, local governments, universities and colleges, and an earned tax credit. He calls his plan the Upward Mobility Act.

The new tax burden will likely fall on taxpayers with incomes in the $200,000 to $500,000 income range, but all will feel the effects.

The service tax proposal will generate the most heat and attention. A state Board of Equalization report claimed that a tax on services could raise $122.6 billion, more than the entire state's general fund budget.[49] However, many of the services included in the study would be exempted from Hertzberg's proposal.

Hertzberg's plan proposes the classic economic fix of broadening the tax base and lowering the tax rates. However, in seeking a $10 billion increase in revenues, it defies the urge to lower the rates sufficiently.

Board of Equalization Vice Chairman George Runner likes the concept but not the tax increase. "I'd consider a broader sales tax only if it's part of revenue neutral tax reform, such as abolishing California's income tax and the Franchise Tax Board, along with other taxes that destroy jobs…The last thing overtaxed Californians need is another tax."[50]

One goal Sen. Bob Hertzberg hopes to accomplish with his major tax reform legislation, Senate Bill 8,[51] is to improve business conditions in the state. The obvious question: Does that objective have to come with a $10 billion price tag?

If, as Hertzberg asserts, his tax changes will boost the economy and keep businesses from fleeing the state, wouldn't the change to a more robust business climate provide new revenue over time through economic growth? Why set the rates to have an immediate large increase in revenue equivalent to about 9 percent of the current state general fund?

Tying an immediate big revenue boost to the new tax formula probably hurts the economy and threatens the proposal's chances. For many in the state, such a big tax increase is like waving a red flag in front of a bull. Such an add-on seems contrary to the overall tax philosophy that Hertzberg is promoting—broaden the base and lower the rates.

Tax Issues Could Dominate the Ballot in 2016

California voters could face an interesting, if perplexing array of choices on the 2016 general election ballot. Besides voting for president, a US senator, and legislative and local offices, the ballot likely could contain a slew of ballot issues, because fewer signatures are needed to qualify initiatives. The issues may range from public pension reform to legalization of marijuana to transgender bathrooms in public schools. But the dominant theme most likely will be taxation.

With budget surpluses, a thriving economy, and unchecked spending problems such as public pensions, will the voters agree to the tax increases? The real question for California politicians and interest groups that want to increase taxes and spending: Why is it that the only ones held responsible for the way government is working are the taxpayers?

About the Author: Joel Fox

Joel Fox has been involved in California politics for over thirty-five years as a public affairs/political consultant and small-business and taxpayer advocate, including nineteen years with the Howard Jarvis Taxpayers Association. Fox is a frequent commentator on local and national news media. He is a co-publisher and editor-in-chief of the website *Fox and Hounds Daily*, which offers commentary on California business and politics. The *Washington Post* twice named the site one of the top California political websites. The picture in this chapter is of Joel Fox presenting Ronald Reagan with a "Lifetime Tax Fighter" award. Photo credit is John Barr.

Three

CRIME

By Katy Grimes

Oakland's historically high violent crime rate is something no one wants to talk about publicly. Oakland has been a crime-laden city for decades, often with the highest crime *per capita* in California, if not the nation. Hundreds of millions of dollars have been spent on ineffectual antipoverty programs, police sensitivity training, and community-based youth and outreach services. But the violent crime continues to escalate and is probably at its worst now.

As with many urban communities in the United States, the victims and perpetuators of homicide in Oakland are overwhelmingly young men of color between the ages of fifteen and twenty-nine. Although African Americans make up only 28 percent of the total population in Oakland, this racial group represents more than 74 percent of homicide victims.[52] "The blood of those killed in the streets of Oakland is screaming for justice, and if the current elected officials can't or will not help, I and people like me need elected officials who can," said Linda Jones, whose son Brandon Morris was killed on the streets of Oakland in 2008.[53]

Ousted Oakland mayor Jean Quan came under fire for fudging crime statistics for violent crimes downward during her bid for reelection in 2014.

Quan, the mayor from 2011 to 2015, paid the price and lost the mayoral seat to another city council member.

Oakland has repeatedly been named by the FBI as one of the "Most Dangerous Cities in America" and is consistently near the top of violent crime reports with Detroit and Flint, Michigan, because of the high murder rate. Oakland is a terribly dangerous place.[54] Oakland crime statistics report an overall uptrend in the last 14 years with violent crime increasing and property crime decreasing. The violent crime rate in Oakland in 2012 was higher than the national violent crime rate average by 415.23%.[55]

The FBI's statistics for US cities show violent crime in Oakland occurred at a rate of 19.77 per 1,000 residents. With a population of 406,000, Oakland had 7,984 instances of violent crime in 2013. There were 92 murders and 180 rapes. The city had 4,922 robberies and 2,792 reports of aggravated assault. Property crime is very high in Oakland at 62.33 per 1,000 people. There were 25,176 total property crimes in Oakland in 2013, including 5,058 burglaries, 6,833 vehicle thefts, and 13,285 nonvehicle thefts.

During the eight-year tenure of former Oakland mayor Elihu Harris, 1991–1999, there were 1,104 slayings in Oakland. During Jerry Brown's tenure as mayor of Oakland, 1999–2007, a total of 771 people were the victims of homicides. Despite sixteen anticrime initiatives during his eight years as mayor, Brown's final year in office saw more slayings than in any year since he held the mayor's job. "The 148 homicides in 2006 represent a 57.4 percent increase over the 94 homicides occurring in 2005," the Urban Strategies Council reported. "This represents an increase of 49 percent in the number of homicides compared to the five-year average of 99.8 and the ten-year average of 99.6 homicides per year." The Urban Strategies Council produced quarterly reports on homicides in Oakland throughout 2006, with the cooperation of the Oakland Police Department Homicide Section.[56]

Why does Oakland's ineffective response to crime matter? With two new radical experiments in criminal justice, Oakland's story is about to go statewide.

*　　*　　*

California embarked on a "grand experiment" in 2011 with a massive prison downsizing. Responding to a 2009 order by a federal three-judge panel, California had to reduce its overpopulated prisons by 25 percent within two years. This amounted to a reduction of nearly forty-six thousand prisoners within a very short time period. The state appealed, but the US Supreme Court upheld the mandate in May 2011 in a 5-4 decision. In a dissenting opinion, Supreme Court Justice Antonin Scalia said it was "perhaps the most radical injunction issued by a court in our nation's history."

Assembly Bill 109, referred to as "prison realignment," was the legislative vehicle for compliance with the order to reduce the prison population. However, unlike the court's orders, the bill required the state to shift a substantial share of the corrections responsibility to the counties. Many legal experts have called realignment the "biggest penal experiment in modern history."

California state government refers to the law as the "cornerstone" to reducing "overcrowding, costs, and recidivism" in state prisons.[57]

Prison realignment might be a moot point. Whatever prison realignment failed to accomplish will be further achieved with Proposition 47.[58] By November 2014, a ballot initiative struck a bigger blow to California's public safety system. Dubbed "the Safe Neighborhoods and Schools Act," Prop 47 was successfully sold to the public as the way to decriminalize drug offenses. The initiative ushered in the reclassification of "nonserious and nonviolent property and drug crimes" from a felony to a misdemeanor in order to continue to decrease prison population. Law enforcement and justice officials say the result is more crime, fewer criminals in custody, and more victims.

Growing the Prison System

In reaction to the escalating murder rate in California from 1966 to 1980, a series of voter initiatives increased prison sentences for habitual violent offenders. During this same time period, there is no coincidence the crime increase coincided with an ill-informed decision to divert "lower-level" criminals from state prisons into county facilities.

Most noticeably, following passage of California's "Three Strikes" law in 1994, the prison census nearly doubled. But the state legislature lacked the political will to order the repurposing of juvenile incarceration facilities for adults or to approve prison construction to adequately address the problem. Ultimately, that led to the federal judges' orders to reduce prison overpopulation.

Passed by the Democratic-controlled California Legislature and signed into law by Democratic governor Jerry Brown in 2011, AB 109 made fundamental changes to the California prison system. AB 109 freed thousands of "low-level inmates" or "less-serious felony offenders" onto the streets of California. Realignment also shifted thousands of inmates from state prisons to county jails. Realignment radically reduced the state prison population by diverting newly sentenced and paroled offenders to county jails and probation.

But jails were forced to release criminals early because of the volume of new offenders redirected their way.

There are no current statewide crime statistics available, and there are unlikely to be until after the 2016 election. However, some cities have maintained crime record keeping. The Los Angeles Police Department released statistics in January 2015 showing violent crime was up overall by 14.3 percent in 2013 and 2014. Violent crime is up 22 percent in San Francisco, according to the Federal Bureau of Investigation. Oakland, California, is still the number two most dangerous city in the United States, only behind Detroit. Oakland's crime rate is about five times the state average and more than double San Francisco's rate, according to the FBI's annual crime report. More than 80 percent of violent crime in Alameda County, home to Oakland, occurs in Oakland or affects Oakland residents.

Assembly Bill 109: The Criminal Justice Experiment

Prosecutors interviewed throughout the state were troubled by AB 109's definition of "low-level offenders," saying it grossly understated the seriousness of many crimes included under prison realignment. Police officers interviewed said there are more criminals on the street as a result of AB 109 and attribute rising crime rates to the law. And they said AB 109 threatened progress made through community policing and other proactive techniques.

When criticized over the plan, Gov. Jerry Brown and his administration blame realignment on a US Supreme Court ruling. Although California was ordered by a federal court to reduce the prison population by forty-six thousand prisoners, assembly Republicans warned that the governor's scheme would increase the target population by over 40 percent.

"For too long, the state's prison system has been a revolving door for lower-level offenders and parole violators who are released within months—often before they are even transferred out of a reception center," Brown said in his AB 109 signing message. "Cycling these offenders through state prisons wastes money, aggravates crowded conditions, thwarts rehabilitation, and impedes local law enforcement supervision."

Brown claimed that shifting inmates to the counties would save money and relieve prison overcrowding by returning "lower-level" offenders to local authorities, which can manage them in "smarter" ways. Brown promised that under AB 109:

- No inmates currently in state prison would be released early.
- All felons sent to state prison would continue to serve their entire sentence.
- All felons who are convicted of a serious or violent offense—including sex offenders and child molesters—would go to state prison.
- Felons who are not eligible for state prison can serve their sentence at the local level.

This was a pretext, according to Republican state senator Jim Nielsen. The US Supreme Court directed the state to fix health care services and reduce prison overcrowding. Nielsen said the US Supreme Court did not order the state to reduce sentences, nor did the court order the state to shift responsibility for habitual felons to counties.

"In fact, the US Supreme Court reviewed a state plan which included already funded plans to add sixteen thousand new cells at existing prisons," Nielsen said. "These plans and projects to convert unused juvenile facilities for adult use have been largely abandoned by the Brown administration. The governor signed legislation to reverse bond authorization for new prison facilities—preferring to dump the problem on counties."

According to a 2012 FBI report, California's realignment ushered in an increase in the crime rate in the first six months of 2012, following the first wave of inmates released. Predictably, there was an increase of 7.6 percent in homicide rates and double-digit increases in burglary and arson rates. Violent crime in California increased at more than twice the national rate, rising 4.0 percent, with the rise in property crime at six times higher than the national rate.

"Nationally, property crime was down 0.9 percent in 2012; in California, it was up 7.6 percent," reported Heather MacDonald in *City Journal.* "Car theft nationally was up 0.6 percent; in California, it jumped 14.6 percent. Burglary nationally was down 3.7 percent; in California, it was up 6.6 percent. Violent crime also showed a disparity: murder rose nationally 1.1 percent, compared with 4.7 percent in California; robbery was down 0.1 percent nationally, while California saw a 3.9 percent rise." Since the 2012 report, state statistics show crime is down overall, but not in California's largest cities.

What California Sheriffs Say about Realignment

AB 109 was supposed to shift "low level" offenders to counties. However, in reality, it has shifted high-risk and ultra-high-risk offenders, because the law ignores the offender's prior criminal history, including serious and violent offenses, according to sheriffs around the state. AB 109 considers only the last offense committed, according to Sacramento County Sheriff Scott Jones.[59]

Jones said passage of California's "Three Strikes" initiative statistically worked, and the state saw a significant downward trend in crime. Passed by voters in 1994, California's Proposition 184 "Three Strikes" law doubled the penalty for a second felony if the first one was serious or violent, and it carried a mandatory prison sentence of twenty-five years to life for a third felony.

In 2010 San Francisco's Golden Gate University published a law review article and independent study on Three Strikes sentencing and concluded that Three Strikes did serve to deter the commission of crime, as well as to incapacitate habitual offenders.

In the first ten years following passage of Three Strikes, crime decreased approximately 45 percent. The California Attorney General's office found that between 2005 and 2010, violent crime declined over 17 percent; homicides decreased 30 percent; arson dropped 38 percent; property crimes declined 22 percent; and theft crimes decreased 16 percent. "However, people forget—it was because of the Three Strikes measure that crime dropped," Sheriff Jones said. "And because people forget, they do things like water down the Three Strikes law."

In 2004, California Proposition 66 tried unsuccessfully to modify some of the provisions of the Three Strikes law. Legislative attempts failed as well.

But the 2012 ballot initiative, Proposition 36, succeeded in modifying Three Strikes by imposing a life sentence only when the third-strike felony conviction is "serious or violent."

"County" Prison Systems

Under realignment, each county has become a county prison system, according to the state's sheriffs. Following passage of AB 109, crime rates in Kern County spiked. Kern County Sheriff Donny Youngblood said supervisory responsibility for these offenders has been shifted to counties without the resources or capacities to do the job.[60] Youngblood said drug and gang problems are endemic in the Central Valley, with troubling trends increasing in drug-related crimes. According to the state's sheriffs, incarceration used to be one of the very few ways the system was able to treat and help detox addicts. Most counties had very effective drug treatment programs.

Now drug abusers and even dealers spend only days in prison under the sentencing guidelines of AB 109—if any time at all is served. Law enforcement and district attorneys say there is an increase in the frequency of drug abuse, as well as a prevalence of hard drugs.

Orange County Sheriff Sandra Hutchens said her county received three times the reassigned prisoners she was told to expect following passage of AB 109. Orange County ended up with one thousand AB 109 inmates from state prisons to house in its county jails.[61]

Realignment: Early Release or Not?

Supporters of prison realignment claimed it was not an early release program. However, this is a deceptive argument. Realignment not only changed penalties but also changed the level of parole supervision for most felons convicted after November 1, 2011.

Realignment shifted the responsibility for tens of thousands of felons to counties where jail space is already filled to capacity and changed the definition of who qualifies for community service programs.

Sen. Jim Nielsen served as the chairman of the California Board of Prison Terms from 1990 until 2007. Nielsen said the convicted felons currently sentenced to county supervision instead of state prisons include:

- Career drug dealers,
- Career burglars,
- Habitual auto thieves,
- Identification thieves,
- Criminals with long criminal records including felonies involving assault and firearms.

"Serving a county sentence is not the same as serving a state prison sentence for these career criminals," said Nielsen. Felons sentenced to jail rather than prison may be released early and only required to have "day reporting," wear an electronic ankle bracelet, or undergo other noncustodial treatment programs.

However, many in law enforcement say AB 109 forced them to work more closely together, and with parole and probation departments. AB 109 established that local Community Corrections Partnerships develop an implementation plan that addresses the major issues involved with local implementation of AB 109 and public safety realignment. These county committees around the state are comprised of the chief probation officer, the district attorney, public defender, a court representative, a chief of police, the sheriff, and the head of the Department of Social Services. "This literally changed how to work together to deal with inmates and treatment," Nick Warner with the California State Sheriffs Association said. Warner also said since the passage of AB 109, the governor sponsored two construction bonds for local jails. "The purpose is to rebuild the types of beds in the facilities, addressing the longer-term inmates' rehabilitation," Warner said.[62]

In a 2012 report by the Public Policy Institute of California, *Corrections Realignment: One Year Later*, preliminary data indicated some counties are experiencing an increase in property crime, particularly burglary and motor vehicle theft. "Unfortunately, the cause-and-effect relationships within these communities are confounded by a prolonged recession and severe budget cuts to local law enforcement and social service programs," the PPIC said. "Crime rates and realignment need to be closely monitored and carefully analyzed."

Additionally, a damning report from the Los Angeles County Probation Department found that the state is decertifying "mentally disordered" offenders just prior to release from prison and moving them to local supervision instead of state supervision. Or they are released from prison directly to a state hospital, but are later decertified by the state hospital and, again, shifted to local supervision instead of remaining on state supervision.

Prop 47: "A Spectacular Example of Orwellian 'Doublespeak'"

In November 2014, voters passed a ballot measure to downgrade so-called nonviolent drug violations and other nonviolent crimes from felonies to misdemeanors. Sponsored by retired San Diego police chief Bill Lansdowne and San Francisco District Attorney George Gascón, Prop 47 carried the misleading official title of "The Safe Neighborhoods and Schools Act" and reclassified certain felonies to misdemeanors. The initiative created a new penal code section, §1170.18, which allows offenders currently serving felony sentences for specified crimes to petition the sentencing court to have their sentences reduced to misdemeanor sentences.

Proponents claimed drug crimes and theft are crimes of poverty and people shouldn't be punished for being impoverished. The promised savings under Proposition 47 won't be calculated until 2016, nor will statistics showing higher or lower crime rates. "Heroin and cocaine as misdemeanors? Date rape drugs, too? Gun theft as a misdemeanor? Just how gullible are California voters?" the *San Diego Union Tribune* editorial board asked. "Proposition 47 will test the question. In the end, we think voters will see the 'Safe Neighborhoods and Schools Act' for what it really is: misguided, wrong-headed public policy."

"Reject Prop 47, the 'catch-and-release' law: This proposition has been titled 'The Safe Neighborhood and Schools Act' by proponents—a spectacular example of Orwellian 'doublespeak.' It is anything but safe,' " said the *Modesto Bee* editorial board.

But proponents of the initiative glossed over potential ramifications of such a sweeping change in the penal system. Prop 47 now undermines the laws against sex crimes because it reduces the penalty for possession of drugs used to facilitate date rape to just a simple misdemeanor. The date-rape drug gamma hydroxybutyrate, or GHB, is a horse tranquilizer. How can administering a horse tranquilizer to an unsuspecting date be considered a misdemeanor?

"This is all part of a larger effort to decriminalize drug use," said Orange County Sheriff Sandra Hutchens. "It's sending the wrong message to kids and young people, that it's okay to use. Look at the Colorado stats to see what is happening with the legalization of marijuana and kids using."

Hutchens said the increase in heroin use is staggering. "People get addicted to pain medication but then can't afford it, so they turn to heroin, which is cheaper," said Hutchens. "Jail is the worst place to get off drugs. Some people need to be kept off of the street as they are a danger. But jail is not the answer." Hutchens said the county drug courts have been very effective in keeping most nonserious drug users out of jail and prison.

"Nearly nine out of every ten offenders who received felony convictions in 2012 for crimes affected by Proposition 47 were sentenced to county jail and/or county community supervision," the California Legislative Analyst's Office reported. "Under Proposition 47, these offenders will continue to be handled locally. However, the length of sentences—jail time and/or community supervision—will typically be less."

Sheriff Youngblood said the other escalating problem for most counties is high numbers of street people with mental health issues who self-medicate with illegal drugs; they often end up behind bars for the crimes associated with supporting a drug habit—property crimes, theft, burglary, or worse.

"Our jails are the biggest mental health facilities," Youngblood said. "Sixty-eight percent of the inmates in my jails receive mental health care." Youngblood added that the escalation of drugged-out street people is largely a result of prior drug generations with decades of "recreational use." Sheriffs Jones and Hutchens reported the same. "We still have mental health facilities,"

Hutchens said. "But they are called jails." She said mental health isn't just a sheriffs' problem, but has been made so. "It would be helpful to have mental health teams with us. These people need housing and treatment, but not in jail."

Creating Victims With Prop 47

Days after passage of Prop 47, the *Los Angeles Times* ran a story about rising crimes rates in San Francisco. "In San Francisco, [there was] a more than 20 percent jump in both the rate of property crime, such as thefts and burglary, and the rate of violent crime, such as robbery and assault, between 2012 and 2013," the *Times* reported.

"Early release has been a near-constant policy in Los Angeles since 1988, when a federal judge allowed sentenced inmates to be let out early as a temporary solution to overcrowding," the *Los Angeles Times* said. "Many inmates were freed after serving only 10 percent of their time. A 2006 *Los Angeles Times* investigation found that nearly sixteen thousand were rearrested for new offenses while they could have been finishing out their sentences. Sixteen were charged with murder."

The New List of Prop 47 Misdemeanors

Sacramento Sheriff Scott Jones explained that in most instances, many crimes that were previously "arrestable" as felonies are now only "citable" as misdemeanors. "That means they [suspects] may not be booked into jail but rather given a citation, like a traffic ticket, with a court date to appear, and released." Jones outlined which felony crimes are now misdemeanors:

- Commercial burglary (theft under $950)
- Forgery and bad checks (under $950 value)
- Theft of most firearms
- Theft of a vehicle (under $950 value)

- Possession of stolen property (under $950 value)
- Possession of heroin, cocaine, illegal prescriptions, concentrated cannabis, and methamphetamine

Inmates awaiting trial on any of the reclassified felony charges in most instances are able to have their charges immediately reduced to the new misdemeanor level and will be let out of jail on a citation.

And thanks to Prop 47, Jones said inmates sentenced already on the reclassified felonies can petition the court for reduction of their felony convictions to misdemeanors, and many of them would be also be eligible for immediate release. Felons convicted of the qualifying felonies can petition the court to have their prior felony convictions reduced to misdemeanors. Jones warned that if they are successful, many of the prohibitions they faced as felons would then be revoked, restoring their right to vote, their right to purchase a handgun, and even their ability to apply for a job as a peace officer.

Will More Ever Be Enough?

Proponents of Prop 47 claim the State of California disenfranchises people through the criminal justice system by incarcerating people for " 'victimless' crimes such as drug possession." But what is enough? At what point will they declare a victory? According to the 2013 prison census data from the California Department of Corrections (the most recent data available), prior to passage of Proposition 47, California was aligned with the top states for proportion of incarcerations for violent crimes. If the goal was to lock up only serious and violent criminals, California is near the top for this standard.

In 2013, prior to passage of Prop 47, the PPIC reported the most recent national data showed California's violent crime rate of 422 per 100,000 residents was higher than the national rate of 387, and ranked sixteenth among all states. In 2013, 59 percent of violent crimes in California were aggravated assaults, 35 percent were robberies, 5 percent were rapes, and 1 percent were homicides.

However, Prop 47 actually reclassified felons with prior convictions for armed robbery, kidnapping, carjacking, child abuse, residential burglary, arson, assault with a deadly weapon, and many other crimes. That reclassification ultimately eliminates jail time for some serious offenders.

Voters Got Bamboozled

Fresno County District Attorney Lisa Smittcamp said the voter approval of Proposition 47 is the biggest thing impacting the criminal justice system today. "Everybody got bamboozled with Prop 47," Smittcamp said in a recent speech to the Fresno Chamber of Commerce. "It's not working out."

"It's a sham," Orange County Sheriff Sandra Hutchens said of Prop 47 "It's a paradigm shift to include a guy on the street with a pocket full of heroin and only give him a ticket," Hutchens said. Orange County and most other counties already had significant drug treatment programs in place. "These guys get three, four, five bites of the apple before they'd ever see prison," Hutchens said. "Judges had a hook to order them to a drug program, and eventually drop the case following treatment."

Because drug possession is now a misdemeanor, each of the sheriffs interviewed said the very effective drug treatment courts may dry up. "There is no incentive for drug criminals to work toward rehabilitation because there's no price to pay if they don't," said Sheriff Jones.

"Proposition 47 is far more dangerous than realignment with the potential for rising crime and victims," Sacramento County District Attorney Anne Marie Schubert said. "It's not stopping crime—they've just changed the name of it. Prop 47 will have a far greater impact in creating victims."[63]

According to numerous police officers, Prop 47 caused police departments across the state to lose their negotiating power with these reclassifications of felonies to misdemeanors.

Kern County's Sheriff Youngblood said the drug and gang crimes are endemic in California's Central Valley. "We have eight thousand square miles and only thirteen substations in the county," Youngblood said.

DNA Collection Hampered

Proposition 47 is responsible for a drastic reduction in the number of DNA samples being collected for analysis. "DNA is the greatest tool ever given to law enforcement to find the guilty and exonerate the innocent," District Attorney Schubert said. Schubert started the Sacramento County cold case unit in 2002, leading to dozens of criminals being charged, prosecuted, and convicted using DNA. "There is a statistically high correlation between drug crimes, theft crimes, and violent crimes," Schubert added. DNA matches have solved many crimes, including those by "low-level" crime suspects, often linked to past violent crimes. Schubert said prior to passage of Prop 47, the California Department of Justice statistics showed police submitting fifteen thousand DNA samples each month to the state for analysis. "Now, the state receives only about five thousand DNA samples a month."

"Recidivism" Redefined Hampers Record Keeping

The California Department of Corrections and Rehabilitation reports that 75 percent of recidivists commit their reentry crime *within a year* of release. With AB 109 and Prop 47 statistics potentially exploding with recidivist offenders, the legislature passed a bill authorizing the Board of State and Community Corrections to redefine "recidivism" in an obvious effort to manipulate recidivism statistics.

Assembly Bill 1050 by Democratic Assemblyman Roger Dickinson ordered the BSCC in 2013 to "develop definitions of key terms, including, but not limited to, 'recidivism,' 'average daily population,' 'treatment program completion rates,' and any other terms deemed relevant…."

The BSCC's new definition of *recidivism* is defined as "conviction" of a new felony or misdemeanor committed *within three years* of release from custody or committed within three years of placement on supervision for a previous criminal conviction. District Attorney Schubert said the previous definition of *recidivism* was "arrests" rather than "convictions," and it was *within one year*, not three years.

Sheriff Jones said the attorney general and BSCC have different definitions of *recidivism*. "There is no meaningful way for me to show recidivism rates now," Jones said.

Prop 47 Bankrolled by Billionaire George Soros

Why did a New York billionaire contribute millions to pass Prop 47? "The biggest chunk of Proposition 47 funding came from New York hedge fund billionaire George Soros, whose Open Society Foundation contributed $1.4 million directly," the *Los Angeles Times* reported in 2015.[64] But this wasn't reported until after the election. "An Open Society spokesperson acknowledged to the *Times* that one month before Election Day, the Soros foundation made a $50 million grant to the American Civil Liberties Union. The ACLU gave $3.5 million to the Proposition 47 campaign in the weeks before the election. The Soros grant will not be publicly disclosed until the organization's federal tax filings are due more than a year from now."

Opponents of Prop 47 spent a total of $550,000, with most of it raised from law enforcement groups.

Possible Legislative Solutions

Several members of the California Legislature have authored bills to try and undo the worst aspects of Prop 47.

- Senate Bill 333 and Assembly Bill 46 would allow felony charges to be filed against suspects accused of having certain date-rape drugs. Proposition 47 reduced the personal use of most illegal drugs to misdemeanors.
- Assembly Bill 390 would require persons convicted of specified misdemeanors to provide DNA samples. California law requires only individuals convicted of felonies to provide DNA samples. Proposition 47 reduced a number of felonies to misdemeanors.

- Assembly Bill 150 would make stealing a gun a felony crime. Proposition 47 made stealing an item that is valued at less than $950 a misdemeanor. Therefore, stealing a gun valued at less than $950 would be a misdemeanor.
- Assembly Bill 1104 would allow the issuance of search warrants for misdemeanor crimes that were previously classified as felonies before Proposition 47's passage.

Released Inmates Back in Custody

There is little data showing recidivism rates yet, and what's reported may not ever reflect real recidivism rates due to the redefinition of *recidivist*. Yet plenty of inmates have been released. A few days after Prop 47 passed, the Sacramento sheriff warned that as many as 420 inmates could be released immediately from his county jail system alone,[65] and KCRA News in Sacramento followed-up with a report of hundreds of criminals being released from jail within a week of passage of the law, angering victim's rights advocates, including 39 criminals released from Yolo county jail, 60 from Stanislaus county jails and up to 50 from Sacramento county jails. Ten thousand criminals were estimated to be released soon under the law, according to the report.[66]

In March 2015, KCRA News in Sacramento did another report on whether inmates released under Proposition 47 ended up back in custody.[67] The news site noted the following:

- In Placer County, 28 inmates have been released since November 2014, and four ended up back in custody. Thus, 14 percent of those released ended up back in custody.
- In Stanislaus County, a total of 127 inmates have been released and twelve ended up back in custody. That is a 9 percent return rate.
- In Sacramento County, 42 inmates have been released and 25 are back in custody. In other words, 60 percent ended up back in custody.

Where Do We Go from Here?

"Only time will tell," said Nick Warner with the Sheriffs Association about realignment and Prop. 47. Others interviewed echoed his sentiments.

A 2012 PPIC report evaluating the effects of realignment on public safety concluded, "If all goes well, California will serve as an example to the rest of the nation on how to reduce the prison population in a manner that maintains public safety." But all is not going well. The PPIC said "the research community must have access to timely and accurate data if it is to provide reliable and sound evaluations of realignment." Yet current data is not readily available. The California Department of Corrections and Rehabilitation has data only from 2013. Some of the counties are able to compile data, but not all. And with recidivism having been redefined, data will be skewed.

Joan Petersilia, Stanford professor and co-director of the Stanford Criminal Justice Center, offered several recommendations:

- Create a statewide tracking database for offenders under probation supervision in the counties.
- Allow an offender's criminal history to be considered when determining whether the county or state will supervise a parolee.
- Cap county jail sentences at three years.
- Impose a prison sentence for certain repeated technical violations. Currently, violators are sent only to county jail.

Petersilia concluded: "Without consistent, honest evaluation of the progress and problems by those guiding the ship, realignment will crash against the rocks, just another failed correctional initiative run aground."[68]

About the Author: Katy Grimes

Katy Grimes is an investigative journalist, senior correspondent with the FlashReport.org, and senior media fellow with the Energy and Environmental

Institute. A longtime political analyst, she has written for the *Sacramento Union,* the *Washington Examiner,* CalWatchdog.org, the *San Francisco Examiner,* the *Business Journal, E&E Legal,* and the *Sacramento Bee,* and can be heard regularly on many talk radio shows.

Four

INCOME INEQUALITY

By James V. Lacy

O n the surface, California's economy is booming. The state's unemployment rate in May 2015 was an impressive 6.4 percent—one of the lowest rates in seven years. Our employed population is helping refill state coffers.
After years of chronic budget deficits, state lawmakers had to figure out how
to spend a surplus in 2015. Of course, it never crossed lawmakers' minds to
refund state taxpayers, especially the state's struggling and diminishing middle class, for the surplus collected by Gov. Jerry Brown's multibillion-dollar
Proposition 30 tax increases, approved narrowly by voters in 2012. In 1987,
Republican governor George Deukmejian returned $1.0 billion in state sur-
plus in the form of rebates to California taxpayers.

Instead, California politicians went on a spending spree—approving a
$167.5 billion total spending plan. State government spent an extra $6.0 billion on K-12 education, compared to last year. It froze tuition rates at all
University of California campuses and established a new special earned income tax credit. From his initial budget proposal in January to the May revise,
Governor Brown increased spending by an extra $2.0 billion.

"I can say very simply the state is definitely on the rebound from just a
few years ago, when the state was mired in red ink," Governor Brown tri-
umphantly proclaimed. "The finances of California have stabilized, we are

balancing our budget, and just since January, several billion dollars have come into the state treasury."[69]

In fact, Brown used his reelection campaign as an opportunity to herald the new "California comeback." This reelection theme may have worked in appealing to the state's elite members of public employee unions, but in reality, California continues to be a state of extreme poverty. According to the official poverty rate released by the US Census Bureau, California has 6.1 million people, or 16 percent of our population, living in poverty. That's if you use the official rate.

Last October, the Census Bureau released an updated poverty figure under its more accurate supplemental poverty rate. This calculation is considered by economists to be more accurate because it factors in taxes, government benefits, and day-to-day costs such as child care. By this more accurate calculation, California had the highest poverty rate in the nation, with nearly one in four state residents living in poverty. The raw numbers are astounding: approximately 8.9 million Californians live in poverty.[70] That poverty level has been virtually unchanged since the Census Bureau began using its updated supplemental poverty calculation.

The reality is that California has become a Dickensian tale of two cities. Rich liberal elites rule the state, while the middle class is either driven out of state or further into poverty. An analysis by the nonprofit California Budget and Policy Center found that middle-income earners have seen their inflation-adjusted wages remain virtually unchanged since before the Great Recession. The median worker in California earns less than $20 per hour, a paltry $39,800 per year, according to the analysis by the California Budget and Policy Center.

"Typically you've seen the middle class as the key to economic mobility, a way to climb the economic ladder," Luke Reidenbach, a policy analyst at the California Budget and Policy Center, told the *Los Angeles Times*. "They are feeling a very specific pinch right now."[71]

Californians want state officials to address the issue of income inequality. According to a recent survey by the nonpartisan Public Policy Institute of California, 72 percent of Californians are concerned about the growing gap between the rich and the poor. In comparing the state's results to the national average, Californians are more likely to believe that things are getting worse.[72]

The middle class no longer exists in the Bay Area. A recent study by a Bay Area consulting group examined the region's income inequality. The top 20 percent of households make $263,000 more than the poorest 20 percent of households. "The Bay Area has the greatest loss of households in the middle-income ranges, which is $35,000 to $150,000," said one economic expert. The Bay Area's middle class is disappearing as a result of the high cost of living, which forces people to leave the area. "Technology has made it where companies no longer need a secretary or administrative assistant or clerk," one consultant explained. "Many of the support positions are gone."[73]

Public Employees and Real Income Inequality

While these middle class private sector workers have been squeezed by higher taxes and higher housing prices, public employees have reaped the benefits of electing liberal Democrats to state and local offices. The problem of income inequality is most apparent in the Bay Area. Average citizens must struggle with daily muggings and outrageously brazen criminal acts, while public employees live like kings. In February 2014, an *Oakland Tribune* photographer was robbed at gunpoint at 11:25 in the morning while on assignment in West Oakland.[74] It wasn't the first time that an *Oakland Tribune* photographer had been robbed. It's become common for photographers and camera crews to be attacked. As recently as this March, two people were robbed while filming a music video in Oakland.

Oakland is one of the poorest cities in California, but its local governments offer public employee union jobs that pay such high salaries that they alone could be the focus of an income inequality debate among student activists at nearby UC Berkeley. Then again, these public employee unions might not even find support among their liberal friends at Berkeley. A recent study by the university found that Oakland spends a greater percentage of its budget on public safety compared to cities of a similar size and crime rate. It is unable to make any progress on its crime rate because the city spends more money than other cities but gets less. Oakland police officers are among the highest paid in the nation, according to research from UC Berkeley.[75]

In a city with one of the highest crime rates in the nation, it might not be a surprise that because of higher risks, police officers would be well-paid. But Oakland police officers are not the exception to the rule in Oakland. The highest paid worker at Oakland City Hall is surely not a police officer, and receives a lot more, in fact, a whopping $436,000 in salary and benefits. A 2012 compensation analysis by the Bay Area News Group found ten employees making more than $318,000 per year in total compensation. These salaries are often a case of egregious payouts and special perks. One civil engineer received a base salary of $70,330, which ballooned to $435,686 through extra perks and payouts. In total, 279,017 Bay Area government employees earned $17.6 billion in total compensation in 2012, for an average government salary of more than $63,000.[76]

A Bay Area Rapid Transit District employee who operates the train maintenance yard in Oakland made $271,000 in 2012, which is more than the chief justice of the US Supreme Court is paid. When city electrical workers went on strike, their public employee union representative told the press "the working class in Northern California are mad as hell, and we're not going to take it anymore." What the union representative didn't tell the press was that the electrical workers were already making an average salary and benefits package of $133,825 per year, much more than the average salary in California, and far exceeding the average real "working class" salary of $30,672 in Oakland, where tens of thousands of people live in poverty. Of course, all of this is at public expense, doubly adding to the inequality problem.

BART Workers: Highest Compensation in the Country

To understand the dual worlds between the public employee "haves" and the dwindling middle-class taxpaying "have-nots," check out the outrageous salaries and benefits for employees of the Bay Area Rapid Transit, known simply as BART. The transit system, which serves the San Francisco Bay Area, has watched as employees have driven up costs to an unmanageable and unsustainable level.

An independent review of more than two dozen Bay Area government agencies found that BART workers received the highest average pay for government employees in the region. But BART transit workers weren't just the best paid in the region. According to the *San Jose Mercury News*, "BART employees also topped the list of the highest-paid transit operators in California."[77] Despite their high pay, BART workers twice went on strike during contentious contract negotiations in 2013.

"We're scrimping by, and sometimes the public treats us like we're above everybody else," one BART employee said in justification of the 2013 strike. "We're not the 1 percenters." The facts about BART salaries and benefits prove the opposite. Just look at the outrageous salaries from 2012, the year prior to the union going on strike.

- The highest paid BART train operators made more than $155,000 per year.
- The highest paid BART electrician made $149,957 per year.
- The highest paid BART janitor made $82,752 per year.
- The average blue-collar BART worker received a salary of $76,551.[78]

During the 2013 contract negotiations, BART administrators offered to raise these salaries even higher. One of their early proposals included a salary increase of between 5 percent and 8 percent, which was rebuffed by the labor union. Instead, the union countered with a demand for a 20 percent salary increase phased in over the next three years. If you aren't angry about the outrageous salaries, let me add two more relevant facts. First, BART employees, under their old contract, had been contributing nothing to their lucrative public employee pensions. Second, BART employees were paying just $92 out of their monthly paycheck toward their first-rate health care benefits.

At the time of the contract dispute, the transit system had little difficulty finding employees to fill those well-compensated positions. BART union workers rarely left their jobs, and when they did, more than enough people applied to fill those vacant positions. A review of BART job application information found that in one span from 2007 to 2013, there were sixty-five thousand job applications for just eighteen hundred line-level union positions.[79]

"I don't know if it's an urban myth or just a saying that the BART contract is held up in union halls around the county as the gold standard," BART spokeswoman Alicia Trost said. "We have to bring our compensation packages more in line with what others have. Years of protecting the employees have caught up with us."[80]

What BART employees lacked in the moral high ground during contract negotiations, they more than made up for with political leverage. In contrast to the rest of the state, the Bay Area has grown dependent on public transportation. "(BART unions) have a degree of leverage from a strike perspective that many other industries don't, and this is a classic example of them capitalizing on it," one economics consultant told the *San Jose Mercury News*. "If you ask me, it's a tiny bit short of blackmail: 'Give me the money or the commute's going to get it.' "

Shrewd negotiators, BART workers walked out on their jobs twice during negotiations—effectively grinding the nation's fifth largest commuter rail system to a halt. The strikes stranded roughly two hundred thousand people, or the 5 percent of Bay Area commuters who rely on the transportation system to get around town. BART management was in no position to negotiate. It caved after a tragic accident during the second strike, when two workers were killed when a trainee was operating a train.

The new contract mirrored all of the union's demands. On salaries, BART workers received a 16.4 percent pay increase over four years. That pay hike doesn't include an annual $1,000 bonus tied to ridership levels.[81] Management's attempts to contain rising health care costs yielded an insignificant but face-saving concession. The new contract required workers to pay an extra $37 per month of their health insurance. Perhaps the only area in which management made minor progress was on pensions. Workers are now forced to pay a portion of their retirement for the first time. That contribution will peak at 4.0 percent in 2017, the final year of the new contract agreement.

It is estimated that the BART strikes cost the Bay Area $73 million per day in lost worker productivity.[82] "Mass transit strikes take a huge economic and environmental toll, not including the disruption and inconvenience they cause for hundreds of thousands of commuters," said Jim Wunderman, the president and CEO of the Bay Area Council, a liberal business advocacy group. "Holding the public hostage over a contract dispute is unfair, unreasonable, and unnecessary. We need to find a better way to resolve BART contract disputes." Is there any doubt about who paid the most for the BART strike? Many Bay Area tech workers ride on company buses to work every day. Other wealthy Bay Area residents, who may have been inconvenienced by more cars of the road, still drove to work or used alternative forms of private transportation services. The people who were left without any options were the poor and working classes that still had to get to their jobs.

GOP Lawmaker's Attempt to Reform Broken Strike System

If there's any consolation from the 2013 BART strikes, it's that the Bay Area residents responded by acknowledging the power of the labor unions. For the first time in decades, a Republican candidate won a Bay Area seat in the state legislature. During her campaign, Catharine Baker promised to introduce legislation to address the BART strike. Other GOP lawmakers have previously tried to ban or limit the power of transit workers to strike. Baker's bill wisely chose an even more narrow change to close a loophole.

During the 2013 BART strike, when the contract expired, management honored the expired contract, which included a no-strike clause. Workers cashed their paychecks but chose to ignore the no-strike clause, effectively cherry-picking portions of the contract to abide by. Assembly Bill 528 would prohibit BART employees from engaging in a strike or work stoppage after the contract has expired if the transit district board maintains the compensation and benefit provisions of an expired contract and an employee or employee organization has agreed to a provision prohibiting strikes in the expired contract.

"This is a very different and unique approach to preventing future BART strikes," Baker said in explanation of her proposal. "This approach is fair to workers, riders, and the general public, who rely so heavily on our mass transit system." The bill didn't get very far—it was postponed by a legislative committee without a vote.

San Francisco Firefighters Exploit Overtime

Across the bay, liberal San Francisco is no better at addressing income inequality between private sector workers and the public employee ruling class. Nearly fifty employees earned more than the San Francisco mayor, whose salary of more than $270,000 is greater than the governor's. How can the top elected executive manage his or her subordinates when scores of employees cash bigger paychecks and have guaranteed civil service protection? Elected officials come and go, but bureaucrats last forever.

A review by the *San Francisco Chronicle* in 2013 found that most of the top earners "got there through overtime or massive payouts of accrued time off upon retirement, with much of that going to fire and police brass." Oh, and that was an improvement. "The overtime has come down from the peak, which was five years ago," a deputy city controller told the newspaper.

Despite supposed improvements in curtailing the abuse of overtime by city officials, San Francisco firefighters managed to abuse the system. Rank and file firefighters were merely following the example of the top leadership. One battalion chief earned a staggering $393,430 before he retired. His base salary was just $158,000, but he managed to double his take-home pay with overtime and other payouts. The majority of top overtime abusers in the City of San Francisco were found in the fire department. Firefighters can commonly earn more in overtime than their base pay. This overtime abuse occurs despite a rule limiting overtime to no more than 633 hours per employee. If there is a cap on overtime, how are employees clearing incredible salaries? A loophole allows firefighters to exceed the cap if they are volunteering for unfilled shifts.[83] Naturally, firefighters in San Francisco have an incentive to collectively "refuse" overtime in order to exceed the restriction.

One San Francisco firefighter received $191,172 in overtime, despite a base salary of $131,101, and cleared a total of $343,730. In fact, more than ten thousand employees in San Francisco earn six-figure salaries. More than a third of the city's workforce earns at least $100,000 in total compensation. The new elite are the eighty-four employees that earn in excess of $250,000 each year in total compensation.[84]

Los Angeles: Different Positions, Same Public Employee Elite

The Bay Area's higher overall cost of living makes it easy to show the excessive and outrageous salaries paid to government employees. However, the same abuse of taxpayer funds is occurring in Southern California, albeit with different positions. A meager clerk typist for the City of Los Angeles earned more than $300,000 in 2012. You would be hard pressed to ever justify a typist earning such an extravagant salary. Los Angeles officials could not even try to explain the excessive compensation because personnel laws, written by public employee unions, protect the worker from any degree of scrutiny. Media outlets were unable to identify the individual by name. The city couldn't explain why the salary total was so high, other than the breakdown of $53,000 in regular pay with an additional $249,000 paid out in the form of special compensation. The best explanation came after a local television news station asked tough questions. According to the Los Angeles affiliate for NBC News:

> According to an assistant to the city controller, the typist's seemingly disproportionate pay was likely the result of back pay plus interest. A typical scenario for back pay would be when an employee is fired,

then wins [his or her] job back and is awarded pay for the time [he or she was] gone.[85]

Surprisingly (or perhaps not surprisingly for those who closely follow government pay scandals), the typing clerk was not the best-paid employee of the City of Los Angeles that year. That honor went to a police detective who more than tripled his $104,000 salary with special payouts.[86]

Los Angeles Pilots Steer for $374,000 a Year While Long Beach Profits

The most elite group of public employees who have landed the highest-paying jobs in Los Angeles spend most of their time at sea. Port pilots guide cargo and container ships into and out of the port of Los Angeles. As a result of a deluge of Chinese and other imports, the port is the busiest in the Western Hemisphere, moving more than $1.2 billion in cargo every day. Pilots have big-time leverage to grind all traffic in the port to a halt. Under their contract, they get three-day weekends, twenty-seven vacation days, and an average salary of $323,000 per year.

The port pilots have developed a novel approach to preserving their sweetheart deals. Private shipping companies pick up the tab for their high salaries through piloting fees. "The harbor guides make more than commercial airline pilots and air-traffic controllers," Bloomberg News noted in a report on the port pilot pay problem, "and their 'monopoly-like system' is a drain on the economy." By law, ship captains must use a local port pilot to navigate them through the port. That's routine throughout the world. Los Angeles is unique in making the port pilots government employees. Efforts to privatize port pilots have repeatedly been stifled by the labor unions. Unions are simply protecting their interests. Since port pilots joined their current union, the minimum salary for a port pilot has more than doubled, rising from $102,000 to $227,000.[87]

Page Six.

Senator's husband stands to profit big from government deal

By Richard Johnson   January 16, 2015 | 5:48pm

California's Rich Liberal Democratic Politicians
The *New York* Post covers US senator Dianne Feinstein's controversial deal

California's income inequality problems are the cause du jour of liberal Democrats. "I'm going to say something, and it's probably going to get me in trouble, but there are some people who are just too rich," the secretary of the California Democratic Party recently said. "If we don't solve the problem of income inequality, we will lose our souls and we will lose our republic."[88] Extreme wealth redistributionist views by party officials have inspired mainstream Democratic politicians to fall in line and repeat liberal income inequality talking points.

When the clothing company Gap announced plans to raise the minimum hourly wage paid to its workers, California's senior US senator, Dianne Feinstein, used it as an opportunity to lament the country's income inequality. "I have spoken to women in Los Angeles with two children who work two minimum wage jobs just to rent an apartment and put food on the table—and yet still remain at or below the poverty line," Feinstein said in a press statement. "This income inequality threatens to undermine the fundamental fairness and stability of our economy and will impact future generations."[89]

If income inequality is fundamentally unfair, why hasn't the distinguished representative from California handed over her millions to the impoverished quarter of the state? Liberals are often the wealthiest and most elite. In 2012, there were more Democrats on the list of the top ten richest members of Congress.[90] Coming in at number nine: US senator Dianne Feinstein.

Feinstein and her Bay Area colleague, House Minority Leader Nancy Pelosi, are among the wealthiest members of Congress. Their combined net worth exceeded $68 million, as of 2012.[91] Feinstein has accumulated at least $42 million in assets as a result of government contracts bestowed to her husband, Richard Blum. The president and CEO of a private equity firm, Blum runs a company that is set to earn more than $1 billion in commissions from the US Postal Service's decision to sell dozens of buildings.[92] Inexplicably, Feinstein continues to take her taxpayer-funded pensions from her days as a member of the San Francisco City Council and County Board of Supervisors.

Why Income Inequality Is a One-Sided Issue

Given the rank hypocrisy by California liberals on the issue of income inequality, the question remains: Why have conservatives failed to capitalize on the issue? For starters, there is an inherent bias in the mainstream media to demonize any Republican who attempts to address the issue. When California's failed gubernatorial candidate Neel Kashkari spent a week living on the streets of Fresno as a homeless person, the media framed the story as a media stunt. It surely was; Kashkari acknowledged it as such. Yet Democrats who have performed similar actions have been heralded for their courage. In 2013, UnitedNY and the New York Community for Change, two Far Left advocacy groups, convinced New York Mayor Bill de Blasio and seven of his colleagues to live on minimum wage. That same year, the liberals at Think Progress applauded as twenty-six members of Congress lived on food stamps to protest cuts to the federal food stamps program. When Democrats do it, the action is framed as the "SNAP challenge."

The media bias against Republicans and in favor of Democrats will continue. Republicans must press forward in the face of this bias in order to reframe the issue as income inequality created by public employee unions. Every time Democrats raise the issue, Republicans should cite the outrageous examples of government employees receiving pay that is comparable with Wall Street bankers. This income inequality is indefensible given that the poorest California citizens are paying their sales taxes as a result of the Democrats' Proposition 30 tax increases.

About the Author: James V. Lacy

James V. Lacy is a frequent guest on Fox Business News Channel's *Varney & Company* and is the author of *Taxifornia: Liberals' Laboratory to Bankrupt America*, a Politico.com best seller. An attorney, Jim has been recognized by the American Association of Political Consultants with their "Pollie Award" for his work in election campaigns. Jim's law firm, Wewer and Lacy, LLP, represents advocacy organizations, political action committees, and initiative committees. Jim also owns, with his wife, Janice, Landslide Communications, Inc., which is the largest publisher of election slate mail in California, producing fourteen million pieces of mail in the 2014 elections.

Five

Education

By Chris Reed

When Jerry Brown ran for a third term as governor in 2010, nearly three decades after his first two terms, members of the California Teachers Association and the California Federation of Teachers weren't really sure what to expect.

While Brown sought and welcomed the unions' campaign support and had been helpful to them while executing his official duties as state attorney general the previous four years, he tangled with unions over control of the school board while mayor of Oakland from 1999 to 2007. He won a showdown with the CTA and blocked unionization of charter schools. Given Brown's long history as an iconoclast, there was a fear that he would embrace the education reform platform touted by President Barack Obama and Education Secretary Arne Duncan and shaped by think tanks funded by billionaire philanthropists, starting with Bill Gates.

But as Brown moves through the first year of his fourth term, any CTA or CFT apprehension looks silly in retrospect. The governor has either orchestrated or encouraged a series of tax and fiscal maneuvers that prop up funding for teacher compensation. He passed a historic bailout of the California State Teachers' Retirement System on terms that were vastly more generous to teachers than other public employees.[93] He looked the other way as school district after school district diverted funds meant to directly help struggling minority students to teacher compensation—even though he had declared in one of his major policy addresses that helping such students was the most important challenge facing California.

Not only did Brown not execute a Nixon-goes-to-China maneuver on public education in the Golden State—a bold move he was uniquely poised to undertake—the governor has gone the other way, acting on several fronts to further entrench the teacher unions' power.

All this was foreshadowed by his first week on the job. His seven new appointees to the State Board of Education, including Patricia Ann Rucker, the CTA's legislative counsel, all opposed Obama-style reforms.

With Brown as a silent partner, the state education board and newly elected State Superintendent of Instruction Tom Torlakson quickly disavowed the reform agenda of the Schwarzenegger administration. Brown also scrapped the secretary of education position in his cabinet that traditionally had been a counterweight to the superintendent of public instruction. His goal, he said, was to speak with one voice on education—indicating barely a whit of differences with Torlakson, the former Bay Area math teacher whose rise to power had been orchestrated by the CTA and CFT.[94]

Four and a half years later: mission accomplished.

On the issue of teacher job protections, the appalling case of Mark Berndt illustrates that Brown ultimately will do whatever the unions want—they just have to give him adequate cover. Berndt is the teacher at Miramonte Elementary School in south Los Angeles who was discovered in 2011 to have been feeding sperm-laden food to the impoverished Latino students who made up his third-grade class. In 2013, Berndt pleaded no contest to twenty-three counts of lewd acts with children.

But the fact that Los Angeles Unified School District officials concluded they couldn't summarily fire Berndt even while having strong evidence of his grotesque crimes struck a nerve. Public anger grew even more when it was disclosed that LAUSD had paid him $40,000 to quit.[95]

This led to teacher-discipline measures being taken up by the legislature in 2012 and 2013. But the bills supported by union-allied Democratic lawmakers—the only measures with a chance of passage—actually made it more difficult to fire bad teachers and did little to streamline discipline. Brown's aides made clear he could never sign measures widely seen in the media as fake reforms.

When Brown finally did sign a teacher-discipline bill in 2014, it was only after a public-relations campaign that led the public and much of the media to believe it was much tougher than it actually was. Instead, it actually expanded protections for teachers accused of criminal conduct.

A *Contra Costa Times* editorial provided one of the few clear explanations of how the law made teacher discipline even more difficult: It "starts to extend criminal due process protections to teacher employment cases, even though courts have previously correctly said that the same standards should not apply. In a court of law, for example, a criminal defendant can remain silent. But in the workplace, and in discipline cases, a worker is expected to explain his or her actions."

Teachers credibly accused of sexual abuse of students, child abuse, or drug trafficking became easier to dismiss. But the law bans any history of violence from being considered when new misconduct is alleged and requires that teachers who are suspected of crimes as serious as murder be allowed to teach until they are formally charged with a criminal offense.

In the case of the Stull Act, Brown's defense of teachers was in a different vein: choosing to ignore a plainly written 1971 state law requiring that student performance be part of teacher evaluations, even after a judge admonished the state's largest school district.

In 2012, in the *Doe v. Deasy* case, Los Angeles Superior Court Judge James Chalfant ruled that a provision in the LAUSD's contract with United Teachers Los Angeles violated the Stull Act. The passage specifically banned the consideration of student performance in evaluating teachers. "[P]arties may not enter into a contract that violates a statutory law," the ruling observed.

But while LAUSD and UTLA have negotiated new terms on teacher evaluations that the UTLA depicts as concessions, there is little evidence that student performance is actually considered by Los Angeles administrators in granting evaluations, which remain overwhelmingly positive. And Superintendent John Deasy, far too independent for the UTLA's taste, was forced out in 2014. Deasy's testimony in the case was so critical of the status quo that many observers believed he wanted his district to lose the case so he could finally have meaningful teacher evaluations.

The Chalfant decision was ignored statewide. A January 2015 report issued by EdVoice, the reform group that assisted with the lawsuit that Chalfant ruled on, found "too many districts with little or no demonstration in official district documents of complying with critical commonsense and mandatory provisions of the Stull Act."[96]

This amounts to nullification of an important state law—a gift from union-friendly local and state officials to the CTA and CFT.

But as brazen as this was, it wasn't the most outrageously favorable treatment provided teachers in the latest Brown era in Sacramento. That came from a brief filed with Chalfant by the California Public Employment Relations Board after the board was taken over in May 2011 by a union faction appointed by the governor. The brief argued the Stull Act didn't apply to LAUSD because it hadn't been collectively bargained with the UTLA. But teachers were given collective bargaining rights only in 1975. This means it is the position of the Brown administration that laws passed before 1975 affecting public schools are not valid until after they've been subject to collective bargaining between local school districts and their CTA or CFT affiliates. The radicalness of that view is difficult to exaggerate.

When it comes to teacher pay and compensation, the Brown administration has acted in similarly extreme fashion. In early 2012, the governor, Democratic lawmakers, and union strategists came up with a plan to pass a 2012–2013 budget that would only pencil out if voters approved billions of dollars in higher taxes. Because of laws protecting teacher jobs during a school year, districts would be thrown into chaos without new revenue. Privately, even Democratic strategists conceded this bordered on voter extortion.

After a campaign emphasizing the grim fate of schools without more funding, voters by 55 percent to 45 percent approved Proposition 30 in November 2012. It imposed much higher income taxes on the very wealthy for seven years, retroactively to January 1, 2012, and higher sales taxes on everyone for four years—generating more than $6 billion in fiscal 2012–13.

Contrary to promises made in tens of millions of dollars of TV campaign ads, in most districts, the new revenue went at least as much to pay raises as to restoring classroom programs shuttered during the state's 2008–2011 revenue recession. This was exactly what Arun Ramanathan, then head of the Education Trust-West reform group, had predicted in early 2012.

In 2014, the governor took an extraordinary new step to protect and increase teacher compensation. To win teacher unions' support for his ballot measure establishing a state rainy-day fund, the measure included a provision that put a hard cap on how much money most school districts could keep in reserve—6 percent of the operating budget.

In its low-key way, the nonpartisan state Legislative Analyst's Office called this baffling. "Less stability in academic programs, increased fiscal distress, and higher borrowing costs all are notable risks associated with lower levels of reserves," the LAO noted in a January 2015 report.[97]

But unions' desire to make sure operating budgets were better able to accommodate their pay demands trumped elemental common sense—with the help of Brown, who for years has touted support of school "subsidiarity," his fancy term for local control.

Astonishingly, that wasn't even Brown's splashiest 2014 move to boost teachers' compensation. That came when he gave his blessing to a bailout of the California State Teachers' Retirement System that went directly against the core principle of his 2012 pension reform measure.

That principle committed the state to a long-term approach in which, going forward, government agencies and new hires would roughly share the "normal cost" of their pensions—the cost of funding benefits accruing in a given year. This approach has long been advocated by reformers because it creates incentives for public employees to accept cheaper hybrid programs in which they get less generous pensions but bigger paychecks because less money is deducted for pension costs.

But a split-the-cost approach was never seriously considered in CalSTRS talks. The bailout, phased in through annual rate increases that end in fiscal 2020–21, is expected to generate about $5 billion a year. Of that extra funding, only 10 percent is covered by teacher contributions. Taxpayers will pick up 90 percent of the tab—20 percent directly through payments from the state budget and 70 percent indirectly through the budgets of school districts, which are funded by the state government.

Further illustrating the perversity of the cap on district reserves, superintendents and school boards can't put money aside to help deal with this jolt. Barring an unprecedented long-term surge in revenue, in coming years, the state will eventually either need to cut general school spending to pay for the CalSTRS bailout (unlikely, given CTA and CFT clout); cut other state spending (likely); or seek to make the 2012 tax hikes permanent (very likely).

But as bald as these union-boosting power plays are, they can be seen as understandable for a pragmatic Democratic governor in a state in which dozens of lawmakers never vote, even once, against the CTA-CFT agenda.

What the governor is doing with his ballyhooed education reform of 2013, however, carries other dimensions—moral and ethical ones. What Brown sold as a "revolutionary" attempt to get more state resources directly to the millions of struggling, mostly minority students is being openly hijacked.

Under the Local Control Funding Formula, districts received extra state funding based on the number of students who were English learners, were impoverished, or were foster children. The LCFF measure also reduced state mandates on programs that districts must offer to give districts more flexibility to—in theory—help the students who most need help if they are to become productive citizens.[98]

"Growing up in Compton or Richmond is not like it is to grow up in Los Gatos or Beverly Hills or Piedmont," Brown told reporters while lobbying the legislature to approve his plan. "It is controversial, but it is right, and it's fair."

This fit in with his repeated comments about the urgent need to improve the education of Latino students, who now make up a majority of California's K-12 students.

But the high point of this seemingly bold reform came the day it was signed in July 2013. The Brown administration didn't take a hard line when the State Board of Education crafted LCFF guidelines on how the funds could be spent.

Two years later, it appears plain that the primary goal of the LCFF was to provide a large, unfettered source of new money available for teacher raises—especially in Los Angeles Unified, which got the most new dollars because of its concentration of struggling students.

This was made explicit in July 2013, when the *Los Angeles Daily News* reported that UTLA officials defended their request for a one-time, 17.6 percent raise by citing all the new money available because of the LCFF. The UTLA ended up winning a two-year, 10.0 percent raise—an agreement that poses huge long-term fiscal headaches because of the enormous cost of the CalSTRS bailout.

Meanwhile, in January 2015, the Legislative Analyst's Office provided more evidence that the nominal rationale for the Local Control Funding Formula was not the real one. It surveyed fifty California school districts, including the eleven largest, and found not one had adequate safeguards to ensure LCFF dollars were directly helping struggling students.[99]

As with the Stull Act, what the districts and their state overseers are doing amounts to nullification of an important state law.

In January, in a telephone interview the state Finance Department set up with California editorial writers, I got a chance to ask Brown two questions about reports from up and down the state about districts giving substantial raises.

He objected to my use of the term *hijacked* to describe what had happened and depicted my concern as being something theoretical that might someday come to pass. In my follow-up question, I told him anyone with a Nexus account or the ability to do a Google news search would know it wasn't theoretical.

Brown said I was making important points. "I take up your challenge and I'm going to look into it more carefully," he said. The governor has had no more to say on the diversion of LCFF funds since then, at least in public settings, nor has his administration.

The hijacking of Brown's signature reform by teacher unions amounts to a real-time testimonial to the incendiary theory at the heart of the landmark *Vergara v. State of California* lawsuit. It holds that state laws are so rigged to favor teacher interests that they funnel the worst teachers to the poorest schools, denying minority students their constitutional equal-protection rights.

In his June 2014 ruling, Los Angeles Superior Court Judge Rolf Treu accepted the premise. His decision cited the unchallenged evidence that teachers were almost impossible to fire in California public schools, and that laws favoring veteran teachers had led LAUSD to pack its least effective educators into the classrooms that most needed the best teachers.

"All sides to this litigation agree that competent teachers are a critical, if not the most important, component of success of a child's in-school educational experience. All sides also agree that grossly ineffective teachers substantially undermine the ability of that child to succeed in school. Evidence has been elicited in this trial of the specific effect of grossly ineffective teachers on students. The evidence is compelling. Indeed, it shocks the conscience," Treu wrote.[100]

His ruling is on hold pending the state's appeal, which contends that his decision is unsupported by his legal reasoning. Whatever the Brown administration and state Attorney General Kamala Harris do going forward, the decision looks doomed in the long run because of the US Supreme Court's increasing hostility to "disparate impact" theories, which hold that statistical evidence alone of different outcomes for different groups is not de facto evidence of bias.

But the governor's decision to offer only vague comments about improving the tenure system without offering specific reforms speaks volumes about how he uses his considerable political capital. His allegedly overriding concern about struggling, poor minority students in California's public schools is belied by action after action that shows his real priority is protecting the mostly white, middle-class members of the CTA and CFT—whether it's from inconvenient state laws requiring meaningful teacher evaluations, from discipline for bad behavior, or from paying as much toward their pensions as other public employees.

And to add to this stupefyingly cynical record, here's one more insult. In the governor's most quoted remarks on education reform—in a tart message accompanying a veto of a bill on school evaluations—he decried the "siren songs" of flighty reformers who switched from one idea to another, willy-nilly.

Brown's insinuation that education reform in America is a charade with no record of success may have some surface appeal. It's undeniable that some reformers, such as Diane Ravitch, have abandoned the focus on teacher quality to talk more about holding parents accountable. It's also undeniable that the success of some reforms, such as charter schools, has been oversold.

But it is simply not true that education reform is impossible, so why bother? That is particularly the case with minority student performance—the issue Brown insists he cares about the most.

In both conservative Texas and liberal Massachusetts, comprehensive reforms—starting with meaningful teacher tenure policies—have improved test scores and graduation rates for African Americans and Latinos. It's also routine for individual school districts to do better than others with very similar demographics and resources, even in California. The converse is also true. A 2007 book released by the Pacific Research Institute and titled *Not As Good As You Think* showed some affluent school districts badly underperforming in measures of education quality.[101]

Plainly, policies matter, schools can be made better, the status quo is not now and forever ineradicable. But rather than acknowledging this, the governor offers up the nihilistic idea that reform can't work. That is a convenient fiction. It covers up the obvious, amply displayed truth that Brown cares far more about keeping teachers happy than improving schools.

About the Author: Chris Reed

Chris Reed has been an editorial writer for the *San Diego Union-Tribune* since 2005. He's written about California politics for *City Journal*, *National Review Online*, and other media outlets and has done pop culture and political essays for the *American Spectator*. He holds a political science degree from the University of Hawaii at Hilo, where he was editor of the student newspaper.

Six

HIGHER EDUCATION

By John Hrabe

Three years after billionaire entrepreneur Mark Cuban first predicted a meltdown in higher education, the industry is still booming. "Remember the housing meltdown?" Cuban asked. "It's just a matter of time until we see the same meltdown in traditional college education. Like the real estate industry, prices will rise until the market revolts. Then it will be too late."[102]

At the end of 2014, the nation's collective student loan debt totaled $1.16 trillion and still shows no signs of decreasing. In the final quarter of 2014, outstanding student loan balances increased by $31 billion, bringing the total increase in 2014 to $77 billion. Student loan debt is still a fraction of the nation's $8.17 trillion in mortgage debt. However, it's the only debt category that lacks a tangible product.

The numbers are increasing for two reasons: new borrowers being added every day, and a slow repayment rate for existing borrowers. Every year, nine million more Americans join the college debt club by initiating new student loans. According to the New York Federal Reserve Bank's analysis, that's actually a decrease in the number of active borrowers from 2010, when twelve million people initiated loans.[103]

Unsurprisingly, many college graduates, who are facing high unemployment or underemployment, are finding it difficult to repay their loans. The default rate has now stabilized at 3.1 percent per year.[104] That's the short-term default rate. Since college debt cannot be discharged in bankruptcy (except in rare circumstances), the annual default rate is not nearly as revealing as the repayment rate. How many people are paying down their debt? A little more than a third. The New York Federal Reserve notes:

> While 17 percent of borrowers are delinquent, only a little more than a third (37 percent) of all borrowers are making regular payments on schedule. The other nearly half of borrowers are either still in school, in deferral, or in one of the various programs that allow students to avoid delinquency. Importantly, these borrowers are not reducing their balances.[105]

America's Household Debt as of Q4 2014

A 2014 Brookings Institution study found that 75 percent of households spent less than 7 percent of their monthly earnings on student loan repayment, for an average monthly payment of $242.[106] With so few former students[107] repaying their loans, there is little overall progress on the outstanding balances. The 2010 graduating class, among the worst off due to the timing of the Great Recession, has a collective outstanding balance of $71 billion, down just 9 percent from the starting balance of $78 billion.[108]

DEBT	QUARTERLY CHANGE	ANNUAL CHANGE	2014 TOTAL
Mortgage	(+) $39 billion	(+) $121 billion	$8.17 trillion
Student Loan	(+) $31 billion	(+) $77 billion	$1.16 trillion
Auto Loan	(+) $21 billion	(+) $92 billion	$955 billion
Credit Card	(+) $20 billion	(+) $17 billion	$700 billion
HELOC	(-) $2 billion	(-) $19 billion	$510 billion
Total Debt	**(+) $117 billion**	**(+)$306 billion**	**$11.83 trillion**

Even going back ten years—before the student debt explosion—the 2004 graduating class has made marginal progress on their debt. "Under a standard ten-year amortization schedule," the New York Fed notes, "these loans would be approaching full repayment, and only about 10 percent of the original balance would remain."[109] In reality, almost two thirds of the outstanding debt remains.

Despite all of these frightening macrolevel figures, young people continue to sign up for new loans. Cuban explains that, just as with housing, students buy into the concept of "flipping" their debt into a bigger payout. "You borrow as much money as you can for the best school you can get into and afford," the billionaire investor explained, "and then you 'flip' that education for the great job you are going to get when you graduate."[110] Flipping an education is more challenging than flipping a house. Unlike a mortgage, the underlying asset with a college degree is nontransferable. Then again, California students can add housing to their list of problems.

Why California's Student Debt Burden is Worse

It's debatable whether all of these degrees are actually preparing students for the workforce or are merely a socially acceptable period of fun and leisure before entering adulthood. But even students with desired degrees who land good jobs in Silicon Valley cannot make meaningful progress on their debt because it comes with a catch. The high-paying jobs are limited to areas with a higher cost of living.

This is, of course, a national problem. However, the long-term burdens are greater in states, such as California, that have a cost of living that is higher than the national average. Millennials simply can't afford to live anywhere but Mom and Dad's basement. Four of the top ten most unaffordable major markets are in California. "Student loan delinquencies and repayment problems appear to be reducing borrowers' ability to form their own households," points out Donghoon Lee, a research officer at the Federal Reserve Bank of New York.[111]

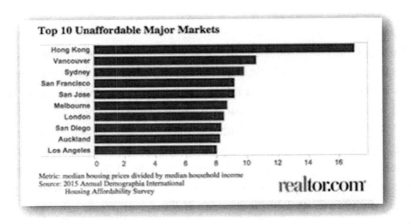

Top 10 Unaffordable Major Markets

Metric: median housing prices divided by median household income
Source: 2015 Annual Demographia International
Housing Affordability Survey

realtor.com

In San Francisco, the average rent in the first quarter of 2015 reached a record high of $3,458 per month, a 13.2 percent increase from the previous year.[112] That figure includes all properties, ranging from tiny studios to spacious three-bedroom townhomes. Even young people willing to live in a shoebox must pay through the nose. A San Francisco studio apartment runs slightly less than $2,000 per month.[113] The high rents have driven people to the greater Bay Area, where rents are also rising. The average rent in the five-county San Francisco metro area, according to the *San Francisco Chronicle*, is $2,370 per month. You'd think that at such high rates, it'd take time to meet demand. The opposite is true. The vacancy rate in San Francisco at the end of 2014 was 3.6 percent. Oakland's vacancy rate was under 3.0 percent.[114] "Property owners get a pricing power that is exceptional when vacancy falls below 5 percent," one California-based real estate analyst explained to *Forbes*. "That's when rent increases accelerate."[115]

People are paying these extortionist rates because that's where the jobs are. The state's job growth, arguably the nation's, has come from Silicon Valley. In August 2014, the Bay Area accounted for half of the state's job growth "The Bay Area not only accounted for half the job gains in the state, it accounted for 15 percent of the job gains nationwide," Michael Bernick, a research fellow with the Milken Institute, told the *San Jose Mercury News*.[116] Yet these high-paying jobs aren't creating long-term wealth.

Millennial Debt Burden: Six-Figure Pauper

Take a young millennial who lands a six-figure job in Silicon Valley. She's made it. She's an elite member of her generation. And even she can't get ahead. Her salary slowly disappears with a morass of high debt service, higher taxes, and the highest cost of living in the nation. After state and federal withholding taxes, let's assume she makes the national average payment of $242 per month on her student loans.[117] Her take-home pay is nearly $5,200 per month.

In Focus: Why a Six-Figure Job Doesn't Build Wealth

Salary	$8,333.33	$100,000.00
--Federal Withholding	$(1,634.51)	$(19,614.13)
--Social Security	$(516.67)	$(6,200.00)
--Medicare	$(120.83)	$(1,450.00)
--CA State Income Tax	$(565.36)	$(6,784.32)
--SDI	$(75.00)	$(900.00)
--Student Loan	$(242.00)	$(2,904.00)
Net Pay	$5,178.96	$62,147.55
--Retirement	$(458.33)	$(5,500.00)
--Restaurants	$(438.71)	$(5,264.52)
--Going Out	$(33.94)	$(407.28)
--Food at Home	$(388.64)	$(4,663.68)
--Car and Gasoline	$(260.00)	$(3,120.00)
--Public Transport and Taxi	$(70.00)	$(840.00)
--Gym Membership	$(67.50)	$(810.00)
--Utilities	$(94.25)	$(1,131.00)
--Clothing and Shoes	$(29.67)	$(356.04)
--Rent	$(2,273.53)	$(27,282.36)
--Other Goods and Services	$(116.93)	$(1,403.16)
--Cell Phone	$(75.00)	$(900.00)
--Vacation	$(200.00)	$(2,400.00)
Down Payment Fund	$672.46	$8,069.51

Using Numbeo, an online cost-of-living calculator, it's easy to see how quickly her paycheck disappears. At the end of the month, she's left with less than $700 of disposable income that could be used for a future down payment on a house. Most Bay Area residents will find these figures ridiculously low. For example, it's hard to imagine anyone in the Bay Area spending less than $34 per month "going out," $400 per month for groceries, and $500 per month eating out.

It will take six years with this model of frugal living to save enough money for a 10.00 percent down payment on the $470,000 median home in Contra Costa County, where she'll no doubt spend additional time on the road commuting. A home in San Francisco or San Jose is decades out of reach. She'll be making student loan payments for nine years and pay $16,500 toward interest at the national interest rate of 4.66 percent.[118] Again, this scenario is the best off—the most elite millennial—who lands the dream job at a tech company. And even she has no room for error, no safety net, no emergency fund.

When she enters the workforce with debt, she's left chasing the highest salary in the most expensive region, which prevents her from building wealth. She certainly can't start a business out of college. This is the new normal as a result of student loan debt: the day they enter the workforce, the American Dream is out of reach for most millennials.

Some conservatives may question why the student loan crisis merits a government solution. "Students agreed to borrow thousands of dollars," a cynical conservative might say. "Repayment—that's their problem." There's just one big problem with that thinking: the federal government is the largest student loan lender. In lieu of a free-market solution to the student loan crisis, more young people will embrace reckless alternatives. "I defaulted on my student loans," one *New York Times* opinion columnist recently wrote. "As difficult as it has been, I've never looked back. The millions of young people today, who collectively owe over $1 trillion in loans, may want to consider my example."[119]

California Educating a Movable Population

In California, the higher education debt problem has a multiplier effect. Higher rents mean more money spent while in college. Consequently, California millennials have more debt out of college, which makes it harder to save for the down payment in what is already a sky-high real estate market compared to the national average. A survey by Wells Fargo found that, after student loan debt, millennials say their top priority would be buying a home. In fact, millennials without debt have ownership rates on par with previous generations at the same stage in life.[120]

California has yet to experience its biggest problem. The state is spending billions educating a population that could move out of state once they earn more money. Jobs in the knowledge-based economy, which are driving California's economy, are inherently vulnerable to outsourcing. There are very few reasons why most new jobs in Silicon Valley couldn't be done from Texas, Tahiti, or Tbilisi. For now, workers in the tech sector seem content with their luxury campuses isolated from the rest of their impoverished state. You have to wonder how much longer it lasts. A person in San Francisco earning $100,000 can live in Austin, Texas, on just $56,560 and experience the same quality of life.[121] After a few years building their Rolodexes and gaining work skills, tech workers have an incentive to hop off the hamster wheel and build a family out of state.

"At some point potential students will realize that they can't flip their student loans for a job in four years," Cuban warned. We still haven't reached the tipping point on the perceived benefits of a college degree. This year's graduating class enters the workforce with an average of $35,000 in student loan debt—the most of any graduating class in American history. The overwhelming majority of students—71 percent—will graduate with some debt.[122] Whether the higher education bubble bursts or slowly deflates, ever-resilient young people will find a way to adapt.

Knowledge has never been more freely available in the history of mankind. Free online universities, YouTube video libraries, and crowd-sourced encyclopedias will continue to educate and inform future generations. Young people, who have never had wealth, can live in cramped dorm rooms and eat Top Ramen. Young people are better positioned to make sacrifices. Young people will start businesses and pursue their big idea.

If the bubble bursts, it's the higher education institutions that will suffer the worst consequences. As Cuban notes, "(Universities) will have so many legacy costs, from tenured professors to construction projects to research, they will be saddled with legacy costs and debt in much the same way the newspaper industry was. Which will all lead to a de-levering and a de-stabilization of the university system as we know it."[123]

Lack of Cooperation in California Higher Education

If colleges are burdened by legacy costs, so are taxpayers. California has three higher education systems: the University of California system, California State University system, and California Community Colleges system. Combined, these colleges teach 2.7 million students every year. One out of every eight college students in the United States is enrolled in a public college or university in California.

Yet, aside from a few transfer agreements between two-year and four-year schools, the state's three systems work in isolation from the others. Instead of cooperation, the systems compete against one another for funding and prestige. All three systems are guilty of an inferiority complex. UC campuses try to improve their national ranking to compete with private universities and Ivy League schools. Cal State universities want to emulate their UC rivals. Even community colleges have begun to mimic their UC and CSU counterparts. Legislation that took effect in 2015 has granted fifteen community colleges the authority to offer four-year degrees in the coming years.[124]

This lack of cooperation among the state's three higher education systems is largely the result of the outdated Master Plan for Higher Education. Created by a special session of the legislature in 1960, the Master Plan for Higher Education established a hierarchy of students for the assembly line economy. The UC system was reserved for the top eighth of high school graduates, who were destined for careers as top managers and professionals. In the next rung, Cal State campuses accepted the top third of high school graduates, with community colleges accepting the rest. Classifying students based on aptitude and standardized testing works well for an industrialized economy. In a world of finite resources, the best professors were intentionally reserved for the best students.

CCSF: Case Study in Higher Education Provincialism

California's split system, which mirrors others throughout the country, encourages a provincialism among campuses, which is exacerbated by accreditation agencies that further inflate the higher education bubble. The state's 112 community colleges are governed by seventy-two elected community college districts. These boards receive little outside oversight and often serve at the pleasure of local unions with a vested interest in the college's decisions. Consequently, candidates run for the college board to gain their own fiefdom for enriching themselves or their political allies.

In 2004, the state took over control of Compton Community College after several cases of wrongdoing, fraud, and misappropriation of public funds by college officials. One former college trustee pleaded guilty to pilfering more than $1 million in public funds by enrolling students in dummy classes. The college lost its accreditation. The state legislature ordered an "extraordinary audit" of the college district. Eventually, the college closed with the neighboring El Camino College District taking over Compton's jurisdiction.[125]

The story of Compton College should have served as a warning sign to other districts. Instead, it was merely a precursor of more problems to come. Only a few years after Compton College closed for good, City College of San Francisco experienced a similar crisis. "This is deja vu all over again," Arthur Fleming, a retired Compton professor, told the *San Francisco Examiner* of the parallels between the two scandals. "It's as if we're replaying the same drama, so far with no difference in the script."[126]

CCSF's problems began after a critical report by the community college accreditation commission. Every six years, all 112 community colleges in California must receive accreditation by the Accrediting Commission for Community and Junior Colleges. After its March 2012 site visit, the accrediting agency issued a scathing report on CCSF's management. That led to the California Community Colleges Chancellor's Office deploying its own Fiscal Crisis and Management Assistance Team to evaluate CCSF.

The chancellor's crisis management team compared CCSF to schools of comparable size and found major disparities.[127] The college employed twice as many tenured faculty members, had substantially more total employees per student, and provided part-time faculty with full-time benefits, all while college enrollment was declining. Over the preceding seven years, faculty salaries increased by 25 percent. According to the state analysts, part-time professors earned an average of $113.51 per hour. It's no wonder that overall expenses at CCSF were $17.00 million more than districts of similar size.

"CCSF has for many years operated based on power, influence, and political whim rather than reason, logic, and fairness," the chancellor's analysts wrote in their report. "Interviewees indicated that CCSF's focus and purpose, which should be serving students, has been lost and is not the basis for decision making. Rather, the emphasis has been on keeping individuals employed and ensuring that they receive benefits."[128]

Outside auditors were most concerned about the long-term financial outlook. Ninety-two percent of CCSF's unrestricted budget was dedicated to employee salaries and benefits. In a decade, CCSF's retiree health benefits payments were slated to double from $6.9 million in fiscal year 2011–12 to $13.0 million annually by 2020–21. The school's unfunded retiree health benefit obligation as of July 2011 was $235 million. "City College of San Francisco (CCSF) has not developed a plan to fund significant liabilities and obligations such as retiree health benefits, adequate reserves, and workers' compensation costs," the management team concluded.

The overwhelming evidence of CCSF's mismanagement led to state intervention. In order to keep the school open and temporarily accredited, the California Community College Board of Governors stripped the elected trustees of all authority and appointed a special trustee to govern the school. Unelected state-level appointees stripped a local elected jurisdiction of its decision-making due to mismanagement. Because faculty unions controlled the outcome of community college board elections, unelected leaders were more capable of acting responsibly.

The special trustee has since helped the school get back on track. CCSF has remained open and accredited. School trustees are slated to regain power this year, but the college still faces reviews until 2017.[129]

Compton College and City College of San Francisco are not anomalies. Buried in the Fiscal Crisis and Management Assistance Team's report was a telling note of how dangerously close other community colleges are to insolvency. CCSF spent 92 percent of its discretionary funds on employee salaries and benefits. Statewide, that figure for most community college districts is 86 percent.[130]

Accrediting Commission Inflates the Bubble

CCSF's problems began with a critical audit by the community college accreditation team. While it may have helped in this instance, the accrediting process is causing its own share of problems in California's higher education systems. Accrediting committees are made up of faculty members and college administrators that have an incentive to preserve the unsustainable status quo.

Anyone can start his or her own college or university. But to get access to state and federal funds, schools must receive accreditation. Neither the state nor federal education departments directly handle accreditation; rather, independent nonprofit entities, often consisting of college professors and administrators, step in to review colleges. That makes the accreditation process an almost quasi-governmental function: the review, which is mandated by law, is frequently guided by public employees, but is formally governed by the guidelines and rules of a private organization.

This nonprofit organization of college bureaucrats evades public scrutiny while enforcing their demands on public colleges. In 2014, the Bureau of State Audits published its audit of the accreditation process, which found an inconsistent application of the accreditation process, few rights for colleges to appeal, and a lack of transparency in accreditation decision making.

Even in the case of the CCSF accreditation report, one of the findings that required a response was the need for CCSF to "revise the college's mission statement." The fate of a public college's accreditation rested on the whims and private deliberations of a private entity of college administrators. CCSF's accreditation ultimately led to litigation, which concluded with Superior Court Judge Curtis Karnow ruling that ACCJC broke the law. Among the court's findings: the committee failed to adequately address conflicts of interest by commissioners, did not include enough academics on its site visit, and violated federal regulations on accreditation.

It would be shortsighted for conservatives to embrace accrediting agencies as the vehicle for holding schools accountable. Conservative-leaning higher education institutions are most vulnerable to the accreditation process. Hillsdale College, a private college in south-central Michigan, has shunned all federal funds—including financial aid and grants—to secure its independence. That independence is currently being threatened by the college accreditation process.

Restructure Higher Education to Prioritize Cooperation

California's higher education problems aren't unique from the rest of the nation, but the state is uniquely positioned to solve this crisis. For starters, California taxpayers have enormous buying power to force changes in the higher education industry. It's time that California restructured its higher education institutions in a way that prioritized cooperation.

One option is a single unified higher education agency—UCLA under the same system and governing board as Chabot Junior College. Our economy is no longer built around a factory worker mentality. We no longer need to isolate the top tier of high school graduates from the community college plebs. Moreover, technology makes it possible to share information among all students for negligible additional cost. UC Berkeley has seven Nobel laureates on its faculty, all of whom are state government employees. The technology exists to make it possible for a community college student in Los Angeles to watch a lecture by a Nobel laureate at UC Berkeley for almost no extra cost to taxpayers. California taxpayers foot the bill for both the community college and UC campus. Why shouldn't the community college student have access to the same course materials, lectures, and videos as the UC student? Part of the problem is structural. Right now, there's no incentive for the UC system to share its Nobel laureates with a Cal State campus or community college, which is under a different bureaucracy that answers to a different board of trustees.

A unified system doesn't require centralization. The state could embrace a regionalized college system, similar to the current community college district model. Under such a system, the local UC and CSU campuses would be transferred under the authority of the state's existing elected college boards. This unified system would allow students to complete coursework at any of the schools under a regional authority.

Regardless of a major structural shift, the California State University and University of California systems should stop teaching all lower division classes. Instead, all lower division general education course work should be required to be completed at a community college. This requirement would break down the elitism currently found in higher education and put the focus on reducing costs.

California's community colleges have their share of warts. Contrary to the faculty union's talking points, not all of the system's problems are owed to budget cuts, poor administration, and Proposition 13. Like all higher education institutions, community colleges are vulnerable to the coming disruption in academia. They're guilty of the mission creep, tenure problems, and fiscal mismanagement that plague all schools. These problems have to be addressed.

Even with its problems, California's community colleges are the low-cost jewel of the state's public higher education system. These institutions deliver a high-quality education at the lowest cost to students, while providing professors a better wage without the pressure to publish or perish like their four-year counterparts. Unlike four-year institutions, community colleges may be the solution to the looming crisis in higher education. If a student were to complete two lower division years at a community college, it would significantly reduce America's student loan debt. A California community college student pays just $46 per unit in tuition. Remember, the average monthly student loan payment is $242 per month. A community college student pays half that amount if she pays for her tuition outright.

Community Colleges: Solution to Higher Education Meltdown

Community colleges have an image problem. They're viewed as the first choice for the second rate. A student body of dropouts. A faculty of middling professors whose research careers stalled. A haven for those looking for the easy way out in life. "If I wanted to learn something," says Jeff Winger, the main character played by Joel McHale in NBC's community college-themed sitcom, *Community*, "I wouldn't have come to community college."[131]

And nowhere is this condescending attitude more prevalent than among the ivory towers themselves. The data shows that professors who begin their career at a community college rarely "move up" to four-year institutions. Four-year faculty look down on their community college counterparts as professionals who couldn't make tenure at a four-year institution.

"I've spent twenty-five years working at five different community colleges, and I can count on one hand the number of people I know who have left and gone to four-year institutions," Rob Jenkins, an associate professor of English at Georgia Perimeter College, wrote in a piece featured at the *Chronicle of Higher Education*. "It's very easy for search committees to pigeonhole candidates with community-college experience as not worthy of serious consideration."[132]

It's a problem among not just professors, but other members of academia too. "I had not even thought about community colleges other than as the place you go for school when you can't succeed at a four-year institution," writes Kim Leeder, director of library services at the College of Western Idaho and a self-described "recovering snob" toward community colleges. "Shall we say it together? *S-N-O-B*."[133]

Yet, the list of community college success stories is endless. Santa Monica College taught a future governor how to read, write, and speak English.[134] San Joaquin Delta College introduced an influential labor leader to the world of community activism.[135] The force was with an aspiring Modesto Junior College film student long before he dreamed up a galaxy far, far away.[136]

"That place made me what I am today," Academy Award-winning actor and community college advocate Tom Hanks said of his two-year alma mater, Chabot College. "Over the course of my career, I've only continued to reap the benefits of the classes I took there."[137]

Community college successes aren't limited to a few anecdotal examples of Hollywood bigwigs and tech moguls who caught their lucky break. Half of all Cal State graduates, 70 percent of the state's nurses, and 80 percent of our firefighters, law enforcement officers, and emergency medical technicians learned at a community college.[138] "I'm a big believer in community colleges," says rocket scientist Adam Steltzner, who led the team at Jet Propulsion Laboratories that designed NASA's *Curiosity* mission to Mars.[139] "It's not about prestige, it's not about your SAT scores. It's from-the-heart education, and I really resonated with that."[140]

About the Author: John Hrabe

John Hrabe writes on California politics for CalNewsroom.com. A proud community college graduate, Hrabe also has degrees from the London School of Economics and University of Southern California.

Seven

TRANSPORTATION

By Michelle Moons

G ov. Jerry Brown's attempt at a legacy achievement ranks among the more disastrous projects in a long line of public transportation debacles in the Golden State's history. Known to some as the bullet train to nowhere, the mammoth government endeavor can be compared to past clunky projects that have sent Californians barreling toward ruin while unions and the politically well connected are financially boosted.

Consider the San Francisco Bay Area's commuter rail system, BART. This system was once seen as the transportation marvel of the future. Today, the dilapidated, union-dominated system more resembles a relic of the past, certainly not the bill of goods sold to taxpayers at the price of "just a little bit more." Yet BART's public employee union workers receive the highest compensation in the nation—with average salaries toping even New York's and Chicago's public transportation employees for similar jobs.[141] Or take the unbelievably botched Bay Bridge update, part of which was contracted out to a Chinese company that had never built a bridge before. Safety concerns and long delays have been hallmarks of such budget-busting projects. The state relentlessly green-lights the behemoth government ventures while suppressing attractive, free-market alternatives through more regulations and higher fees. Innovative companies, such as Uber and Lyft, have succeeded in identifying the public's wants and needs and then have provided a desirable service. Consequently, their success has drawn the attention of the politically well connected as they seek to maintain their gains through state-sponsored systems. As we'll see in the case of these ride-sharing companies, government regulators often swoop in claiming hero status for not shutting the businesses down, instead regulating them to death in the twisted proposal, "I'm from the government and I'm here to help."[142]

California's High-Speed Boondoggle

California's High Speed Rail (HSR) Authority drafted a 2014 business plan that claims partial completion by 2029. A trip on the planned San Francisco to Los Angeles Basin section is supposed to take under three hours, but that is not a realistic projection, say insiders. An additional "eventual" section is proposed for Los Angeles to San Diego, though without even a projected completion date. Hopes of that coming to fruition carry little credibility.

Initial rail debt funds were sold to voters in 2008 under a well-marketed project package. Proposition 1A requires not only high speed capability, but also a connection between all the state's major population centers to spur economic development. In the face of a crushing $68 billion cost estimate, questions arise about the possibility of private rail financing. To this Jeff Morales of the HSR Authority says, "If somebody were coming in looking just to make a profit by running trains, (the current plan is) probably not how they would have done it. And they would have bypassed all those population centers." His comment undresses one of the key assertions of the project: that it could run without government subsidies. If it could, then why would a private investor needing to turn a profit to keep things rolling not choose the route mapped out? The answer is because it's not expected to turn a profit, and thus would require government subsidies to maintain its existence.

As Californians look forward, HSR officials claim that civil engineering projects will be complete in the year 2018. This is assuming they can procure the necessary properties from Central Valley owners in time. As of mid-April 2015, the state has procured only 192[143] of the 1,066 properties needed for portions of the initial 130-mile Central Valley HSR segment. Additional properties are in the process of being condemned through eminent domain. Should an owner not be amenable to the price offered or not wish to relinquish his or her right to the property, the state initiates a condemnation process. Estimated timelines for acquiring the properties are highly optimistic, according to rail critics and comments from a rail representative. The rail authority's press secretary has conveyed that some owners have been fighting the agency for three years.[144] Many landowners have filed lawsuits fighting condemnation, considering the project remains uncertain.

Owners facing condemnation have criticized the HSR Authority for announcing the path of the railway before valuing their properties. They assert that such an announcement prior to valuing the properties drives down their valuation. The state, they say, is using illegal tactics in order to offer property owners less than the property would otherwise have been worth.

Delays resulting from troubled financing and land acquisitions have resulted in what construction project one contractor Tutor Perini Corporation. CEO Ron Tutor says is an eighteen-month delay. Tutor expressed plans to seek compensation from the state for the delay in starting construction, adding cost onto the already underfunded project.

High speed rail was sold under the premise that the line would be high speed. Voters were promised that a trip from San Francisco to Los Angeles would take less than three hours. That promise, however, is now being lost in the realities and excused under the claim that the rail doesn't technically need to make the trip in two hours, forty minutes or travel at 200 mph, it only has to be "capable" of doing so. That claim is still up for debate in court proceedings.

If a traveler seeks speed, why not use cost and time efficient commercial air travel? Breitbart California Editor Joel Pollak wrote an April 2015 comparison between a prospective high speed rail trip from San Francisco to Los Angeles and a private commercial airline alternative on the basis of cost and time. Pollak noted that total time from door to door on the bullet train, if it actually meets the projected rail time, would take an estimated four hours after adding in "last mile" travel to and from the stations. That's the same amount of time it took him to travel the same route door to door via airline and public transportation on a recent trip using Southwest Airlines. In the analysis, Pollak also notes the estimated cost of a train ticket, $86.00. Remember that this is the projected cost and will likely end up being subsidized. His trip using commercial air travel: $77.50. "The train will lose money and require a subsidy," National High Speed Rail Association former president Joseph Vranich stated, according to the *Los Angeles Times*. "I have not seen a single number that has come out of the California high speed rail organization that is credible. As a high speed rail advocate, I am steamed."[145]

In checking commercial airline rates in early May 2015 for a one-way LAX to San Francisco ticket, the cost was $77.00 or less for many options across six different carriers. Each one of the six carriers posted travel times between one hour, ten minutes and one hour, thirty minutes.

With seemingly no time or cost benefit to using rail over air travel between Los Angeles and San Francisco, little incentive exists to choose rail over air. An Amtrak trip in 2015 between Los Angeles and Fresno requires switching from a bus to a train in Bakersfield. Some have suggested the more responsible alternative to the bullet train would be to complete the traditional rail line between Los Angeles and Fresno.

Further rail concerns involve safety. Airports offer stringent security screening, while rail has none. Terrorists thus have greater opportunity to effectively strike rail lines. In 2005, four Islamic terrorists bombed London trains and a bus, leaving[146] 52 dead and 770 injured. Travelers may be motivated to choose commercial air travel over rail for the higher level of security screening. Much of the rail is expected to operate at an elevated position and across major fault lines. Should the "big one" hit, an elevated rail line could result in deadly high speed crashes.

Fully aware of HSR funding shortfalls, Governor Brown has moved to use an estimated one quarter of cap and trade funds to further fund the project. Directly after being sworn in for a historic fourth term as governor of California, Jerry Brown gathered a handpicked crew in Fresno for an invitation-only, symbolic groundbreaking. Public officials signed an emblematic piece of track. During the carefully choreographed event, Brown reportedly told the crowd of some seven hundred dignitaries, rail enthusiasts, and union representatives, "I wasn't sure where the hell we were going to get the rest of the money," then turned slyly to reassure the masses banking on the project, "Don't worry about it. We're going to get it."[147]

With $2.7 billion in 2009 federal stimulus funding that must be spent by September 2017 or be lost, Brown has no time to lose. Rail representatives say construction is still at least three years from seeing actual tracks laid, and acquiring almost thirteen hundred properties from the Madera to Bakersfield segment is one of the first major hurdles. Only 137 properties needed for the smaller Madera to Fresno CP1 section had been acquired.[148]

Even if they meet the 2018 deadline for completion of civil engineering construction projects (CP) one through four, Madera to Bakersfield, the subsequent rail construction would only then begin for the 90–130 mile portion of test track. No rail builder had been chosen as of May 2015. That means we could see a repeat of the Bay Bridge boondoggle, like the hiring of Chinese contractors that had never built a bridge before. Once CP one through four are completed, there would be another three years of testing before the system would be ready for operation, rail representatives have said.

It's worth recognizing that nine of the top fourteen donors to the Proposition 1A high speed rail funding campaign were seven construction unions, one public sector union, and one union-affiliated, labor-management-cooperation committee.[149] Prop 1A was the bond measure approved by voters in 2008. Each gave $50,000 or more to the campaign, according to California Secretary of State records.[150] Additional questions have persisted over ownership interests held by Richard Blum, US senator Dianne Feinstein's husband, in Tutor-Perini, the civil engineering contractor on HSR's $1.2–$2.0 billion CP1. In reviewing SEC filings, Blum was a 10 percent owner in Tutor-Perini until December 2005. At that time Blum disposed of many but not all shares, according to the filings.[151] Blum's available filings since that date don't appear to include sale of the over four hundred thousand shares remaining, leaving Blum with a residual interest in the rail contractor. This is not the first time Blum has held stock in a company that won a bid for a government project that he or his wife had influence over. URS, a company that Blum owned an interest in at the time, won a contract with the University of California while Blum sat as a regent for the UC.[152]

Many Central Valley farmers will not benefit from the rail but, like other Californians outside urban areas, will nonetheless pay for the rail with their tax dollars. "Higher prices discourage demand. If carbon pricing doesn't sting, at least a little bit, we won't change our habits," then state senate leader Darrell Steinberg said in 2014 when introducing a carbon fuel tax bill. State climate change opportunists have repeatedly used the issue to cycle special interest and union money back into politicians' bank accounts.

Under Steinberg's assertion, many lower income Central Valley residents for whom rail is not an option would face higher fuel prices and taxes to pay for the bullet train. Those in the agricultural industry would be among those Californians disproportionately burdened. Farmers use significant amounts of fuel in running equipment necessary to their operations. Rural Californians may travel longer distances daily that require the use of a vehicle. These Californians would face disproportionate financial burdens as a consequence of taxpayer-funded rail spending. It's a burden that the select Californians who could potentially use the rail would not be forced to bear as heavily. The project and resulting tax burden would put the needs of city residents over rural Californians, as urban dwellers will have greater access to and efficient use for established rail routes.

Central Valley farmers are already feeling the water squeeze between a prolonged drought, high water prices, eminent domain property lawsuits, and environmental regulatory burdens that keep those farmers from using valuable water. Environmental regulators have restricted these farmers in accessing Sacramento-San Joaquin Delta water on the assertion that the three-inch Delta Smelt must be protected.

Republican assemblyman Jim Patterson of Fresno brought[153] forth legislation that would protect farmers and Central Valley residents in the rail path from unjustified condemnation of their properties. AB 1138 would have required[154] California's HSR Authority to prove certain minimum requirements before being allowed to pursue acquiring property through eminent domain. They included proof that the project had the money to pay for the property, an estimate of when those funds would be available to pay the owner, and verification that environmental clearances to use the land had been cleared.

Only $6 billion of the currently $68 billion estimated cost to build the San Francisco to Los Angeles line has been procured. Patterson told the *Sacramento Bee*, "Eminent domain is absolute and irrevocable. If the funds fall short or the litigation succeeds, there is a real possibility that all this property won't be utilized." Nevertheless Democratic legislators fell in line with Brown's push and killed the bill in April 2015.

Yet another bullet train concern is the sinking Central Valley. The region has faced the issue for years, but a 2008–2010 USGS report measured sinking of one foot a year as intensified through times of drought.[155] During times of drought, increased restrictions on surface water usage forced farmers to seek another source, one that they found in underground water. In late 2013, CHSRA Chief Program Manager Frank Vacca attempted to waylay concerns, simply asserting that the fact was being factored into the design. But remember, we don't know for sure yet who the manufacturer will be. Should the winning rail-laying contractor perform as the inexperienced Chinese company used for the already corroded Bay Bridge, public safety concerns would be more than justified. Vacca commented, "This is just one more box to check on our list of engineering considerations."

Multiple lawsuits are expected to extend into 2016. Phase two of a lawsuit against the 2008 voter-approved Proposition 1A high speed rail funding measure is slated for court in fall 2015, but could be pushed back to 2016. Depending on the result, the case could face another year in appellate courts. Lawsuit proponents brought the case under evidence that the rail will not meet the requirements of the proposition that were sold to voters to get the measure approved.

Prop 1A authorized $9.95 billion in bond debt to build HSR, linking the California regions of Sacramento, the San Joaquin Valley, the San Francisco Bay Area, and Los Angeles. The Legislative Analyst's Office (LAO) estimates a final Prop 1A cost of $19.40 billion[156] after factoring in $9.50 billion in estimated interest, assuming a thirty-year payment schedule.

Prop 1A funds won't cover the $68.00 billion estimated cost the high-speed rail project has ballooned to from the $11.00–$16.50 billion estimated back in 1996.[157] The LAO estimates over $1.00 billion in additional unknown costs to operate and maintain the system every year. The mere $6.00 billion in funding procured for high speed rail as of early 2015 consists of $2.60 billion of the Prop 1A bond debt matching funds and $3.30 in federal stimulus funds. Prop 1A funds can be used only in proportion to funds from outside sources.

The $68.00 billion only covers the San Francisco to Los Angeles segment. Additional extensions to Sacramento and San Diego have indeterminate completion dates somewhere beyond 2030. Adding on those segments could drive the rail cost to upward of $150 billion. Considering the history of similar big government projects all but ensures that the government estimates sit at the low end of the scale for total cost and time to complete. The Bay Bridge and Bay Area Rapid Transit system are ample pictures of such projects.

Additional lawsuits lodged against the rail project involve alleged violations of the California Environmental Quality Act (CEQA) and alleged illegal practices in the taking of landowner property through eminent domain.[158] The authority has been accused of certifying a "legally inadequate" environmental impact report. A 2012 Government Accountability Office (GAO) preliminary analysis of portions of the HSR project noted "environmental review process and acquisition of necessary rights-of-way for construction could increase the risk of the project's falling behind schedule and increasing costs."[159]

In its report, the GAO referenced a study of sixty-two rail projects; fifty-two of those projects were found to have demand forecasts that fell short of actual demand. "Research on ridership and revenue forecasts for rail infrastructure projects have shown that ridership forecasts are often overestimated and actual ridership is likely to be lower."

GAO issued a follow-up report in 2013 that was touted by rail proponents for a "forecasts are reasonable" analysis of ridership estimates.[160] However, the report strongly emphasized the current lack of established criteria for estimating these forecasts for intercity high-speed rail and stated that updates to current HSR estimates are necessary. The report further noted, "If the California high-speed rail project is unable to generate the necessary ridership and revenue to cover the system's operating costs, the project may not be able to operate without a subsidy—as required by Proposition 1A."

Bay Bridge Debacle

The San Francisco-Oakland Bay Bridge stands as another rusty example of public projects failing to meet the lofty promises used to sell them to the public. "Cost-cutting" attempts led to the use of Chinese subcontractor Shanghai Zhenhua Port Machinery Company Ltd. (ZPMC) in 2006. The company had never built a bridge before, and Caltrans Senior Materials Contractor Jim Merrill called the company "high risk," but they attractively bid $250 million less than any competitor.[161] One of the reasons cited for hiring ZPMC was the company's reputation for speed, a reputation not realized in the Bay Bridge construction. As the project progressed, Caltrans paid hundreds of millions and eased US bridge construction standards and welding codes to make up for continual delays.

From early on, the new bridge project yielded repeated problems. Within months of winning the job, ZPMC was seen operating without basic quality control, according to notes from Gary Pursell, a Caltrans engineering supervisor. The Chinese-based company also provided key documents printed only in Mandarin Chinese, not English, as their contract required.[162]

Bad directions were merely foreshadowing big problems to come. In March 2013, breaks were found in thirty-two of the bridge's rusty anchor rods, resulting in compromised earthquake safety gear. The retrofit fix cost millions more.

Grossly negligent errors and oversights continue to plague the bridge. In February 2015, the California Department of Transportation released an update on 424 high strength steel anchor rods from the tower foundation that protect the bridge tower during an earthquake.[163] High strength steel is prone to corrosion more than regular steel, according to retired Bechtel engineer Yun Chung Long, who has criticized Caltrans's use of the more vulnerable material.

Caltrans, knowing of the vulnerabilities of the high strength steel, chose to use it anyway. [164] The unusual design of the bridge was used as justification for the steel's use. When the thirty-two broken anchor rods were found back in 2013, review of Caltrans's records failed to turn up any evidence of manufacturing process oversight or preinstallation testing of the tower rods.

Upon deeper review of preinstallation records, Caltrans found additional process errors that may have seriously compromised the integrity of the rods. Contrary to instructions, rods were exposed to potentially crack-inducing materials, then in transit the rods were scraped, further increasing the probability of cracking.

In late 2014, steel tubes surrounding the rods were found to be missing inches to meters of grouting essential to protect the rods from water corrosion. A 2015 Caltrans release stated, "Unfortunately, the state's contractor failed to properly fill all the 424 tubes with grout. In September 2014, Caltrans inspectors observed water at the base of the SAS tower beneath caulking that was placed around the rods."

Water has continued to reappear within the tubes, with no clear source. Experts have suggested gaps or cracks in the concrete at the base of the bridge as a possible source. Caltrans and prior contractor American Bridge/Fluor continue to fight over who may be at fault.

Discovery of the gross oversight led to an emergency meeting. During that meeting the oversight committee for the bridge project chose to move forward with testing water from one hundred flooded tubes. Price tag to test the contractor's "unfortunate" failure: $400,000.

That is just the tip of the proverbial iceberg. Once the tower was installed in 2011, the ability to remove damaged rods without destroying them or to replace them with new ones was rendered impossible.

In a March 2015 report, the *San Francisco Chronicle* cited Caltrans officials who indicated a need for millions more in bridge testing. The $6.4 billion project is already over budget and expected to hit $10 million in deficit spending.

All $6 million budgeted for bridge testing was spent before budget year-end 2015, halting further testing, according to Caltrans officials. [165] The oversight committee suggested Caltrans look in other parts of the budget to fund additional testing of potentially compromised rods.

BART Pension Problems

Next we look to the fifth largest transportation agency in the nation, the Bay Area Rapid Transit System (BART). The system opened in 1972 with the promise to voters that it was the future of transportation. But since coming out with visions of quiet, relaxing trips, the system has fallen into disrepair, consumed by crushing costs of union contracts and extremely overdue maintenance.

BART railcars today are busting at the seams. Ridership has ballooned to an estimated 420,000 for weekdays, rising sharply in recent years. The ailing system is suffering from an outdated train control system, dilapidated railcars and tracks, too few crossover tracks, and a shortage of railcars in light of demand. But overcrowding and safety concerns are taking a backseat to labor contracts, including some of the highest transit employee compensation packages in the country.

Labor and benefits alone make up $470.00 million of BART's $1.57 billion preliminary budget for 2016.[166] That's up 12 percent from 2015, significantly more than any other expense category in the budget. The district also contributes the great majority of the employee portion of pension contributions in addition to the employer portion. BART contributions jumped 12 percent from 2015 to the 2016 budget. The 2016 budget memo stated increases in pension expenses are expected to continue rising into future years. Expenses for employee medical plans are expected to increase 9 percent in 2016, due in part to higher insurance premiums.

In 2013, BART budgeted approximately $379.2 million for labor, almost $100.0 million less than budgeted for 2016. The increase follows 2013 labor negotiations that devolved into strikes and plunged Bay Area commutes into chaos. BART employee compensation was examined in the first edition of *Taxifornia*. It was noted that the top train operator alone, pre-union-labor contract renegotiation, took home over $193,000 in salary, overtime, and benefits in 2013. An employee overseeing train storage and maintenance yard traffic remarkably took home over $270,000, and the top-paid janitor received over $80,000 for the year. Since that time labor unions have secured new contracts and the budgeted BART salaries for 2016 have jumped 24 percent.

BART representatives held a teleconference on the 2016 budget in May 2015. One caller asked about the rising costs of riding BART that were later echoed by another caller. She conveyed that she now spends $160 a month between fares and parking to ride the BART. In 2013, BART faced a $3.0 billion shortfall over the coming decade. BART's ten-year unfunded capital shortfall is now projected at $4.8 billion as listed in the 2016 preliminary budget.

Looking to make up the funds needed to repair and update BART's equipment, officials are looking to push a property tax increase on the November 2016 ballot in Alameda, Contra Costa, and San Francisco counties, according to the *Contra Costa Times*.[167] A separate half-cent sales tax measure from the Contra Costa Transportation Authority could compete with the potential property tax push in a high profile presidential election. The competition could kill both if moderate voters split. BART polling of likely voters has shown insufficient support for a measure increasing property taxes to serve a $4.5 billion bond. That's even with substantial frustration over BART; a 2014 survey showed only 28 percent were very satisfied and 46 percent somewhat satisfied.

Riders faced transit turbulence when labor union contract negotiations in late 2013 between BART and its two largest unions, SEIU Local 1021 and Amalgamated Transit Union Local 1555, drew heated arguments and strikes. Arguments peaked at the end over whether or not union employees would be granted six weeks of family paid medical leave as part of a labor contract package. What BART called mistaken language not ratified by its board, the unions called nonnegotiable. After seven months of negotiations, two strikes, and two worker fatalities, the unions filed a lawsuit against BART's board of directors.[168] The move was met with additional concessions from BART, which led to final contract approvals in January 2015, nine months after the tortuous drama began. Four years later they'll get to do it all again.

For eight days during the two 2013 strikes, BART's four hundred thousand daily riders were left to seek out alternate transportation. Republican assembly member Catharine Baker (San Ramon) introduced[169] a bill in early February 2015 that would prevent future BART strikes. As one justification for the bill, Baker cited[170] a $73 million per day lost worker productivity cost to the Bay Area economy during the strike.[171] Under the new legislation, BART employees with no-strike clauses would continue to be paid under those contracts if union contract negotiations extended past the prior contract's expiration; however, they would not be permitted to strike.

Whether legislators believe in the merits of AB 528 or not, it's nearly assured to fail. Labor union strongholds in the state capitol are known for their controlling influence over Democratic legislators. Those union influencers aren't likely to allow Democrats to weaken their power.

Democratic mayor of Orinda Steve Glazer faced union backlash for responding positively to Baker's bill on the basis that the workers still get paid and area residents don't get slammed with a BART strike. Glazer's city is home to a heavily used BART station. But Glazer was frank concerning the climate in Sacramento. "Her bill is going be a tough sell, because the Democrats are more fearful of the union than the people."[172] Labor union strikes haven't been the only disruption to BART service. The protest-prone region has seen a number of shutdowns as a result of protester actions. In late November 2014, approximately two hundred Black Lives Matter protesters flooded an Oakland station and fourteen chained themselves to the train, effectively shutting down service in the area. The arrest of and charges against the fourteen spawned a January 2015 protest that shut down two San Francisco stations.[173] It's worth noting that the public is solidly opposed to the BART strikes. The *San Francisco Chronicle* noted that "even in the labor-friendly Bay Area, one of the nation's most-liberal bastions," people are annoyed at disruptions in their daily commute.[174]

Dangerous maintenance issues have also interrupted service. On one day in May 2015, a ten-inch gap of broken track, a helium balloon that short-circuited electrical lines, reports of a person on the tracks, and a power outage each caused hours of delays and shutdowns. Stranded riders looked to ferries and ride-sharing companies Uber and Lyft as alternatives. With the unpredictable uptick in demand, ferry lines lingered and ride-sharing rates surged.

Should rail enthusiasts see their bullet train system materialize, what happens when labor union workers decide to strike from HSR positions? Hordes of commuters could be forced to seek out last-minute alternative transportation, as they have with BART shutdowns. California's economy could face much greater losses than the $73 million daily worker productivity losses seen during the BART strikes. What caused public outrage, economic disruption, and commuter chaos during the Bay Area BART labor union strikes could hold hostage thousands of commuters between San Francisco and Los Angeles. And under threat of such a fight, the bargaining power of those labor unions could be exponentially increased.

The BART system gives us an opportunity to see a rail system once seen as the shining star of the future, but that has fallen victim to the political spectacle that befalls big government programs. But the BART serves residents within one region and could be effectively turned around if respect for taxpayer dollars is put ahead of political expediency. Allowing innovative companies and free-market competition to thrive by removing government stumbling blocks could further serve the regions' commuters and ease transportation congestion for all.

Ride-Sharing Regulations

Poor Bay Area transportation options are rumored to have birthed the innovative ride-sharing company Uber. Along with fellow rideshare services such as Lyft, they are pioneers of a new industry and fresh opportunity for potential drivers and riders. But as happy customers increasingly choose the streamlined and often more cost-effective travel providers over other more regulated options, government is looking to get its hands on some of the profits and bureaucratic control.

Taxis are highly regulated and pay significant sums in government fees. The first edition of *Taxifornia* referenced the steep $100,000.00 that San Francisco collects when an official taxi operator sells its medallion, the license to operate a taxi. Drivers in Los Angeles see median hourly income of $8.39 after working an average seventy-two hours a week.

In January 2015 the Los Angeles Taxicab Commission decided[175] to "help" city taxis out. With the unanimous passage of a new order, Los Angeles taxis will be required to use new Uber-style, commission-certified mobile apps or face daily fines of $200.00 starting in August 2015.[176] A *Los Angeles Times* article noted that between nine licensed cab companies, there was a 21 percent drop in trips in the first half of 2014 following years of increases. As of December 2014, Los Angeles had over twenty-three hundred licensed taxis.

Los Angeles has also moved to require increasing numbers of qualifying "green taxicabs" within operators' fleets.[177] By December 31, 2015, each operator's non-wheelchair-exempt fleet must contain 80 percent qualifying green taxis.

In fact, California is already trying to take an adjusted approach to the new business model. Instead of just banning the operations, they are easing the companies into regulation. With a move in late 2013, the California Public Utilities Commission agreed to "allow" the companies to continue to operate under the new category of business "Transportation Network Companies" (TNC) if they submit to certain regulations. At that time the PUC indicated it would issue licenses to these drivers as they do with taxis.

As of early 2015, a host of new "TNC" or ride-sharing bills faced the state legislature. Some of these bills seek to regulate TNC fare structure (AB 1360), safety and background checks (AB 24), customer records (AB 886), and ongoing checks of driver DMV records (AB 1422).

As TNC legislation has boomed, district attorney's offices in Los Angeles and San Francisco went after Uber and Lyft with lawsuits attacking the companies' background-check claims.[178] The San Francisco district attorney indicated that at $2,500 per violation, the "tens of thousands of violations" could add up. Expect to see more legal action as these companies see growing success.

In early 2015 the California Department of Motor Vehicles issued an advisory suggesting ride-sharing service providers would be required to acquire commercial license plates or face noncompliance fines.[179] An old law had allowed the TNC companies to be threatened with shutdown before. Lyft was quick to denounce the move, and apparent pressure on the DMV led the agency to retract the advisory in favor of sorting out new PUC regulations.

If this rate of regulation continues, ride sharing could easily become just another taxi system, beholden to government regulators and bleeding profits as they pay regulatory compliance and government fees. With increased costs, rising fares would likely be close behind. The attractive free-market competition that brought customers over to the new concept would likely soon fade under the government machine.

Looking to the future, companies like Uber are looking to expand their business model. One idea that's been floated is the natural extension to delivering not just people to their destinations. Pilot programs delivering meals, providing moving services, and even bike courier services have been launched in select areas.[180] More proposed regulation is likely to follow in favor of political benefit.

Los Angeles's Subway to the Sea

After decades of talk, failed attempts, and political maneuvering, Los Angeles's "Subway to the Sea" is making waves again. But what Los Angeles Mayor Antonio Villaraigosa has billed as access to the sea will end miles from the coast, even if it does reach its twenty-plus-year timeline.

Some have billed the resurgence in rail projects as a rail "renaissance." Perhaps that was echoed in the choice of the Los Angeles County Museum of Art for the new Purple Line subway extension's November 2014 groundbreaking. This rail rebirth, however, comes in at an estimated cost of over $6 billion for nine miles of track. Interestingly enough, that's similar to the fraction of funding procured thus far for the $68 billion HSR cost estimate.

Extending the Purple Line closer to the ocean has drawn the warning of Metro officials cited in a *Los Angeles Times* article saying the addition would cost billions more. One Metro representative indicated that the light rail would eventually take its Purple Line parallel route all the way to the coast.

Funding for this multibillion-dollar project comes in the form of a $1.2 billion grant, almost $1.0 billion in federal loan funds and voter-approved county sales tax funds. Segment one alone of the three making up the line extension will cost an estimated $2.8 billion. Segments two and three will heap on another estimated $3.5 billion.

UCLA transportation expert and urban planning professor Brian Taylor was also cited by the *Los Angeles Times* as he questioned the exorbitant $600 million–$700 million per-mile cost of extending the line as opposed to more cost-effective transit improvement options. Complicated utility lines, oil fields, and gas and seismic factors are noted obstacles to this project's success. Area residents are being told that Purple Line riders are supposed to jump in number by 215,000 with the extension. Let's remember, however, that in a review of historical ridership estimates, a study cited by the GAO showed fifty-two of sixty-two projects experienced actual demand short of forecasted ridership estimates.

Environmental analysis indicates that the extended Purple Line would only marginally alleviate traffic concerns for the area with little or no freeway relief.

Santa Monica's mayor said at the groundbreaking ceremony that she is holding out hope that the line will be live as *soon* as 2035. Like the high speed rail groundbreaking, it seems public officials host transportation project groundbreakings to convince the public to look at the magic wizard and "pay no attention to that man behind the curtain." All is well, dear constituents.

Anaheim's Transit Hub

ARTIC is Anaheim's completed monument to poor government planning and using inflated projections in selling big government projects to the public. In anticipation of two high-speed rail lines, the infamous California bullet train and another, the California-Nevada Super Speed Train, Anaheim built what looks like the pinnacle of over-the-top transit centers. Funding for the $184.2 million station came largely from Orange County taxpayers through half percent sales tax Measures M and M2.[181]

Billed as a "significant vision" and "the future of transit in Orange County," the Anaheim Regional Transportation Intermodal Center (ARTIC) celebrated its grand opening in December 2014. ARTIC's website heralds it as a public-private partnership outfit serving "three million Orange County residents as well as more than forty million visitors annually." A lofty statement given four short months of troubled operating revenues.

Six-month total revenue projected for ARTIC is $391,548, falling monumentally short of the $2.38 million estimated operating cost.[182] Property management costs for just the first six months of 2015 are reported to be $1.00 million of that operating cost. The next fiscal year isn't looking promising either. Documented initial estimates made in 2014 project $5.20 million in operating costs for the fiscal year starting July 1, 2015—with city officials indicating they aren't even close to securing the naming-rights sponsor or advertising revenue that were supposed to make the environmentally friendly "LEED Platinum designed" transit hub self-sustaining.

Keep in mind that in California's best-case scenario, the state's high speed rail line won't reach Burbank until 2022. The HSR Authority timeline doesn't even give dates for completion of the Burbank to Los Angeles segment or extending the Los Angeles to Anaheim segment.[183]

Described by the *Los Angeles Times* as ARTIC's biggest advocate former Anaheim mayor Curt Pringle also served as chairman of the High Speed Rail Authority.[184]

Priority parking is reserved for those possessing California DMV HOV lane stickers or driving zero-emission or hybrid vehicles. Parking spaces from spaces leased to a restaurant tenant are estimated to bring in $46,800 for the six months ending June 30, 2014, while parking staffer and supply costs are estimated at $92,456.

Ridership numbers aren't panning out either. Reports say that Anaheim officials promised the public nearly three thousand train boardings alone would start from day one. In reality, daily ridership didn't even hit eight hundred by the end of the first month. Estimates from city officials ran as high as ten thousand riders combined between bus, taxi, airport shuttle, and trains by ARTIC's opening day.

"I think it's certainly a beautiful piece of architecture," Transportation Authority Board Director Michael Hennessey said of the transit station according to the *Voice of Orange County*.[185] "But I don't think the project has done anything to facilitate transportation…in my view the case was never made for it. And the numbers show it."

One might wonder, well, where are those funds going to come from to make up the shortfall between revenues and operating costs? City officials are scrambling to find an answer and could tap ideas for more government projects, including turning next-door city-owned property into housing, retail, or office space. But in the short term, Anaheim spokeswoman Ruth Ruiz has been cited as suggesting use of the expected city reserve surplus of $1.5 million, still only a portion of ARTIC's projected shortfall.

The center appears to be shaping up as yet another testament to politicians and special interests dictating to the people what they should want and not responding to what people actually need and want. Actual travelers through this and the previous center often say they prefer the old transit center or complain of bad planning in the new one. Income and ridership projections have fallen far short of preconstruction promises and don't appear to be looking up despite efforts to make the government-serving system work.

Ask a rail enthusiast, big government politician, or rail construction contractor in California and you might hear that we are in the middle of a rail "renaissance." The sound of it evokes a sense of romance, historic art, and culture. The reality of bloated government projects, however, is a history of asset mismanagement, government overreach, and neglect for the freedom and best interest of hardworking Americans.

So are these projects a testament to an ever-growing system of madness—or a deliberate effort to grow government and enrich the political elite and well connected? Considering that project contractors and unions carry on, their financial interests served whether or not a project ultimately succeeds, history would suggest the latter.

One of the worse parts of the high speed rail project is, should it manage to reach the stage of laying tracks and then face failure, the tracks cannot be used for low speed rail. The high speed rail tracks would become an enduring monument to failed government-pushed projects that grease the hands of unions and the politically well connected with hardworking taxpayer dollars. Whether or not the rail fails, many public sector unions and friends and associates of the political elite will come out financially benefitted, often with little to no particular investment in the ultimate success of the project.

About the Author: Michelle Moons

Michelle Moons is a native of California. She has volunteered building homes in Mexico and aiding in Hurricane Katrina relief. A graduate of Seattle Pacific University, she worked in public and private accounting before work on a state assembly campaign in 2012 led her into political reporting. She joined the Breitbart News team in 2014 with the launch of Breitbart California.

Eight

By Shawn Dewane

B en Franklin once said, "We'll know what the water is worth when the well runs dry." It is important to understand that water is incorporated into every product and service each of us relies on every day. A recent analysis found that "in an average year, 50 percent of the surface water from rain and snow goes to environmental purposes, 40 percent toward growing food and farm products, and 10 percent from urban needs."[186]

However, and in spite of this assurance, farmers in the Central Valley are suffering unemployment rates not seen since the Great Depression. Land remains fallow instead of being farmed. "Food prices surge as drought exacts a high toll on crops,"[187] because water that would otherwise be used for farming and urban use is allowed to flow to the Pacific Ocean.

Half of the state's water supply is reserved for environmental purposes—and environmentalists get first priority. In times of drought, everyone else takes a cut first. Because of the environmental regulations in the water business, it is often said that more water flows underneath the Golden Gate Bridge every day than Southern California uses in an entire year. And as Mark Twain once said, "Whiskey is for drinking, water for fighting." That's where the debate about water use in California begins. How much water is reserved for what use, and in what order of priority is it allocated?

Californians passed the Burns-Porter Act of 1960 and said yes to the future. The passage of this bill brought to life the State Water Project that would quench the thirst of Southern California. That vote begins the development of the State Water Project and what is now "the nation's largest state-built water, power development, and distribution system."[188] Today, this project delivers water supplies for twenty-five million Californians and 750,000 acres of irrigated farmland.

Under normal operations, water from the Sacramento River Delta is pumped into the State Water Project, where it is shipped through 701 miles of open canals and pipelines to thirty-four storage facilities, reservoirs, and lakes. The system pumps water from the Sacramento River Delta through the series of canals and pipelines to be stored in the reservoirs and lakes as a backup reserve supply for times of drought.

But normal operating conditions changed on December 15, 2008, when the US Fish and Wildlife Service issued a biological opinion regarding the operation of the State Water Project as it was designed. That decree stated that continued operation of the service "was likely to jeopardize the continued existence of the delta smelt and adversely modify its critical habitat."[189] This opinion forced the shutdown of the State Water Project and thereby the ability to refill the storage facilities, reservoirs, and lakes.

Lower than average precipitation followed this opinion, which caused the withdrawal of water from storage to provide for the current needs of Southern California. As the drought continued, stored supplies were further drawn down to meet local demands. The current situation—the lack of available water—can trace its roots to this biological opinion and the decision to shut down the pumps that feed the State Water Project.

California Water and Power

Clean, affordable water is fundamental to the economic development of our communities. There are two requirements for peace in the world, water and power, and the two are inextricably linked—without one you cannot have the other.

According to the California Energy Commission, "Water-related energy consumes 19 percent of the state's electricity, 30 percent of its natural gas, and 88 billion gallons of diesel fuel every year—and this demand is growing."[190] The University of California tells us that it takes about 3,600 kilowatts to move one acre foot of water one foot in elevation. A water pump is similar to a straw in a glass of water.[191] To get one drop out of the top of the straw, you must move the entire column of water from the bottom of the glass. Water is heavy, about 8.345 pounds per gallon. Lifting a column of water from hundreds of feet below the earth is very heavy and requires a lot of energy.

Water not only consumes energy but produces it as well. Water stored behind Hoover Dam provides the energy to move the turbines that create the electricity the Southwest depends on—no water, no power. Now consider that "two thirds of the state's precipitation occurs in Northern California while two thirds of the state's population resides in Southern California."[192] Moving this water from north to south uses a lot of energy.

In 2006, the California State Legislature passed Assembly Bill 32. "AB 32 requires California to reduce its greenhouse gas emissions to 1990 levels by 2020."[193] According to the California Public Utilities Commission, the 33 Percent Renewables Portfolio Standard, Implementation Analysis of Preliminary Results, estimates that the cost of AB 32 compliance will cause the cost of electricity to rise 10 percent. Then on April 29, 2015, Governor Brown went even further, signing an executive order to advance the policy goals of AB 32, by signing an executive order, that "greenhouse-gas emissions be 40 percent below 1990 levels, by 2030."[194] This is an ambitious goal that will require the installation of vast amounts of renewable energy.

The impact of the state's water policy can be felt far and wide. According to IBM, it takes roughly 10 liters of water to create a sheet of paper, 140 liters of water for a cup of coffee, and 15,500 liters of water to make one kilogram of leather. When the price of water increases, the price of all goods and services that use water as a component of supply must rise as well. As the per-unit price of water increases, so must the cost of all goods and services that incorporate water as a component of its production. In turn, that causes regional price inflation in California.

Add all this up, consider the cost of the climate change bill, then note how much electricity it costs to move water, and you will get an idea of the scale of the importance of water pricing in the California economy and the nation.[195] Herein lies an opportunity to harness these policy goals of greenhouse gas reduction with water supply policy to help relieve the drought.

Why Water Is a Commodity

Something magical happens as water flows from the water main in your street, through your meter at the curb, out of your tap, and into the glass for you to take a sip and quench your thirst. The act of taking that one little sip allows you to exercise your liberty with respect to your private property, the water in the glass.

By turning the tap, you chose to purchase the water in your glass, and you are now obligated to pay for it. The water district that provided the water lived up to their end of the contract by providing you the water on demand. And since it is your private property, it should be your choice as to what you do with it.

To further prove the point that it is your property, consider what might happen if you choose not to pay your water bill. When your bill is late, the water district will use the full force of the government to collect payment. First will come warnings, and if those go unheeded, penalties and fines will follow, and if those too are ignored, your meter will eventually be shut off.

Those who advocate for fairness in water supply will subjectively say that the government should pass a law that restricts how you use the water you purchased, ignoring the private property principle granted to you by the Constitution of the United States. Restrictive rules designed to impose control over the use of water will be introduced, such as a prohibition against hosing your driveway, washing your car, or watering your lawn. Just because you purchased your water from a government agency doesn't make it less of your own property.

It has been said, "From the taste of wheat, it is not possible to tell who produced it, a Russian serf, a French peasant, or an English capitalist."[196] We need to recognize that there is no shortage of water; it is an abundant commodity, the same as any other commodity, such as corn, soybeans, wheat, gold, or silver. Water can neither be created nor destroyed. Through the hydrologic cycle it naturally recycles itself, covers two thirds of the earth's surface, and flows by gravity from the headwaters of the river, where it falls as rain, to the river's mouth, where it is deposited in the ocean. The availability of water where and when it is needed is what is in short supply, and ironically it is not for the lack of a delivery system.

Water, with private property rights tied to it, has intrinsic value. This value, once established, can be traded and bought and sold. The commodities market provides a mechanism where such trades could occur. Through the commodities market, the economic value of the water could be realized, and thereby the highest and best use of the intrinsic value would be found. Today, some say the price of water is too high, some say too low. How is anyone able to determine what the water is worth without a market mechanism to find the price where the market will clear and the right amount of water will be traded at the right price and delivered to a user willing to pay for it? It seems logical that a farmer would gladly trade his water to an urban dweller if the transaction produced greater economic benefit than the farm product he is laboring to grow.

The bottled water industry provides an example of the free market and market mechanisms for the commodity water. In this market water is neatly packaged and delivered to every store and corner gas station across the country, at a price everyone is willing to pay.

And the difference in price is staggering. My local water provider sells me 748 gallons of water for $3.40 and delivers it to my tap, on demand. The equivalent amount of Fiji bottled water would cost about $800.00—and consumers readily pay this. The water in the package is not significantly different from the water that comes from your tap. The question is why a consumer is willing to sacrifice his or her scare economic resources when the pricing disparity is so dramatic.

The answer is that price is only an obstacle in the absence of value. Here the consumer is not only buying the water but also purchasing convenience. The convenience comes from an extraordinary supply chain that delivers not only the bottle and packaging, but the water itself, gathered in the Fiji Islands and transported across the ocean to every street corner in America.

What is the difference between the water from your tap and the water in the Fiji bottle? One is supplied by the private market and one by the government. Today the government maintains near monopoly control over the supply and distribution of water in California. Does it have to be this way?

We can look to another liquid commodity for an example. Today, there are over one million miles of oil and gas pipelines in the United States. Oil and gas are both liquids transported via pipelines. The pipes deliver a commodity to every corner gas station in the country at a price everyone can afford. Yet gas and oil are much more difficult to extract and refine. They must be of extraordinary quality and they must be handled very carefully, as they are explosive, and a drop is never wasted. Water supply and distribution systems share many of the same characteristics.

Margaret Thatcher once said "the government should be in the business of providing services, not owning assets." The water pipelines and distribution systems could be sold to the private sector, with the capital that is recovered returned to the ratepayer. A portion of the water rate going forward could be used for the future repair and maintenance of the distribution system that would be contracted to the pipeline owner. The private sector would have to compete for the government contract, bringing economic value and a basis of cost comparison for the ratepayer. The proper role of the government is to define the water quality that the private sector would deliver into the distribution system. The pipeline distribution systems could be interconnected so that there would be competition for the price of water that enters it. The system would move the water from where the water is abundant to where it is needed, on demand.

San Francisco's main water supply, Hetch Hetchy in Yosemite National Park, was more than 90 percent full in June 2015, despite drought restrictions.

As a matter of public policy, water rates should be fair, understandable, cost effective, and good for the economy.[197] In 1996 Californians voted to amend the California State Constitution by passing Proposition 218. This constitutional amendment, also known as the "Right to Vote on Taxes Act," limited the ways in which government can raise money for operations without taxpayer consent, including charging higher water rates to those users who consumed the most water. Prop 218 requires that the user be charged no more than his proportional interest in the water delivered to him or his parcel.

Tiered rates and budget-based or allocation-based water rates are a popular way to further incentivize water conservation; however, they have recently been found to be in violation of Proposition 218 when they don't conform to the "proportional cost of service attributable to the owner's property."[198]

These rules compare your water use to that of other water users, and when the average of all users is defined, a water budget is designed where a consumption above a subjective threshold causes the user to pay more per unit for the water he purchases, increasing his total water bill.

All of this ignores the fact that you already have an economic signal to reduce consumption, as the more water you use, the more you will pay, under any set of circumstances. A rational consumer will, acting in his own enlightened self-interest, automatically conserve water to reduce his bill to maximize his own economic resources. In addition, the consumption of the water generates the revenue the district will use to build the infrastructure to replace the supply that was consumed in the first place.

Other economic incentives will be offered, such as government rebates for turf removal. Turf removal rebates and other such financial schemes are Robin Hood in reverse. In this case we take from the poor and give to the rich. The reason is that the money to provide the rebate for the removal of the turf is embedded within the water rate that all users pay. As a proportion of the total household budget, the poor pay the most for water service, yet they are the least able to avail themselves of government rebates to relandscape their yards, while the wealthier are the most likely.

In addition, allocation-based rate structures exacerbate the Robin-Hood-in-reverse problem by further distorting the pricing mechanism. The users in the highest tiers benefit most from their reduction in water consumption. Imagine two consumers, one in the highest tier at $9 per unit and one in the lowest tier at $2 per unit. The high tier user is being given $9 from the district treasury, while the low tier user only gets $2, with each reducing his or her water consumption by the same amount. Ironically, this water conservation does not come for free; it simply comes at the expense of another, and ironically the consumer that is hurt the most is the poor one, because water service consumes a larger portion of his or her household budget.

A secondary effect of this policy is that it requires the district to hold in its reserve the private property, money, of the constituents it serves by charging a higher than normal price for the water to provide for the turf removal rebate. The turf rebate is simply a portion of the water rate that everyone pays; the cash collected is then reserved at the water district and given back to those who implement water conservation, such as lawn replacement. This further deprives the private sector of its most valuable resource, money, which would otherwise be deployed elsewhere in a more productive fashion.

The most damaging effect of government subsidies and pricing schemes is that they erode the confidence in government, as the poorest among us are as rational as the wealthiest and easily see that the subsidy comes at their own expense. It has often been said that trust leaves on horseback and returns on foot. Trust is difficult to earn, easy to lose, and even more difficult to regain and is not easily measured in dollars and cents.

Supply and Demand

At this point one must ask, what are the economic consequences of government-mandated water use policies? Unfortunately, it would require the repeal of the fundamental laws of supply and demand for them to work in the way they are intended. The fixed costs of operating massive public waterworks are very high. The canals, tunnels, storage reservoirs, plants, and equipment must all be paid for whether the system delivers one drop of water or one million acre feet. As mandated conservations kicks in, per-unit water prices must rise to pay the high fixed costs of operating the waterworks.

As the per-unit cost of water rises, those at the top of the economic spectrum benefit the most because they are most able to take advantage of the government rebates offered to implement water-saving devices, replacing a lawn with artificial turf and retrofitting interior water fixtures of their home with water-saving devices.

Ironically, the poor are hit hardest here again, as the per-unit cost of water increases when they have the least opportunity to avail themselves of the water-saving devices that generate the rebates for implementing conservation and realizing the savings.

As prices continue to rise, the economic signal to conserve grows stronger and more conservation will occur, which will cause the water rates to rise further yet, and on it goes. If water were priced as a commodity, volumetric discounts would be given to the largest customers, as these large customer are in fact covering the largest portion of the fixed operational costs of the utilities and are in fact subsidizing all of the other users.

Under normal market conditions, prices rise when goods are scarce. The rise in price increases profit, which in turn attracts competition. The competition then figures out how to increase supply, which in turn lowers prices. This price-setting mechanism is what is missing from the water pricing formula.

Freedom from Conservation Mandates

Today, we are faced with a drought of biblical proportions and government that is beginning to choose the winners and losers among us; those who will be provided water and those who won't. The arguments will share the same theme as today's other political debates: fairness, waste, cost, necessity, the environment. All of those themes will be played out as the vast silent majority of citizens stands by and, without realizing it, has their liberty stripped away by new government rules and regulations regarding their use of water.

The rules will be thought up by well-intentioned government bureaucrats that are trying to reduce the activities of daily living to a written document that will form the basis of law, with the power of government behind it. Some will advocate usurious fines for those that fail to comply. The small and organized vocal minority will clamor ever louder as the crisis grows deeper for yet more government involvement to right the wrongs of those that don't comply and fairly distribute the increasingly limited resource we all so desperately need, all the time insisting the supply is finite and must be divided among us.

From Scarcity to Surplus

The answer to the drought is to increase the supply of water. The science and technology exist today to create a water supply that is inexhaustible. In some ways the implementation of science and technology and engineering is the easy part. The harder part is changing the mind-set from scarcity to surplus. This is where the politics happen and why politicians should not be involved in controlling the supply and distribution of water. The proper role of government is to ensure water quality. Water quality regulations should be created through the scientific process that determines what compounds that occur in the water supply, naturally or by man, are harmful to the long-term health condition of human beings.

Recently, Prime Minister of Israel Benjamin Netanyahu visited California and spoke with Governor Brown. Israel has made great strides in attaining water security in the last few decades. Netanyahu said that rainfall has dropped by half in the sixty-five years of Israel's existence while the country's population grew tenfold and the economy grew by a factor of seventy.[199] Yet Israel is not experiencing the effects of a drought. Why? Because of the implementation of science and technology at the highest level.

Water Recycling

Water recycling provides for about 20 percent of the supply of the water demands of Orange County. Today the Orange County Water District recycles one hundred million gallons per day of wastewater via the world famous Groundwater Replenishment System. This water would otherwise be dumped into the ocean. The source water is the by-product of the activities of daily living of the 2.4 million people in the district's service area and is dependent on people consuming water. If conservation goes too far, the feedstock for the plant will dry up.

Today the district uses a four-step process to recycle the water to beyond drinking water standards. The process starts with microfiltration, during which suspended solid particles are removed. Next it moves on to reverse osmosis, when it is forced through a solid plastic membrane at the molecular level. Then the water is hit with hydrogen peroxide and ultraviolet light. Minerals are added and then the water is shipped upstream, where it reenters the earth. Sometime later your local water retailer will pump it out of the ground and serve it to you from your tap.

The expert staff at the Orange County Water District estimate that 1.3 billion gallons of wastewater is discharged to the ocean that could otherwise be recycled through a process like this.

Water Reclamation

Water reclamation projects such as the Mesa Water Reliability Facility could also be developed,. This project taps an ancient aquifer, deep within the Orange County Groundwater Basin. Therein lies an ancient redwood forest that is decomposing and leaving behind a stain and slight odor in the water. Using membrane filtration, this project pumps the water to the surface and then forces the water molecules through nanofiltration to remove the color and odor from the water. It is then discharged directly into the drinking water system for consumption by the public. The development of this project allows Mesa Water District to be independent from imported water. By being a good neighbor, Mesa frees up water in the state for other purposes, such as farming. Local water supply and control are important in the context of the state's water supply needs.

Desalination

"If we could ever competitively, at a cheap rate, get fresh water from salt water, that…would really dwarf any other scientific accomplishments," said John F. Kennedy on April 12, 1961. That time has come. The cost of importing water from Northern California has risen dramatically and will continue to rise for years to come. As of April 15, 2012, "rates have risen 96 percent, since 2006."[200]

In the early 1970s, the Orange County Water District Board of Directors, led by Board President Henry Segerstrom, successfully appealed to the Federal Government Office of Saline Water for the construction of a large-scale seawater desalination facility on the property of the Orange County Water District. He appealed to the imagination of Congress by stating, "Americans did not stand on the moon through timidity of action," encouraging the Congress to move forward with the construction of an ocean desalination module in Fountain Valley. Seawater desalination has been discussed as a potential large-scale water source since the days of Aristotle. The technology is proven worldwide and is in use on a large scale in every major industrialized country in the world today.

Ocean desalination uses the same technology as water recycling and water reclamation: membrane filters. The only difference is the porosity of the filter itself. Sodium chloride molecules are small and therefore require a tighter screen.

Today, California requires twenty-seven regulatory permits to design, construct, and operate an ocean desalination facility. Each of those permits is subject to legal challenges. Ocean desalination is remarkable because it create drinking water closest to the people who need it without the necessity of land-based canals and conveyance and storage reservoirs. The ocean itself is the reservoir.

Poseidon Resources is proposing to build the largest ocean desalination facility in the Western Hemisphere in Huntington Beach. Poseidon obtained a land lease from a power-generating station in Huntington Beach to build and operate a reverse osmosis seawater desalination plant. The project as conceived would utilize the existing ocean intake and outfall for the source and disposal of ocean water and the resultant brine. Co-location and redundant use of the existing infrastructure generates significant cost savings and mitigates impact to the environment.

Currently the AES plant takes in five hundred million gallons of seawater per day to cool the electric generating station, currently situated on the shore of Huntington Beach. Poseidon would take 20 percent of that water that is discharged from the electric generating station, remove the salt, and deliver fifty million gallons per day of clean drinking water to Orange County.

Before the brine is discharged to the ocean, it will be diluted with additional seawater. This ensures the increased salinity will not affect marine organisms in the near vicinity of the ocean outfall. When complete this project would deliver 10 percent of the water demands of Orange County. It has been under consideration for over fourteen years.[201] Poseidon has obtained twenty-six of the twenty-seven regulatory permits necessary to build and operate the plant. Each permit was challenged in court by opponents of the project, and in each case the opponents lost the case. The cost to pursue the regulatory permits alone is over $45 million. The same people who oppose the project based on cost continue to litigate the project and thereby increase the cost.

By developing local resources such as ocean desalination, Orange County is doing its part to alleviate the effects of the drought on others throughout the state. By reducing our demand on imported water, we free up the water resource that would otherwise be imported into Orange County for others to use. Therein lies the common ground between urban and agricultural users: we provide for our water supply and they provide us with food.

One of the main objections associated with ocean desalination is energy consumption. Science and technology will provide the solutions here as well. More efficient membrane filters and solar electric generation harnessed with ocean desalination provide an opportunity to solve multiple policy goals simultaneously.

New, more efficient membrane technology on the near horizon promises to deliver even better results. The Perforene membrane, developed by Lockheed Martin, is perforated graphene, where perforations can be as small as a nanometer. These pores are so small that they will trap the salt in seawater and allow for its removal. When commercialized, the Perforene membrane promises to significantly reduce the energy consumption associated with ocean desalination by 10 percent to 20 percent. "As a separation membrane, Perforene offers the tantalizing possibility of changing the relationship between rejection and permeability that limits today's solution diffusion membranes," says Steve

Sinton, Lockheed Martin Fellow.[202] As material science advances, energy consumption associated with membrane filters will continue to decrease.

Governor Brown set an ambitious goal of 50 percent renewable energy for California. The Independent Energy Producers Association estimates that this standard may result in overgeneration of power during peak energy production during the day. This overgeneration will need to be taken up somewhere, and currently the State would have to pay out-of-state entities to take the electricity.

Ocean desalination plants are energy intensive. According to the IEP, "[A]ssuming the State constructed fifteen desalination plants, each capable of producing 50 million gallons per day, these plants would take up 30 percent of the overgenerations forecast to occur by 2030 under a 50 percent renewable standard. Moreover, these same fifteen desalination plants would supply an amount of additional water to meet 12 percent of the state's current public water supply demand; meet 3 percent of the current irrigation supply needs; or equal 37 percent of the current deliveries from the State Water Project."[203]

The Orange County Water District and the Amy Corps of Engineers jointly operate the Prado Dam as a flood control and water storage facility. The dam provides a unique opportunity for a solar installation. The face of the dam is situated in a south/southwesterly direction and provides enough surface area to generate about twenty megawatts of electricity. The electricity generated there could be used to offset the energy consumption of the Huntington Beach desalination project proposed by Poseidon resources. Here we have a shovel-ready project to help alleviate the water supply problem and meet the renewable energy goals as set by the governor.

The Tyranny of Controls

There are three ways to handle the distribution of scarce goods or resources: 1) Take as much as you want at a given price and use it however you see fit; 2) We can only provide a limited amount of the resource at a particular price for you to use however you see fit; or 3) We can only provide you with a limited amount, and you may only use the resource according to a detailed set of rules.

Herein lies a choice: Do we expand our supply of water so that it is pure, plentiful, and affordable for everyone, or do we live with what we have and try to control and restrict its use through tyrannical controls as if were a finite resource?

The way forward is to unleash the private sector and, with market-based incentives, allow the development of a sustainable new water supply on a grand scale that is resilient to drought. Through the application of science and technology at the highest level, water recycling, water reclamation, and ocean desalination and water conservation are all part of the solution.

About the Author: Shawn Dewane

Shawn Dewane serves as an elected director of the Orange County Water District and the Mesa Water District. Shawn recognizes that clean, affordable water is fundamental to our civil liberty and key to the economic development of our community. Professionally, Shawn owns Dewane Investment Strategies (www.dewaneis.com), an independent Southern California branch office of Raymond James Financial Services.

Nine

PENSIONS

By Ben Boychuk

Underfunded and uncontrolled growth in public-employee pension costs are driving California cities into insolvency, imperiling vital services, and threatening to create two distinct classes of citizens: a specially protected minority of well-remunerated government workers and retirees, and everybody else.

Consider the case of San Bernardino. In August 2012, the inland Southern California city filed for Chapter 9 bankruptcy protection shortly after the city treasurer reported there wasn't enough cash on hand to make payroll. San Bernardino's venture into bankruptcy court came just a few months after Stockton made its own trip in Northern California. The East Bay city of Vallejo was just emerging from a painful (and more or less fruitless) Chapter 9 restructuring as San Bernardino and Stockton were getting the process under way.

San Bernardino's fiscal decline was decades in the making. The day after a politically divided city council voted in July 2012 to begin preparing the bankruptcy filing, then mayor Pat Morris, a Democrat and former judge, laid the issue on the line for reporters. "The reasons for our dilemma are multiple and long enduring," he explained. "They began long before the meltdown of our economy. We've been living on the financial edge for a long, long time.

But we were unmasked by the meltdown in 2007 when we lost $16 million in sales tax in one year, when we lost 60 percent of our land value and five thousand homes went into foreclosure."

The city also had relied foolishly on $6 million a year in redevelopment funds—money that disappeared after Gov. Jerry Brown abolished development agencies earlier that same year as part of his budget plan. By the time council members declared a "fiscal emergency" on July 17—a necessary step before formally filing for Chapter 9—the city of 213,000 people had an annual budget deficit of about $45 million.

Morris was unambiguous about what was really dragging his city further downward in an ocean of red ink: out-of-control labor and pension costs. "Years ago, mayors and councils negotiated labor contracts that were far, far too generous for this generation of service," he said. "Those are unsustainable in this current marketplace."

As a result of those deals—along with a bizarre provision of the city's charter—San Bernardino's pension costs rose from $5 million in 2000 to a budget-busting $26 million in 2012. As part of the city's efforts to eliminate the $45 million revenue gap, the city council voted to suspend its payments to the California Public Employee Retirement System (CalPERS). It was obvious to almost everyone—with the possible exceptions of the city attorney and his council allies, as well as the city's powerful firefighters union—that if the city was going to get out from under those crippling costs, something would need to be done about the out-of-control growth in pensions. Bankruptcy, however painful, seemed the best way to do the unpleasant job.

Three years, one mayor, a city attorney, three council members, and tens of thousands of billable hours later, San Bernardino's lawyers in May 2015 submitted the city council-approved, court-mandated "Plan of Adjustment" to a federal bankruptcy judge in Riverside. Under the proposal, which still requires court approval, retired city employees would receive no less than 100 percent of their pensions while investors and underwriters would get just one penny on the dollar for $50 million in outstanding pension obligation bonds. (Naturally, debt holders challenged the city's proposal.) What's more, the city agreed in 2014 to repay $13.5 million plus interest to CalPERS for withheld payments. And as of May 2015, San Bernardino's pensions had a total un-funded liability of $285 million.

What in the world happened?

In brief: the beleaguered, insolvent city took on the powerful, $285 bil-lion state pension fund juggernaut and got crushed. Despite a couple of early tactical victories for the city, the outcome wasn't even close.

San Bernardino is a microcosm of the massive challenges facing California municipalities as unchecked employee pension costs and postretirement ben-efits consume an ever-larger share of government operating budgets.

San Bernardino chose a bold path, born of desperation. Vallejo and Stockton studiously avoided direct conflict with CalPERS. Both cities decided they lacked the resources and wherewithal to wage a lengthy court battle. CalPERS officials had been steadfast: public employees' retirement payments are constitutionally protected and therefore untouchable. But San Bernardino saw employee compensation and benefits consuming 80 percent of the city's budget and concluded that the harsh reality of bankruptcy would surely give the city leverage to take on the giant pension fund and prevail where Stockton and Vallejo hadn't even bothered to try. As city manager Allen Parker would later put it, "We naively thought we could negotiate more successfully, but that didn't necessarily happen."[204] That's putting it charitably.

CalPERS had challenged San Bernardino's right to file for bankruptcy in the first instance. The pension fund's attorney argued the court would es-tablish "a dangerous precedent" if it allowed San Bernardino to remain in bankruptcy. If San Bernardino prevailed, CalPERS claimed, other cities would be tempted to follow suit and use bankruptcy to escape their contractual and constitutional obligations.[205] Federal bankruptcy court Judge Meredith Jury rejected that argument. "I can't see anything other than dissolving the city if they can't file under Chapter 9," she said.[206]

But CalPERS had another way of strong-arming the city, much as it had intimidated Stockton officials into leaving their city's pensions untouched. The pension fund simply threatened to terminate employees' pension plans, which would result in huge reductions in retiree payouts and send current employees scurrying for the exits. When Stockton's bondholders argued the city's workout plan must address pensions in order for the city's other creditors to be treated equitably, Stockton's lawyers essentially took the CalPERS line, telling the court the city would lose employees "in droves" if the pension fund made good on its threat.

San Bernardino's insolvency showed that not every David can slay his Goliath. Bankruptcy also threw a bright light on public employee compensation and the way unions negotiate at the expense of the public good. In a series of court filings in 2014, the city's lawyers presented some fascinating numbers about the San Bernardino fire department. With about 160 full-time emergency personnel, the top 40 employees make an annual salary of $190,000 on average. The next 40 averaged $166,000 a year. And the next 40 averaged $130,000.

Firefighters have a tough job. And a smaller fire department has seen greatly increased overtime hours, which balloon firefighters' salaries. Still, that's an awful lot of compensation in a city where the average per capita income is a little over $37,000 a year and roughly one third of residents live below the poverty line. As it happened, the firefighters' union was the only collective bargaining unit that refused to make any concessions to the city as it looked for ways to restructure its finances.

But there was also a major structural reason for those outsized salaries, and one that San Bernardino's adjustment plan could not touch. Section 186 of the city's charter requires that public-safety workers be paid on a scale tied to the average salaries of workers in "similarly sized" cities—cities such as Irvine and Huntington Beach, where the average per capita income is three times higher than poor San Bernardino's. Section 186 hobbled the city's effort to escape a fiscal cataclysm. In the midst of bankruptcy, the city council had no choice but to approve $2 million in salary hikes for cops and firemen. The people and their representatives had no say in the matter. Judge Jury has said that charter reform is a vital step in returning the city to solvency. But several attempts to revise Section 186, including a November 2014 charter reform initiative, have come up short. With pensions untouched and the city's outmoded charter intact, the only good that might come of San Bernardino's bankruptcy is the city's intention to repay the firefighters' intransigence by outsourcing their jobs.

*   *   *

A few years ago, bankruptcy looked like the cities' salvation. But in every case so far, city officials have blinked in the face of the state's most powerful pension fund.

California, in fact, has 130 state and local pension systems, many of which are in no better shape than the municipalities and agencies they serve. The two largest—CalPERS and the California Teachers' Retirement System (CalSTRS)—serve a combined 3.1 million members, with 750,000 or so retired state and local government workers currently collecting benefits. Both funds carry gargantuan unfunded liabilities: at least $190 billion combined, assuming the state controller's numbers are correct. One doomsday scenario from Stanford University estimated that taxpayers might be on the hook for upward of $500 billion based on lower annual rates of return on investment than CalPERS's overly optimistic 7.75 percent.

Strange as it may seem today, the Golden State's pension system was once a model of fiscal rectitude. California set up its retirement system in 1932, when the United States was deep into the Great Depression. Given the times, the program was necessarily modest. An employee was entitled to a pension equaling 1.43 percent of his salary averaged over the last five years on the job, multiplied by the total number of years of service. So a state worker who retired at sixty-five after working forty years qualified for a pension equal to 57.20 percent of his average final salary. Setting the retirement age at sixty-five for state employees and later for local government workers held down costs at a time when the average life expectancy of an American male was just sixty-six years old.

Legislators began meddling with the system in costly ways beginning in 1968, with a bill that added cost-of-living adjustments to CalPERS's calculus. More pricey perks followed. In 1970, lawmakers lowered the retirement age from sixty-five to sixty and boosted the pension formula from 1.43 percent of an employee's average final salary to 2.00 percent. That meant a government employee who retired at sixty with a salary of $50,000 after forty years on the job could expect a pension equal to 80.00 percent of his average salary, or $40,000. If he stuck it out another five years, his pension would be equal to 95.00 percent of his final average salary. Not bad.

In 1983, the legislature passed a bill offering police and firefighters an even more generous formula, reducing the retirement age to fifty-five and increasing the calculus from 2.0 percent to 2.5 percent of his average final salary. Within the past decade, most public-safety employees have negotiated an even more generous "3 percent at fifty" plan, which has allowed some police and firemen to retire with six-figure pensions while still young enough to launch a second career, often in another police or fire agency.

In 1984, voters approved Proposition 21, which gave CalPERS's governing board wide latitude in allocating investments. The change in rules paid off. Prior to Prop 21, CalPERS's investment income more than doubled from $1.5 billion in 1982 to $3.3 billion in 1985. After Prop 21, investment returns doubled again, reaching $6.1 billion in 1990. The go-go '90s saw an explosion in CalPERS's fortunes, as the fund earned a whopping $68.0 billion between 1994 and 1998 thanks to the dot-com boom, which was really a bubble.

Those huge revenue gains gave pension fund managers and elected officials a sense of invincibility. For a short time in the late 1990s, CalPERS was fully funded. Wealth bred complacency and risk taking, which led in turn to an even more consequential policy change. In 1999, the legislature passed and Gov. Gray Davis signed Senate Bill 400, which offered state and local government employees generous, retroactive benefit increases. The timing was poor, coming just as the tech bubble began to collapse.

CalPERS officials knew SB 400 carried risks. Their worst-case scenario involved a long-term economic slump that would force state pension contributions to rise by billions of dollars—exactly what ended up happening. But state lawmakers either didn't understand the risks or didn't much care. State Sen. Deborah Ortiz, the chief sponsor of SB 400, later claimed that CalPERS staff offered only rosy projections, with the state's costs ranging from $379.0

million to $466.0 million over ten years—a reasonable expense for a state with a budget of around $99.0 billion.[207] In fact, the actual cost turned out to be several times that number, with the taxpayers' tab approaching $10.0 billion halfway through the decade. By 2010, the state was paying $3.5 billion a year into CalPERS. Congressman Tom McClintock, who was a state senator at the time, offered a characteristically blunt assessment of CalPERS's pitch: "They lied."[208]

SB 400 also had the unintended effect of pressuring local governments to match the generosity of the state. In 2001, evidently unmoved by the lessons of the late dot-com bust, the legislature passed a bill that let local government unions bargain for the same benefits their colleagues in state government won two years prior. Many local officials, flush with sales tax and redevelopment money, were only too happy to go along. Suddenly, cities found themselves in competition to see who could offer the most generous benefits packages. Many police and fire unions demanded—and got—provisions in their contracts similar to San Bernardino's ill-advised Section 186. At the same time, many cities took "pension holidays," going several years without contributing to CalPERS because the fund enjoyed record surpluses.

That changed mid-decade. As CalPERS investments in tech stocks and later real estate foundered, the pension fund's directors had little choice but to raise cities' contributions in order to compensate for the losses. And because CalPERS has virtually unlimited power to decide what state and local governments must pay into the fund, cities suddenly faced double-digit increases in their payments. San Jose—which would later become ground zero for reform—watched helplessly as its contributions nearly doubled from $73 million in 2001 to $122 million in 2007. By 2010, the city's contribution had doubled again, topping $245 million.

It could have been worse—and it is. CalPERS has had to resort to all manner of accounting tricks to soften the impact on struggling municipalities. Most pension funds use a three-year average to smooth out variations in rates of return and keep cities' contributions fairly stable. The idea is the good years will generally offset the bad. But CalPERS in 2005 took the unusual step of extending its performance average to *fifteen years*, which incorporated the fund's sizable losses with even more sizable gains. After the stock market collapsed in 2008, CalPERS announced it would allow local governments to finance much higher contributions over *thirty years*, which means a generation yet unborn will pay for the blunders of a generation fading away.

Once the consequences of SB 400 became evident, Gov. Arnold Schwarzenegger floated the idea of an initiative in 2005 to effectively privatize the state pension system by moving most workers away from a defined benefit into a defined contribution plan. With defined contributions, both the employee and the government make a contribution to a worker's retirement account, which he can draw upon tax free upon retirement. The current system of defined benefits means workers are guaranteed benefits whether they're paid for or not. Ultimately, the taxpayers will bear the burden of liability.

Schwarzenegger didn't think that was particularly fair. The unions responded by pillorying him as an enemy of hardworking, middle-class government workers. The state nurses' union was especially vindictive after Schwarzenegger publicly derided them—at an event honoring women's contributions to the state, no less. "Pay no attention to those voices over there," he said. "They are the special interests. Special interests don't like me in Sacramento because I kick their butt."[209] The nurses spent the next year following the governor from event to event around the state and nation, staging more than one hundred protests in the course of his ill-fated "Year of Reform."[210]

Arnold wasn't an especially good governor, let alone a conservative one. But on pension reform he was ahead of his time. When the nonpartisan Legislative Analyst's Office published an assessment in 2011 of a much less ambitious reform package favored by Jerry Brown, it affirmed many of the points Schwarzenegger struggled to convey six years earlier. The LAO chided CalPERS for allowing pension holidays only to wallop cities with contribution hikes when the economy went south: "In the late 1990s, pension systems cut employer contributions to near zero based on short-term investment gains…then increased them substantially…just when governments faced their own problems."[211]

The LAO also warned of another political problem: the rise of the "$100,000 club." While noting that only about 2 percent of CalPERS and

CalSTRS retirees drew six-figure pensions, the LAO pointed out that club will grow considerably in the coming years due to inflation and, more significantly, "the effects of increased pension benefit provisions put in place in the late 1990s and early 2000s."[212]

＊　＊　＊

Apart from the scandalous appearance of retired government workers drawing pensions that in a few cases topped $500,000 a year, the most noticeable consequence of unchecked pension growth was the appearance of the "crowd-out" effect. As a 2011 Little Hoover Commission report explained it, "Government budgets are being cut while pension costs continue to rise and squeeze other government." If the Old Testament prophet Jeremiah had been an academic economist, he might have written something similar to this passage in the Little Hoover report:

> "[T]he tension between rising pension costs and lean government budgets is often presented today in a political context, with stakeholders debating the severity of the problem and how long it will last. In another five years [i.e., 2016] when pension contributions from government are expected to jump and remain at higher levels for decades in order to keep retirement systems solvent, there will be no debate about the magnitude of the problem. Even with the introduction of two-tiered pension plans, barring a miraculous market advance, few government entities—especially at the local level—will be able to absorb the blow without severe cuts to services."

Their conclusion? "Pension costs will crush government."[213]

That time is fast approaching—indeed, it's already happening. Stockton and Vallejo emerged from bankruptcy with their pensions intact—and on no surer fiscal footing than they were in 2012 or 2008. Services continue to deteriorate, populations are declining, and tax bases are shrinking. Vallejo made its creditors accept drastically reduced payments, cut retiree health care benefits, laid off cops and firefighters, and cancelled a project to rehabilitate its decaying downtown. But the city's pension costs are rising inexorably as before. The city estimates its costs will grow 8.5 percent a year through fiscal year 2020, eventually consuming one-fifth of the budget. And as Steven Malanga noted in a 2013 story for *City Journal*, "To employ a cop in Vallejo still requires $230,000 a year, including $47,000 in annual CalPERS costs."[214] It's essentially the same story in Stockton, where a once vibrant downtown resembles a ghost town and the city now vies with Oakland for the state's highest violent crime rate.

The "crowd-out" phenomenon obviously isn't confined to down-on-their-luck cities. It's visible in more prosperous places like San Diego, San Jose, and Los Angeles. The City of Los Angeles projects a $165.1 million deficit in the 2015–16 fiscal year, due in large part to police overtime costs and a decision by the city's pension board last year to reduce its actuarial investment rate of return from 7.75 percent to a somewhat less lofty 7.50 percent. Last year, the city closed its deficit by slashing some public safety services, including 911 emergency operators. Budget cuts forced the San Jose Police Department to eliminate its burglary unit in 2012. A subsequent spike in property crimes, brought on in part by prison realignment, caught the police flatfooted. And there are 1,400 miles of potholed roads in Sonoma County with little money to fix them.

Other cities are on somewhat better footing. Fitch Ratings in June 2015 released a generally positive analysis of San Francisco's creditworthiness ahead of a municipal bond auction set for July. But the firm noted long-term challenges, including a projected $417.9 million budget deficit in the 2020 fiscal year "largely due to more rapid growth for personnel expenses than revenues."[215] The rating company also pointed out that pensions, other postemployment benefits such as health insurance, and debt service consumed about 22.6 percent of the city's budget in the 2014–15 fiscal year.[216]

As Manhattan Institute senior fellow Stephen Eide noted in an April 2015 report on the problems that unchecked pension costs pose to government services, the crowd-out problem is built into the system. "When the value of a pension system's investments drops during recessions," Eide explains,

the employer must increase contributions to stay current on its plan to ensure that it will have sufficient assets during the next twenty to thirty years to fund workers' retirements. Since revenues also drop during recessions, pension systems require employers to spend more on retirement benefits when they can least afford it. Crowd-out is thus a feature, not a bug, of public pension systems.[217]

Eide has documented many of the baleful effects of crowd-out on local governments and services. Between 2004 and 2012, for example, US Census Bureau data show that growth in pension costs outpaced local government spending on key services such as police and fire protection, parks, and libraries.[218]

Crowd-out has also confounded cities' ability to perform routine maintenance on roads and parks. In San Bernardino's recovery plan, for example, the city estimates $180.0 million in deferred street repairs and improvements, up from $88.4 million in 2008. Deferred maintenance on city-owned buildings and facilities is estimated at $123.0 million. "Were localities to devote what they currently spend on pension debt service to basic maintenance instead," Eide avers, "some could reduce all or most of their infrastructure backlog within a few years."[219]

Rising pension costs also led to sharp reductions in staffing. In December 2014, Eide writes, "local government staffing levels in California remained 8.0 percent below where they were in December 2007. Private-sector job levels in California, by contrast, were 2.4 percent higher." Now, there's an excellent conservative argument to be made that government employment *should* be lower than it was before the Great Recession. Among other reasons, staff reductions force cities to reevaluate their priorities. And there is plenty that local government does that would be better handled by the private sector. But Eide suggests that by restricting staffing, "crowd-out also restricts municipalities' policy possibilities."[220]

*　*　*

The crowd-out effect would seem to be an excellent reason to tackle pension costs head on. But reform isn't easy.

Reformers must first contend with what's known colloquially as "the California rule." The state supreme court ruled in a series of cases that the government could not alter or reduce a vested benefit for work performed—not even prospectively. Put another way, once a government employee is hired and given a vested pension right, it cannot be taken away. But that doesn't prevent state or local governments from changing the benefits for *new* hires. After the court's 1947 decision in *Kern v. Long Beach*, for example, the city went five years without offering its employees a pension plan.

Of course, the justices had no reason to think—indeed, they could not have possibly known—that the state's pension plans would one day pose an existential threat to the state's fiscal viability. Yet the court remains firm.

CalPERS and the legislature have resisted anything resembling serious reform.

Its legislative allies keep resisting the one reform that would truly free California taxpayers from this ruinous pension system: moving it toward a 401(k)-style defined-contribution plan, as other states and municipalities, including Utah and Rhode Island, have done.

The legislature did pass some modest reforms in 2012 at the behest of Governor Brown, but they were mostly easy pickings that wouldn't offend the unions, such as higher employee contributions and modest rules discouraging double dipping and pension spiking—the practice of using overtime to bolster salaries in the final years of service. But keeping with the "California Rule," the changes apply almost exclusively to new hires, and a Stanford University analysis estimated the reforms would reduce long-term pension debt by at most 10 percent.

A certain sense of complacency could very well undermine the urgency of reform. Even though the economic recovery has been anemic at best, California's overall fiscal health has improved since the dark days of 2010. The state's credit rating is no longer the worst in the union—that dubious distinction is held currently by Illinois, with New Jersey placing a close second. We're number three.

The state's unemployment rate is better, too. Not great, but better. According to the US Bureau of Labor Statistics, California's U6 unemployment—the "real" unemployment rate which measures total jobless, plus all "marginally attached" and part-time workers—was 14.7 percent in the first quarter of 2015, compared to 22.1 percent five years earlier. And while we can be grateful the state hasn't had a multibillion-dollar budget crisis since 2011, Stephen Eide warns "local services are not improving at a rate proportionate to economic growth. When the next recession hits, more municipal bankruptcies will come."

*   *   *

Given California's cerulean blue political landscape, it should come as no surprise that many of the more promising reforms of the past five years have come from Democrats. Somewhat surprising, however, is that most of the Democratic reformers are dyed-in-the-wool progressives whose efforts to make the most modest of changes to the pension system have been stymied at every turn by their natural union allies. So the progressive reformers have taken up the crowd-out argument with gusto, appealing both to their constituents' liberal sentiments and rational self-interest. Their case is straightforward: the more we must spend on retired government workers, the fewer dollars we will have to devote to welfare, job training, subsidized housing, and education—to say nothing of filling potholes, collecting garbage, and paying cops and firemen.

"There's a difference between being a liberal and progressive and being a union Democrat," said San Jose Mayor Chuck Reed. "If you drain money out of services and pour them into retirements, people suffer."[221] Reed's harsh experience at the union bargaining table taught him a lesson that a certain type of cynic has known forever: "It's always about money, not about the public… The focus on money is different than a focus on public service."[222]

Reed has emerged as one of the foremost champions of pension reform in the state following his mostly successful campaign to pass a ballot measure to radically overhaul the city's pension system. The campaign was "mostly successful" because not all of Measure B survived a later court challenge. But the reforms the measure advanced remain important.

Measure B amended the city's charter to create a hybrid pension system combining a traditional defined benefit plan with a 401(k)-style defined contribution plan. New city employees pay for at least 50 percent of the total cost of the new plan. The initiative also capped the city's contribution to 9 percent of an employee's salary—slashed from more than 50 percent under the old regime. Crucially, the measure gave current city employees two options: contribute significantly more to their existing retirement plan or choose a lower-cost plan. Workers, of course, would keep all of the benefits they had accrued to that point.

San Jose's Measure B faced a ferocious opposition campaign from the unions, who later challenged the initiative in court after voters passed it in a landslide. A Santa Clara County Superior Court judge ruled that the provision requiring current employees to pay more violated their "vested rights." But the surviving provisions saved the city $20 million in the first two years.

In San Diego, Republican City Councilman Carl DeMaio led a similarly ambitious campaign in 2012 to redesign that city's dangerously underfunded pension system. San Diego's Proposition B capped the city's pension liabilities by freezing "pensionable income" for five years and moving all new hires (except police) into a defined contribution plan. The initiative also provided a lump-sum cash-out option to employees, although the IRS has held that up.

Reed and DeMaio joined forces to place an initiative modeled after the San Jose and San Diego measures on the November 2014 ballot. They withdrew the measure after Democratic Attorney General Kamala Harris produced title and summary language so obviously skewed against the measure that it would have had little chance of getting past the signature-gathering stage.

Reed and DeMaio are back in 2015 with a new campaign aimed at the November 2016 ballot. Their new initiative would weaken the "California Rule" by amending the state constitution to provide voters with the right to use future initiatives and referenda to "determine the amount of and manner in which compensation and retirement benefits are provided to employees of a government employer." The measure would specifically require voter approval anytime a pension agency wishes to establish a new defined-benefit plan for new employees hired after 2019. In fact, the Reed-DeMaio initiative—which they're calling "the Voter Empowerment Act of 2016—requires a vote *anytime* a government employer contributes more than half of pension costs for new employees.

But that's just a first step. Public pensions should be more like private pensions, which reward work and prudence, not just time served. Retirement ages need to go up and double dipping needs to end. No longer should state workers—including public safety workers—be allowed to retire at fifty-five or fifty to collect six-figure pensions and unlimited health benefits, only to get a second state or city job and double dip.

Ballot initiatives tend to be blunt instruments of reform. But when legislators are effectively in the pockets of the Service Employees' International Union, the California Teachers' Association, the California Federation of Teachers, the California Correctional Peace Officers' Association, the California Nurses' Association, and the California Labor Federation, what other option do taxpayers have?

Fact is, Californians today are spending more on public employee pension benefits than we're spending on higher education—$6.5 billion a year and counting. The typical Democratic response is to propose higher taxes. But the very idea of raising taxes on productive, private sector workers to pay the pensions of public employees is repugnant, especially to anyone who has prudently saved for his or her own retirement. Besides, higher taxes will do nothing to alleviate the crowd-out problem. As Democrat and former Schwarzenegger advisor David Crane showed after voters approved Jerry Brown's "temporary" income and sales tax increase, money that was supposedly earmarked for education was really going to plug a $4.5-billion-a-year hole in CalSTRS funding. Voters were duped. How difficult is that to understand?

It's an immutable law of politics that when circumstances change, policies must change. Requiring local government workers to contribute substantially more to their retirement plans, as San Jose and San Diego did through their local initiatives in 2012, reflects a profound change in circumstances. And just as voters empowered CalPERS thirty years ago to expand its investment portfolio, it makes sense for voters to empower themselves to impose checks on CalPERS and other pension funds to ensure long-term fiscal viability.

Despite the best efforts of lawmakers, regulators, trial lawyers, union flunkies, environmentalists, and bureaucrats, California remains a prosperous state. But the fruits of prosperity belong to more than just a special class of people. It is wrong to compel Californians struggling to eke out a middle-class life far away from the irenic coast to pay their public servants to live like pashas.

Put another way, government workers would have their fellow citizens—some yet unborn—hand over an ever larger share of their earnings in order to finance a retirement that few private sector employees will ever know or enjoy. However well intended, that's a perversion of public service. Binding contract or no, voters won't put up with such an inequitable relationship for long.

About the Author: Ben Boychuk

Ben Boychuk is associate editor of the Manhattan Institute's *City Journal* and a columnist for the *Sacramento Bee*, the *Press-Enterprise* in Riverside, and Tribune Media. He was previously managing editor of the *Claremont Review of Books* and an editorial writer for *Investor's Business Daily*. He lives in Inland Southern California with his wife and two children.

Ten

DEMOGRAPHICS

By Brian Calle

What is California? It depends on who you ask. Everyone has strong opinions about the Golden State. To outsiders it's a land of larger-than-life people and places: Silicon Valley's techies and Malibu's sun-kissed surfers, Hollywood's movie stars, the Bay Area's iconic landscape, and the home to Disneyland. In a 2013 Business Insider survey, Americans nation-wide chose California as their favorite state, the craziest state, the state with the hottest residents, and (on the flip side) the most overrated state in the union.

These colorful strokes of opinion are perhaps painted most broadly in the realm of politics. In the eyes of much of America, California's political climate can be summarized in four words: blue, and getting bluer. There are many reasons for this. Prominent liberals, such as *New York Times* columnist Paul Krugman, tend to praise California's progressive tax structure, wide-ranging regulations, and environmental consciousness; conservatives, on the other hand, decry the state's regulations on business and roll their eyes at ubiquitous warning labels on buildings, motor oil, air fresheners, and luggage sets "known to the state of California to cause cancer."

California tends to reinforce this hard-Left stereotype in national politics. Both of California's US senators and thirty-nine of the state's fifty-three congressional representatives, including long-time party leader Nancy Pelosi, are Democrats. The state has not gone Republican in a presidential election since George H. W. Bush's first run for commander in chief; since then, every Democratic candidate has carried the state by a margin of 10 percent or greater. It is thus unsurprising that citizens outside the Golden State, depending on their political viewpoints, consider California either a shining example of responsibly compassionate government or a nightmarish laboratory experiment in one-party politics.

But these easy stereotypes fail to tell the whole story of California's rich political and social landscape. In reality, both the past and the future of this remarkably important state are much more nuanced. As California demographics continue to shift due to immigration, education, an aging population, and public policy, these often overlooked, underexamined, and misunderstood pressures will sculpt the Golden State's political landscape over the years to come.

Race and Immigration

Regardless of political bent, no one can deny that California's changing racial and ethnic landscape will be one of the key determinants for future state elections. Demographic shifts over the past fifty years have permanently changed the game for political players here.

California is one of only four "majority minority" states (along with Texas, Hawaii, and New Mexico)—as well as the District of Columbia—in which more than half of the population belongs to a minority racial or ethnic group. In March 2014, California became only the second state after New Mexico whose Latino population outnumbered its non-Latino white population. Further diversity is found in California's Asian American population, the highest concentration of any state.

This diversity is unsurprising. California, after all, boasts an ideal geographic location for immigration both from the South and from across the Pacific, not to mention a picturesque landscape and famously desirable climate. What is surprising, however, is just how quickly these demographics have shifted. Only thirty-five years ago, in 1980, whites made up 67.0 percent of California's population, while Latinos accounted for 19.0 percent.

Asians, who had been officially permitted to immigrate in large numbers to the United States only following the passage of the 1965 Immigration and Nationality Act, contributed another 5.3 percent of the population. Within ten years, however, the Latino population had bloomed to 26.0 percent of Californians, and the Asian population had reached 9.0 percent (a full 40.0 percent, incidentally, of all Asian Americans living in America).[223]

Two main factors contributed to California's diversity boom. The first, of course, was high levels of immigration. According to the Immigration Policy Center, the foreign-born share of California's population, already at a significant 15.1 percent in 1980, shot up to 21.7 percent in 1990 and had climbed to 26.9 percent by 2010.

Immigration has slowed somewhat in recent years, particularly for Latinos, and especially since the housing bubble burst in 2007. Although Latino immigrants still outnumber their Asian counterparts in California, new arrivals are more likely to come from across the Pacific: in 2013, the *New York Times* reported that more than twice as many new immigrants now come to California from Asia as from Latin America. Projections from the USC Sol Price School of Public Policy estimate the foreign-born share of California's population will stabilize at 27.2 percent.

While California has always been a prime destination for immigrants, however, it also has a much-higher-than-average rate of people leaving the state. Out-migration swelled with the housing bubble; in 2005, the Census Bureau reported, 160 people moved from California to another state for every 100 from another state that moved in.

This high rate of domestic out-migration has further narrowed the gap between California's white and Latino populations, given that the bulk of domestic migration in America tends to be white. Some alarmist commentators have linked this to the cultural-avoidance phenomenon of "White Flight," but there is no evidence to suggest that whites as a class are more eager to leave California than they are to enter it. Whites have long entered and exited the state in roughly equal proportions; the 1990 census (the last census where such data was collected) reported that, while 75 percent of California's domestic out-migration was white, so was 74 percent of its domestic in-migration. It should thus surprise no one that when California began to register net out-migration, the percentage of white Californians sagged correspondingly. Even if out-migration were spread evenly across ethnic groups, the sharp spike in foreign immigrants over the past thirty-five years would still ensure California's minority-majority ratio.

The second main factor contributing to California's climbing minority populations is high birth rates among Latinos that far outstrip both white and Asian American rates (though this, too, has slowed in recent years). Starting in the midnineties, the lion's share of California births have been Latino, accounting for 46.0 percent of all births in 1995 and topping 50.0 percent each year between 2004 and 2010, before slightly receding to 48.6 percent in 2012. Over a similar period, white births hovered between 25.0 and 30.0 percent, while Asian American births modulated between 10.0 and 13.0 percent.[224] (Asian Americans have historically had birth rates significantly below replacement, with population increases attributable almost exclusively to immigration.)

The result is that, as of 2014, Latinos represent 40.0 percent of California's population, while whites make up 39.0 percent and Asian Americans contribute 14.0 percent. These trends may be slowing, but they have had a permanent effect on California's demographic climate. In 2014, 51.7 percent of California's children were Latino, 27.0 percent white, and 10.7 percent Asian. The California Department of Finance projects that Latinos will make up the majority of California residents sometime after 2060; in the meantime, Latinos are already California's largest ethnic plurality.

These trends account for much of the perception that California is set to become yet more Democratic in the coming years. After all, California's Asian and Latino voters have long leaned Democrat. In California's 2014 gubernatorial election, for example, Gov. Jerry Brown won 73 percent of the Latino to Republican Neel Kashkari's 27 percent.[225]

Projecting how Asian voters will behave in future elections is a murky endeavor, because Asian voters tend largely to abstain from pledging allegiance to a particular political party. In 2012, only 53 percent of Asian Americans identified as either Democratic or Republican; that number shrank to 45 percent among non-English speakers.[226]

Further complicating matters is the relatively small sampling of demographic data compiled on California's Asian voters. While heavyweight organizations like the Pew Research Center have entire wings of researchers devoted to compiling Latino data (Pew Hispanic Center, in this instance), research on California Asian Americans is often a more scattered, smaller-scale affair.

It is worth pointing out, however, that the 2014 gubernatorial election saw the state GOP gain ground among Asian voters. In two of the state's most hotly contested political bouts, Asian American Republican women triumphed against Democratic opponents. Vietnamese American Janet Nguyen bested Jose Solorio for a seat in the state senate, and Korean American Young Kim defeated incumbent Assemblywoman Sharon Quirk-Silva. Also, Taiwanese American Ling Ling Chang won a state assembly seat in Southern California's San Gabriel Valley.

The large numbers of Asian Americans currently unaffiliated with a political party indicate an opportunity for both Left and Right. Ideological polling puts a majority of Asian Americans on the Left end of the political spectrum, but within more targeted and specific subsets of the broader Asian community, the GOP retains an opportunity to woo new immigrants to their cause.

Where Asian Americans lean toward Democrats, Latinos are considered by many to be a solid blue voting bloc. Research from the Public Policy Institute of California, however, reveals that the Latino vote may be less of a lock for the Democratic Party than it appears at first glance.

In a series of seven polls of likely Latino voters conducted between September 2013 and July 2014, PPIC found that while Latinos identified as Democrats by a commanding margin (59 percent, versus 18 percent who identified as Republicans), they also identified as conservatives (33 percent) nearly as often as they identified as liberals (34 percent). This suggests that for Latinos, political allegiance to the Democratic Party is not entirely based on loyalty to its platform but more on concern over perceived Republican stances on some issues.

A quick study of California politics helps explain what has driven Latino voters to the Democratic Party. The simple and unsurprising answer is immigration. More specifically, it was Proposition 187, the Republican-backed 1994 ballot measure that barred undocumented immigrants access to public services ranging from education to health care.

Termed the "Save Our State" initiative, Prop 187 turned the issue of illegal immigration, previously a largely bipartisan concern, into a political slugfest during that year's gubernatorial campaign. The Republican incumbent, Pete Wilson, supported the proposition, promising to enforce it fully if passed by the voters. Democratic challenger Kathleen Brown took Wilson fiercely to task on the issue as a bully who would throw a politically unpopular group under the bus to score points with his constituency.

Prop 187 and Wilson triumphed on Election Day, but it was a pyrrhic victory for Republicans. During Wilson's first run for governor in 1990, Latinos favored his Democratic challenger by a mere 6 percentage points. After he declared his support for Prop 187 during the 1994 campaign, however, Latino voters favored his opponent by a whopping 46 points.[227]

Prop 187 passed that year with 59 percent of the vote, but this too was partisan: 78 percent of Republicans supported the measure, while 64 percent of Democrats—and 77 percent of Latinos—opposed it. It was a watershed moment for California politics, one whose long-term impact on GOP support has long been overlooked. In the twenty years since, Republicans have consistently failed to regain the ground lost to the "Prop 187 Effect."[228]

What made Prop 187 so enduringly devastating for Republicans was the unprecedented way in which the measure energized Latino youth to political action in 1994. In the days leading up to the vote, high- and even middle-school students boycotted school or walked out of classrooms across the state to protest the initiative. I was among them.

In 1994, I was in eighth grade at Magnolia Junior High school in Chino. As one would imagine, politics was not a frequent topic of conversation for my friends and me—we were more concerned with Pogs, comic books, and music. But Prop 187 captured the attention of students, particularly Latinos. Many of us talked about ditching school, walking out, or just not coming at all in protest over the harsh proposition. I was fourteen then, and my peers were as well.

Although Prop 187 was immediately struck down in court and never fully implemented, these students—voters now—have proven to have long memories. A Tomás Rivera Policy Institute survey of California Latino voters during the 2000 election found that 53 percent still associated the Republican Party with former governor Wilson. In 2010, when Republican gubernatorial candidate Meg Whitman appointed Wilson her campaign co-chair, a full 80 percent of Latino voters reported that they were somewhat or very concerned with the appointment.[229]

Prop 187 and, more importantly, the vitriolic rhetoric used to bolster its passage have not been forgotten, and their residue continues to impact the California electorate.

But while Republicans have clearly dug a deep hole for themselves in the Golden State, all is not lost for the GOP, which has begun to adjust to the realities of California's new demographics in its policies, its branding, and the demographics of its own elected officials. Helping their cause is the fact that immigration is today far from the most significant of Latinos' political concerns. In one 2014 survey, 21 percent of California Latinos termed education their biggest policy issue, while 16 percent picked jobs, 15 percent picked government spending and the deficit, and 13 percent picked Social Security. Immigration came in seventh place, with 8 percent.

Yet while most Latinos have other matters on their mind, immigration remains a "threshold issue," according to the Dan Schnur, the director of the Jesse M. Unruh Institute of Politics at the University of Southern California. If Republicans are to have any credibility with Latino voters, immigration is still an area they must thoughtfully address.

The Golden State's Golden Girls and Boys

Another factor that promises to create socioeconomic challenges for the Golden State is the age of its population. The problem is twofold. First, California is top-heavy. The state is home to over four million baby boomers, those born between 1946 and 1964, who make up the largest generational cohort in American history and the eldest of whom have just begun to retire.

Second, not only are California boomers numerous, but California children are remarkably scarce.

While children made up 33.4 percent of the state's population in 1970, they accounted for only 25.0 percent of the population in 2010. By 2030, as demographers such as the University of Southern California's Dowell Myers have projected, they are likely to constitute only 20.9 percent of all Californians.

Over the next decade and a half, the majority of California's boomers will slide gradually from the golden years of their careers—statistically, the age range of maximum earnings and largest house purchases and, thus, the age range of greatest economic stimulation—into retirement and reliance on Social Security. It is hard to overstate the economic impact of this shift.

The clearest indicator of these economic consequences is the "senior ratio," the ratio between California's senior citizens and men and women still of working age. For four decades, this ratio remained at an almost static twenty seniors per one hundred working-age residents; by 2020, however, the number is projected to climb to twenty-eight, and to thirty-six by 2030.[230]

To reduce this to crude terms, the average taxpayer of working age has, for the past four decades, been responsible for the upkeep of one fifth of a senior citizen. As the senior population mushrooms and the workforce shrinks at both ends, however, this responsibility will double over the coming years.

Interestingly, this enormous spike in the senior ratio would be far more catastrophic were it not for one mediating factor: California's immigrant populations, who tend to be younger than average and thus will help to bolster the workforce against the added senior burden in the years to come. Demographers estimate that immigrants will account for 40.8 percent of California workforce entrances in the 2020s and only 20.1 percent of all workforce exits. Even with this fortuitous stabilizing force, however, the economic forecast remains cautious.

For both their own sakes and for the sake of the seniors who will rely on their economic productivity, it will become increasingly important for the workers of the coming decades—today's children and young adults—to possess the tools required to bear this heavier financial burden. In today's policy terms, that means a solid commitment to education and a focus on the economy, which will need to grow by leaps and bounds over the decades to come to support the weight of public retirement funds and health care costs for the aging masses.

In the decades to come, Californians will be forced, like the rest of the country, to confront the real statistical problems of an aging population.

California's Changing Landscape

The past 30 years have seen dramatic economic reverberations throughout California. The recession of the early 1990s, the dot-com bubble at the turn of the millennium, the housing boom and bust of the 2000s, and its subsequent limping recovery all contributed to the biggest shakeup to the Golden State's economy since the Gold Rush.

In the late 1980s, the central hub of the California economy was Los Angeles, then, as now, the second-largest city in America by population and home base for America's juggernaut aerospace and entertainment agencies. The region at that time housed fifteen of America's twenty-five largest aerospace companies: one out of every four aerospace workers in the country lived in Southern California, with one out of every ten in Los Angeles County.[231] At the height of the Cold War, the local economy reaped huge benefits from the industry.

California's aerospace industry peaked in 1987, however, and has dropped precipitously ever since. In 1990, Los Angeles County had 130,100 aerospace workers; by 2000, that number had fallen to 52,400, and again to 39,100 by 2010.[232]

Struggling with this and other blows, the Los Angeles economy has stagnated over the past few decades. In fact, between 1990 and 2013, although the population of Los Angeles grew by 13.0 percent, nonfarm job growth actually declined by 1.3 percent, with 2006 and 2007 being the only two years with growth slightly above 1990 levels. The data is even more dramatic when government jobs are eliminated from the snapshot: 2014 was the first year in twenty-four years where Los Angeles broke above 1990 levels in private job creation, by a margin of 1.1 percent. [233]

As Los Angeles, Southern California's economic hub, has stumbled, the San Francisco Bay Area has become the much-ballyhooed economic powerhouse that successfully rode the technology boom to a position of state and national prominence. This shift has given Northern California significant clout both economically and politically.

The Bay Area is of course by no means a new economic player, or one limited to the tech industry. In fact, in 2014 health care was the largest industry for the city of San Francisco.[234] Other major fields include finance and (like Los Angeles) a booming tourism industry. It is tech, however, that has pushed the Bay's meteoric rise to California economic supremacy over the past three decades.

While Los Angeles's population rose by 13.0 percent between 1990 and 2013, San Francisco's population increased by 22.8 percent. But while Los Angeles has only 1.1 percent more jobs now than it did in 1990, San Francisco boomed to a 21.2 percent jobs increase. And there's more: While Los Angeles performed more poorly when government jobs were factored out, San Francisco's private sector actually outstripped public job creation. Private job levels are a staggering 25.3 percent higher in the Bay Area than they were in 1990.[235]

This shift in economic power has brought in its wake corresponding political realignment. Much ink has been spilled over California's east/west political dynamic: the densely packed urban coast tending (as densely packed urban coasts do) to vote Democratic while the sparser, more rural inland communities lean Republican.

Less attention has been paid, however, to the political geography *along* the Democratic coast. This geography is less visible because it does not appear in voting maps, which are the easiest type of political demography to compile. Nevertheless, it is this geography, of north and south coast, on which the thought-leadership and powerbases of the political landscape have begun to shift.

When faced with the common electoral question of Democrat versus Republican, voters from the Bay Area and Los Angeles tend to behave the same way: decidedly Democratic. In the 2012 presidential election, President

Obama carried San Francisco by an eye-popping margin of 83 percent to 13 percent and Los Angeles by a commanding 69 percent to 29 percent. This would at first glance seem to indicate a wide unity of political opinion in California's two economic centers.

This unity breaks down, however, when one considers political ideologies rather than simple candidate preference. In other words, while Los Angeles and San Francisco may both favor Democratic candidates, they differ substantially when it comes to the flavors of Democratic policy they prefer. This can be seen clearly in a 2012 Public Policy Institute of California survey entitled "California's Political Geography," which placed Californians from every region on a five-point spectrum: Loyal Liberal, Moderate Liberal, Conservative Liberal, Moderate Conservative, and Committed Conservative.

The PPIC data showed that while every segment of the Bay Area and its environs identified strongly with the Loyal Liberal label (indicating strong liberal views on both social and fiscal policy), Los Angeles County contained no Loyal Liberal areas and only one Moderate Liberal area, with most areas identifying as Conservative Liberal (conservative on social issues and mildly liberal on fiscal issues) or Moderate Conservative (moderately liberal on social issues and conservative on fiscal issues).

The takeaway is that Los Angeles Democrats gravitate toward more moderate political positions than their Bay Area counterparts.

As economic power has shifted from Southern to Northern California over the past decades, political power has, to a large degree, followed suit. Today, Democrats of the Bay Area variety hold all but one of California's most important statewide political offices, including Gov. Jerry Brown (the former mayor of Oakland), Lt. Gov. Gavin Newsom (former mayor of San Francisco), Sen. Dianne Feinstein (former mayor of San Francisco), Attorney General Kamala Harris (former district attorney of San Francisco), and Controller Betty Yee (a San Francisco native). One notable exception is Secretary of State Alex Padilla, the only Latino elected to statewide office, who previously served on the Los Angeles City Council.

This shift also impacts the ethnic diversity of California politics. Unsurprisingly, the bulk of California's Latino population resides in Southern

California; at the time of the 2010 census, 44.6 percent of Los Angeles County residents were Latino versus 14.1 percent of San Francisco County residents. This diversity in the south has had demonstrable political consequences: all nine of California's Latino congresspersons represent Southern Californians.[236]

But even San Francisco is seeing a slight movement rightward in political ideology. This is due in part to the tech boom and skyrocketing housing costs pricing lower income earners out of the city. But that's not the only cause, as University of San Francisco Politics Professor Corey Cook told Salon. com: "Absent the tech boom and population change, we're seeing a significant change in the local political context." From Cook's perspective San Francisco "has moved in a pro-growth, pro-business direction."

In 2014 the Bay Area even elected a Republican, Catharine Baker, to the Sixteenth State Assembly District—the first time a Republican has prevailed in an election in a state legislative or congressional district formerly in Democratic hands in eight years.

Some of the credit for the shifts in political outcomes is also due to a pair of reforms to the electoral process passed by California voters: a top-two primary system and citizen-led redistricting. The top-two system advances the two highest vote getters from the primary election to the general election regardless of party affiliation. That has caused a number of more competitive general elections where Republicans face Republicans and Democrats face Democrats. The second reform, a citizens' redistricting commission, sought to end gerrymandering by politicians and instead created a Citizens Redistricting Commission to draw legislative boundaries. The result so far has been more competitive races.

The 2016 US Senate election for Sen. Barbara Boxer's vacated seat will be the next big test for changing electoral dynamics in the state and could be a predictive moment for state politics. The two early frontrunners to fill the seat are Kamala Harris, a multiracial Bay Area Democrat, and long-serving Democratic Congresswoman Loretta Sanchez, a Latina from Southern California. This race has the potential to be a defining moment for the future of the Democratic Party and for California's entire political landscape.

Looking Ahead

While it is easy to glance at California's political geography and history and assume that the state will forever remain a bastion of the Left, some hard demographic facts give pause to such a confident prediction. The Democratic Party has made substantial gains in the Golden State while simultaneously swinging its power base northward and thus Leftward. Conversely, many of the wounds suffered by Republicans, such as Latino distrust for the party, have been self-inflicted and linger. But this isn't your grandmother's California, or even your mother's, for that matter. Northern California is in the midst of a major socioeconomic shift, Southern California continues to change demographically, and the electorate is rapidly changing—all of which will cause unique challenges and opportunities in the political, cultural, and economic spheres.

About the Author: Brian Calle

Brian Calle is opinion editor for the *Orange County Register* and the *Press-Enterprise* and the cohost of Fox 11's special election broadcast *You Decide SoCal 2014*. He is also editor in chief of CalWatchdog.com and a Presidential Fellow at Chapman University. Andrew Egger worked as a research assistant and contributed to this chapter.

Eleven

DIRECT DEMOCRACY

By Stephen Frank

Put aside all previous thoughts about how public policy is developed in California. Laws are certainly not formulated and passed as students are taught in school. The traditional Democratic and Republican Parties are essentially dead and replaced by the very rich, unions, and special interests. Voter disenfranchisement is very real. Elected officials and the courts have an ever-increasing impact on policy. The exploding field of technology has already changed the business of politics at its core and will continue to do so in ways not yet imagined. Social media, cable TV, and investigative reporting will keep us more informed but won't answer the question, "How can the grassroots political activist get a piece of the policy action in this more complex, more legalistic, and massively more expensive system?" This chapter will explore those topics in this ever-changing environment of public policy development.

If you believe your high school government class, the process is sequential and relatively simple. A legislator in Sacramento notices a problem and determines constituents need help. Then the assembly member or state senator has staff draft a bill. The bill is introduced and assigned to a committee. The committee holds a public hearing and all sides are heard. Then a vote is taken. If passed, the bill goes to the floor for a vote of all members.

If passed, the bill now goes to the other legislative body for more hearings and possible amendments. If passed by committee, the bill goes to the floor, is voted on, and passes. The bill, having been passed by both legislative bodies, now goes to the governor. The governor's staff looks at the bill and recommends to the governor to sign or veto the bill. If signed, the bill becomes law. A veto by the governor means the bill goes back to the legislature for a veto override or a rewriting.

The textbooks make it a simple process. It is open, transparent, and fair. That is the textbook version. It is not real life. Reality shows that bills are usually initiated not from a constituent concern but from an agenda introduced by a lobbyist. According to the *San Jose Mercury News*:

> A lobbyist has an idea to make life better—but only for his client. The lobbyist writes the bill, shops for a willing lawmaker to introduce it, and lines up the support. The legislator has to do little more than show up and vote. This is the path of the "sponsored bill," a method of lawmaking little noticed outside California's capital but long favored on the inside. In many states lobbyists influence legislators; in California, they have—quite baldly—taken center stage in lawmaking.[237]

This is not a partisan state of affairs. Republicans and Democrats alike use lobbyists to write and promote legislation. It is not new; the process goes back to the days of Artie Samish, the well-known lobbyist of the 1920s to the 1950s. "Samish thus had a political machine, but it was organized through interest groups rather than a political party organization," notes the San Jose State University Department of Economics. "These interest groups could deliver a large bloc of votes of friends and relatives at Samish's command. The interest groups also gave Samish control over large funds, what are now called 'slush funds,' which he could spend at his discretion."[238]

The lobbyists of today operate in a more sophisticated way, staying within the law but still arranging for money for candidates and officeholders. Lobbyists work diligently to build relationships with legislators. In fact, most of the Sacramento lobbyists of today, like Artie Samish in the past, once worked for the legislature or a legislator. Lobbyists understand that most officeholders mean well, but are looking for the next office, so need doors opened to the moneyed class.

With Prop 14 as law, political parties have very little leverage with office-holders or candidates. Under this initiative, passed in 2010, political parties are outlawed from nominating candidates for office. Now registered voters choose the candidates. Democrats can vote for Republicans and Republicans can vote for Democrats, both in the primary and general elections. Also, since Prop 14 creates a November election with the top two vote getters in the primary, few third-party candidates are on the ballot for the general election. In 2014, out of 150 legislative races for assembly, state senate, Congress, and constitutional office, only *three* had third-party candidates on the November ballot. Indeed, in 2012 and 2014, there were twenty-eight districts with only one party on the ballot (this includes the spring 2015 special elections for three state senate seats). This is like God showing only Eve to Adam and saying, "Now choose a wife." Indeed, the system actively suppresses the votes of the traditional Democratic and Republican Party members.

In twenty of those twenty-eight districts, the voters were given a choice of a liberal Democrat or a very liberal Democrat. In those districts, why would a Republican vote? Republicans were forced to choose the lesser of two evils. The same was true for the eight districts of Republican versus Republican. The choice was between conservative and very conservative—why would a Progressive Democrat want to vote?

What about those who believe that the Democratic and Republican Parties are actually the problem? The system is even worse for them. The system results in third-party voters not voting at all and not participating in a system that excludes them at the November general election.

Voter Suppression in Thirty-Ninth Assembly District

One of the best examples of voter suppression can be found in the Thirty-Ninth Assembly District in the San Fernando Valley. In 2012 California held the first "Top Two—Prop 14" election under the new law. In this election, when Republicans, Decline to State, Democrats, and Third Parties were beginning to understand the ramifications, the primary ballot listed seven candidates, including a Green Party member. By the 2014 primary only three candidates—two Democrats and a Libertarian—were on the ballot. The primary winners were the two Democrats.

For many, Prop 14 is the California version of the "Jim Crow" laws of the old South. It certainly discourages people from voting. Why even bother to vote for a candidate you oppose? Choice is limited, resulting in voter suppression.

In the 2012 general election, the district saw a turnout of roughly 107,000 voters, or 56 percent of registered voters. By November of 2014 the turnout dropped to 22 percent, or 45,000 voters.[239] The vote total was so low that the incumbent was actually defeated. Looks like the Republicans and third-party folks decided to punish the incumbent, since he had the endorsement of all the unions and the Democratic Party.

Ultimately, Prop 14 has changed the role of the California Republican Party and the California Democratic Party. Instead of running voter registration drives, developing candidates, and promoting party values and principles to the general public, both parties are well on their way to becoming super PACs. The parties have become these legal entities to collect and distribute money.

The Democratic and Republican Parties have been replaced by three new parties, the *very rich*, the *unions*, and the *special interests*. Let's explore the impact of each.

The *very rich parties* have major donors such as Tom Steyer, who spent over $68 million on the 2014 elections, though much of that was spent out of California.

One candidate, Bill Bloomfield, was a Republican who changed parties and in 2012 ran unsuccessfully himself as an independent for Congress against liberal Democratic incumbent Henry Waxman on the west side of Los Angeles. In a 2015 special election for the Seventh District state senate seat, he spent more than $1 million as an independent expenditure to support a candidate in a Democratic-dominated district who was considered by most observers to be the more moderate Democrat. His candidate, Steve Glazer, won the election. He also gave vast sums of money to help both Republicans and Democrats running for partisan offices in 2014. In the 2014 election, he personally spent more than $1 million in a losing effort to support a Democrat who was trying to unseat the California Teachers' Association–backed incumbent running for superintendent of public instruction, Tom Torlakson.

Torlakson won his race with big teachers' union support, and the *unions* are making their influence evident in other races as well. In the Seventh Senate District special election in 2015, the unions spent over $2 million to support one Democrat who was running against another Democrat. "Their" Democrat (Susan Bonilla) always supports the union position. "The bad Democrat" (Steve Glazer) believes public employee union members should not be allowed to strike. Yet on key issues, neither candidate provided a real choice for voters. Both support higher taxes. In 2012, Glazer ran the Prop 30 campaign, the measure that raises $6 billion a year for seven years, for Governor Brown. Bonilla supported this. Both Bonilla and Glazer support the requirement that public school teachers must pay dues if they want to teach.

One candidate is a complete Progressive; the other candidate is certainly in the Progressive court. In this race financed by the unions, why should a Republican, American Independent, or other conservative party member vote for either candidate?

The major funders of the California Democratic Party are the unions and major corporations. The major donors of the Republican Party are the very rich and the major corporations. The *very rich* and *unions* are dominating the financing of campaigns. Neither party depends on the small donor any longer. The result is little interest in the issues of the individual.

Special interests are a third factor in the decline of the political parties and voter suppression. Special interests are often financed by officeholders who keep large sums of money in the bank. Gov. Jerry Brown ended the 2014 election with $24 million in the bank. Under California's campaign finance laws, "That money can go toward a ballot measure if he chooses."[240]

Republican and Democratic legislative leaders have millions in campaign accounts to spend to stay in leadership or to move to higher office. Some of the money is used to elect to office fellow party members who support the *special interest* of the day. In addition, the Democratic Legislative Caucus and the Republican Legislative Caucus have their own political action committees, collecting and spending money without approval and, in many cases, without consultation with their official parties. These caucuses identify, prioritize, and support favored *special interests*.

In the midst of these extremely influential dynamics, the legislators in Sacramento still adopt laws and regulate policy. The process can seem to be unpredictable. Though Democrats have almost a "supermajority" in both the state senate and assembly (two thirds of the membership is a supermajority), some Democrats may vote with traditionally Republican priorities and support business interests or help dilute job-killer bills and policies.

The *initiative process* can be greatly influenced by the legislature. The legislature, by a simple majority vote in both houses, can put an issue on the general election ballot, bypassing the signature requirements necessary for initiatives. This process certainly aids the *special interest groups.*

It is estimated to take $2.5 million to obtain the signatures needed to qualify an initiative for the ballot. Rather than spending money from the bank account of the special interest group to obtain signatures, any special interest group can use substantially less money to influence a simple majority of the legislators to vote to put the initiative on the ballot. This has absolutely favored special interest groups that are congruent with traditional Democratic issues, since the Democrats have held the majority in one or both houses of the California Legislature for more than fifty years.

It was a Republican governor, Hiram Johnson, more than one hundred years ago, who reformed California government, making it more open and transparent. Governor Johnson created the initiative, referendum, and recall processes. At the same time he gave voters more power, he also opened the door to the corruption of the legislature by lobbyists, such as Artie Samish. Samish was able to raise the money to put his people into office and keep them there. Until recently there were no term limits, so, once bought, a legislator was a long-term investment.

The initiative process has generally been used by the special interests, not the grass roots. The Initiative and Referendum Institute at the University of Southern California reports:

> The California initiative process gave rise to a new breed of campaign professional: the paid petition circulator. With signature requirements doubling nearly every decade, citizen groups were unable to rely solely on volunteer effort. As early as World War I, Joseph Robinson was offering his organizing services to initiative proponents. His firm, which paid its employees a fee for each signature brought in, had a virtual monopoly on the petition business from 1920 to 1948—a period during which, Robinson estimated, his firm was involved in 98 percent of the successful statewide initiative petition drives. Robinson stayed in business into the late 1960s, when he offered his services to Ed and Joyce Koupal, but by then he had competitors.[241]

Today petition gatherers receive up to $15 a signature for a ballot measure. If you want to create a ballot measure you need approximately $2.5 million just to qualify the measure. Then, if it is controversial, you might need to spend another $20.0 million to get it passed.

The big question is always, "How many signatures do I need to qualify a ballot measure?" The state law says you need 5 percent of those that voted in the previous gubernatorial election. So, for 2012 and 2014, a little over 504,000 "good" signatures were needed to qualify a measure. Since the voter turnout was so low in November 2014, for 2016 and 2018, only 376,000 signatures will be needed, 25 percent less. This does make it easier.

Like learning how a bill becomes law, the creation of an initiative is also simple, but never by the books. For $200 you can file the language of a ballot measure with the secretary of state. That office then sends it to the attorney general for "title and summary." Then it goes back to the secretary of state for the formal approval to distribute the petition for signatures.

Sounds simple. Yet the attorney general can play games with the description of the measure. Usually, he or she plays games with the "summary," what the measure accomplishes if passed. It is here that the attorney general can claim high or low costs, more freedom or less freedom.

For instance, this happened in 2014 with a pension reform measure.[242] Former San Jose mayor Chuck Reed attempted to introduce a measure to reform the state's broken pension system but was thwarted in the title and summary stage. Reed filed a lawsuit, calling the description written by Attorney General Kamala Harris "inaccurate and misleading" because it did not make it clear the initiative would protect pension benefits already accrued.[243]

Then you have the other part of the political games played by an attorney general—failure to obey his or her oath of office. The role of the California attorney general is to defend the laws of the state. A passed ballot measure, when the vote is certified within thirty days of an election, becomes law. It is the duty of the attorney general, as specified in the job description, to defend all laws. Yet Kamala Harris, the twice-elected attorney general, made a determination that she would not defend at the Supreme Court a law passed by the voters, Prop 8. This was the measure the people of California approved stating that marriage is between a man and a woman.

Instead of doing her duty, Harris turned the attorney general's office into a political operation, run by ideologues rather than attorneys doing their duty for the people of California. "I declined to defend Proposition 8 because it violates the Constitution," Harris said in a March 2013 press release. "The Supreme Court has described marriage as a fundamental right fourteen times since 1888. The time has come for this right to be afforded to every citizen."[244]

The governor of California can also refuse to obey his oath of office and not defend ballot measures passed by the public. Prop 187, passed in 1994, tried to control illegal aliens in California. The governor is elected to protect the rights of the citizens and defend our laws. Gray Davis refused to obey his oath of office. Today, the cost of illegal immigrants in California is approximately $21 billion, with crowded classrooms, crowded hospitals, and crumbling infrastructure. Illegal immigrants are holding jobs that honest

Americans cannot have, thanks to state policy. Prop 187 would have stopped this problem more than fifteen years ago.

To summarize, we have political parties that are dead. We have elected officials acting like Lone Rangers, for their own good and prosperity. Officials take their oath of office with their fingers crossed behind their backs, never intending to fulfill the duties of the office.

At least we have the courts to protect us! Wrong! Proposition 8 is evidence of how the courts have determined that the laws passed by the people of California are not worthy of their "constitutional views" from the bench. Prop 8 and Prop 187 were both declared unconstitutional by the courts.

In June 2013, the US Supreme Court ruled in *Hollingsworth v. Perry* that the traditional marriage activists who put Proposition 8 on the ballot did not have legal standing to defend their measure. "We have never before upheld the standing of a private party to defend the constitutionality of a state statute when state officials have chosen not to," Chief Justice John Roberts wrote in the majority opinion. "We decline to do so for the first time here."[245]

In other words, when Attorney General Harris refused to obey her oath of office, the people of California were denied by the Supreme Court the right to be heard on a ballot measure they passed. Millions of voters wanted this. One opponent, Kamala Harris, literally had veto power on the thirty-eight million people of the state. She knew that by refusing to defend the law of the state, the Supreme Court would have to oppose Prop 8. What a waste of money on elections when you have attorney generals and governors casting their one vote, overturning ten million voters. Now that is power.

Is it any wonder folks distrust government, politicians, and policies? A few judges determine if laws passed by the legislature or the people are enforceable. Lobbyists are writing laws, without the legislators being open and telling the public the real origins of their bills. Thanks to an initiative, millions of voters have been prohibited from voting for candidates of their choice. In 2012, in the twenty-eight legislative districts that had only one party on the ballot, the voter turnout was 11 percent less than in the districts with two parties on the ballot.

The actions of our legislature, elected state officeholders, and courts are creating significant economic and personal problems for the people of

California. The 2016 election will be the first election in this new era of politics and public policy for California. What does the future hold for California politics? Four predictions are discussed below.

Voter Influence through the Ballot Box

The people may indeed have a greater voice in the state through the ballot box, if they use it. As legislators shy away from tough decisions in an effort to ensure their reelection, more issues may be left to the voters through the initiative process. Pension reform, assisted suicide, tax policies, legalization of marijuana, even the repeal of the grocery store plastic bag ban will be on the ballot. The future is going to bring more and more measures to the ballot as legislators feel more comfortable letting the public decide rather than casting a difficult vote.

This will give the people a greater voice in the future and direction of our state. Yes, we can talk with our legislators, but only a handful of people in a state of thirty-eight million actually get to see a legislator. Most are too busy with jobs and families to attend town hall meetings or set up a conference with a twenty-three-year-old staffer in a Sacramento office.

We barely have time to read a newsletter or care to see the eleven o'clock news. But, we can have a say on those policy items that matter most to us, that speak to the quality of our lives, or that set the policy for taxes we must spend. This trend could be positive for the people of California.

The Increase in Absentee Balloting

How we vote is changing. The trend toward increased absentee ballots is clear. Presently over 50 percent of voters vote by absentee. There is even a movement to follow the Oregon example, where almost all ballots are cast by mail. Here in California, SB 163 has been introduced to provide every California voter with a mail-in ballot for all elections. Absentee/mail-in ballots are traditionally available thirty days before Election Day. The trend will definitely continue to impact campaign strategy significantly. This trend could be positive if more people actually vote using the convenience of a mail-in ballot. Indeed this could reduce the overall voter suppression discussed earlier.

The Influence of Ideological Organizations

Another trend for the future is the expected increased impact that legal and ideological organizations will have on public policy. Some organizations are old-timers on the scene, such as the ACLU and Sierra Club. Others have appeared more recently, such as the tea party. Some are issue specific, such as the Howard Jarvis Taxpayers' Association and various ethnic associations. Others have more global ideology, such as the Reason Foundation (libertarian) on the Right, and the California Public Interest Research Group (CalPIRG) on the Left. California conservative activists join groups fighting Agenda 21, illegal aliens, local taxpayer organizations, and government schools. The California Progressive grassroots no longer need the Democratic Party to advocate for open borders, less development, higher minimum wage, "social justice," and more. There are plenty of organizations carrying those banners.

The Influence of Ever-Changing Technology

The really good news is that due to the Internet and data mining, it is possible to qualify a ballot measure for under $1 million. Yes, that is still expensive, but a good idea can find financial supporters to promote an initiative. Already there are data firms that have records of those that have signed ballot measures, with key areas of ideology, age, and interests noted. Enhanced data shows every voter the value of his or her home, cost of his or her cars, subscriptions to magazines, degrees, and professional licenses. The enhanced voter database knows about your family, brushes with the law, and your sources of income.

For a price there are enhanced voter lists that include the e-mail address of most registered voters. In fact, several years ago, the State put a line on the voter registration form to add your e-mail address. Since 2012 campaigns and candidates have been e-mailing these voters. For local elections and candidates for legislative office that cannot afford glossy high-price mailers, this is a very inexpensive method of reaching voters.

The Democratic and Republican Parties in California have this information with a few additions. They know if you vote and how often you vote. If a homeowner is not registered, they know that as well. The good news is that large and small political and public policy groups also have most if not all of this information on databases they have been building for years. The Pasadena TEAPAC, a tea party, is creating such a database; it is filing dozens of initiatives in the San Gabriel Valley and Los Angeles County. Several other groups on the Left and Right are doing the same.

By having such a list, the organizations are able to develop computer programs to directly communicate with the targeted voters and gain their support to sign a petition meant for the ballot. Using mail programs they are able to reach voters. This is especially an important strategy for last-minute attack ads. By using the Internet an attacked candidate can respond in a matter of hours. He or she can even respond at midnight before the election for last-minute robocalls.

Maybe the end of the political parties as a voice for activists and policies has come at the right time. While the major parties are raising and passing major dollars around the political arena, the grassroots activists, along with the ideological organizations, single-issue groups, and those that want to be independent but involved in the process have an inexpensive way to use technology. The politics and public policy of the future are for the rich and special interests. Now we can add the grassroots, if well organized and tech savvy, as an effective player. Those with a cause no longer have to worry if developers are trying to take over their city council, or unions are trying to keep control of the school board.

The political parties have lost their voice, their power, and their ability to move an agenda. In the future politics and public policy will be controlled by those with money—the very rich, the unions, and the special interests. The grassroots can have a place in the public policy arena by using the initiative process, fighting voter suppression by encouraging voting, participating meaningfully in ideological organizations, and utilizing the ever-changing technological resources.

The future for California policy and politics is actually very bright for our citizens. That does not mean they are going to win every battle, but at least they are in the ball game with the rich, the unions, and special interests.

Elections will be won in 2016 and 2018 the same way they were won in 1960 and 1984. It will take hard work, communication with the voters, and a message that reaches their values and principles. The method of campaigning has changed. That is to be expected and exalted. Thanks to technology, the activist on the street can be as powerful as an oil company or union.

The power base is switching in California. Power is leaving the political parties, and it is leaving the legislature. If the grassroots activists stay aware of the changing political climate and use the developing technological tools, the grass roots can get a piece of the action. Grassroots activists can be a meaningful and influential participant in public policy leadership in California.

About the Author: Stephen Frank

Stephen Frank is a longtime political and public policy activist and analyst. He has edited the California Political News and Views since 1996. A political consultant, Steve is a frequent guest on talk radio and a public speaker. He has worked on races from water district to president while being a grassroots organizer. Steve is a human-rights activist.

Twelve

CORRUPTION

By Jon Fleischman

It should tell you something that when you do a web search for the terms "political corruption California" you immediately get back a link to a law firm specializing in representing elected politicians who have been accused of a crime. California's newest cottage industry?

California has more than its fair share—a lot more—of political corruption, and corrupt people in political office. Of course, there is no state in the country that is free of political corruption—nor any country on the planet. But the amount of it that takes place in California is staggering, and as one tries to make sense of it, there are some conclusions that one can make as to why it is so prevalent here.

California government is so big and powerful, both at a state and local level, thanks to generations of domination by liberal politicians, that the opportunities for elected officials to use the power of their offices to choose winners and losers in both the public and private sector is staggering.

Built into the system here a vast amount of "sanctioned corruption"—which is where, in return for political favors (referring back to the aforementioned winners and losers), financial contributions are regularly doled out to politicians, sometimes in direct contributions to their campaigns, or to political committees allied with the politicians, or even to shadowy nonprofits who in turn finance global travel to exotic locales for these deserving politicos. While the line between "sanctioned corruption" and illegal corruption can be gray, the highest profile examples clearly stepped over that line.

Mixed into the anecdotal examples you are about to read are some politicians who were corrupt as persons, but the actual crimes for which they were charged and convicted were not public corruption, per se—nevertheless, examples of egregious and illegal behavior that cost individuals their public office or their chance at a future office.

Lastly, before I walk you through a rogues' gallery of corrupt ex-officials, I would say that if you look at how politics is conducted here, you will see that despite the efforts of California's early-twentieth-century reformers such as Hiram Johnson, who restructured much of this state's political process to try and weed out corruption, they were unsuccessful. Machine politics in state-wide races and in lopsided districts means less scrutiny by the public—especially in areas where Democrats and the political structures that support Democrats are dominant.

Of course general voter cynicism, largely caused, I believe, by a state government that is focused on providing "wins" to special interest groups and that is completely out of touch with the average person, no doubt impacted by these ongoing stories of corrupt politicians, is a factor in record-low turnout in elections. Low turnout means even less voter scrutiny of ersatz politicians before they take office.

As we look at some of these scandals, some unfolding, some that have run their course, it is no accident that I have clustered a group of them having to so with ex-Democratic state senators Ron Calderon, Leland Yee, and Rod Wright at the beginning. These cases all point to what can only be described as a "culture of corruption" that is prevalent in the California State Capitol these days.

In the cases of Caldron and Yee, the fact that the level of illegal and corrupt activity that is alleged by federal prosecutors could happen is eye opening and speaks to a legislature where behind-the-scenes deal making and hand shaking must be commonplace. And most especially in the case of Wright, the way that almost all of his senate colleagues circled the wagons around him, many seeing Wright as a victim instead of as an accused felon, was nothing short of stunning.

The Brothers Calderon

The Calderon family has been a fixture in the state capitol for a long time. The first of three brothers elected to the legislature, Charles, served in the assembly and the state senate, and then again in the assembly—retiring due to term limits. His next younger brother, Tom, served in the state assembly for four years and retired from public service after a failed bid for California insurance commissioner in 2004. The youngest Calderon brother, Ron, served in the state assembly for four years and just completed eight years in the state senate last year. Charles's son, Ian, was elected to the state assembly in 2012 and continues to serve. It's worth mentioning that neither Charles nor Ian is implicated in the corruption case I'm about to summarize for you.

In February 2014, federal prosecutors announced a sweeping indictment against then state senator Ron Calderon, charging him with fraud, bribery, money laundering, and other offenses.[246] The Feds allege that Calderon solicited and accepted almost $100,000 in cash bribes—as well as VIP treatment (lavish lifestyle stuff—fancy meals, golf outings, the "usual"). In return for the money and gifts, says the government, Calderon helped facilitate a half-billion-dollar health care fraud, among other objectives.

Ron Calderon's brother, Tom, it is alleged, facilitated the cash bribes through payments made to his consulting firm. Tom Calderon is facing federal charges as well. The government also says the bribe was facilitated by a payment of $30,000 to Tom Calderon's college-aged son for summer employment that lasted only a few weeks.

The nature of the complex policy objectives and outcomes pursued by Ron Calderon give rise to the question of how far this corruption may spread within the capitol. State Senate President Kevin DeLeon has already been questioned by FBI agents, and it is said that for a time, before being publicly charged, Calderon himself was wearing a wiretap. Calderon's attorney, high-profile criminal defense counsel Martin Gallegos, has said that he expects legislators to be called during the trial, which is scheduled to being in the latter part of this year.

Despite the severity of the allegations Senator Calderon was permitted by his colleagues to serve out his term. They could have exercised their power, under the state constitution, to expel him—but did not.

Gun-Running "Uncle Leland" Yee

The criminal case against state Sen. Leland Yee is a stunning indictment, in and of itself, on how deep the culture of corruption extends within Democratic Party circles. Leland Yee was an established and honored part of the party machine, occupying coveted San Francisco-based assembly and state senate seats from late 2002 through end of 2014. Prior to his election to the legislature, Yee served for five years on the San Francisco Board of Supervisors.

Before I go on, as an aside, it seems appropriate now to mention that as a state legislator Yee was extremely aggressive at both sponsoring and supporting gun control legislation. This becomes ironic because in March of 2014, federal prosecutors charged Yee with violating honest services wire fraud statutes by allegedly taking bribes in return for sponsoring legislation. Yee was also charged with conspiracy to deal firearms without a license and to illegally import firearms from the Philippines (apparently by setting up an international weapons trafficking deal with undercover FBI agents). Yee has also been charged with taking "tens of thousands of dollars" in both campaign contributions and in cash payments to help a client with legislation.

According to the charges, Yee and his campaign staff took $42,800 from undercover agents in exchange for carrying out specific requests. A month later, to pile on, the Feds added racketeering charges as well. Yee was arrested and is currently out on $500,000 bail.[247] Yee was facing term limits in the senate, but had filed his candidacy for secretary of state. By the time this scandal broke, it was too late to have his name taken off of the statewide ballot. Yee, despite a suspended candidacy, received nearly 10 percent of the vote—far from what was needed to make the runoff.

The charges are so over the top and outrageous that the first reaction is to say that it couldn't be true. And yet it is all very, very real. This summer, Yee pleaded guilty in federal court to one count of racketeering, with a potential of decades in prison.[248] Given the gravity and severity of the amassed charges against then-sitting senators Ron Calderon and Leland Yee, it is telling about the culture of the state capitol that neither of these senators was expelled. Hiding behind the "innocent until proven guilty" mantra, there was no thought apparently given to the notion that serving as a state legislator is not a right, it is a privilege. Both Calderon and Yee served most of 2014 in a made-up status called being suspended, which in many ways seems to mirror a paid vacation. Between them one out of every twenty Californians was unrepresented in the senate. But there was another Democrat in the state senate who spent most of last year suspended…

Rod Wright's Wrong Residence

.Two prominent Los Angeles area politicians were both successfully prosecuted by the Los Angeles County district attorney for felony perjury and voter fraud. It seems that both of them were very interested in serving in elective office, but both preferred to actually live in tonier neighborhoods than were available in their very economically challenged districts.

There may be no case of a criminal prosecution and conviction of a sitting member of the California legislature that more exposed the culture of corruption in the state capitol. Democrat Rod Wright, a former district director for Congresswoman Maxine Waters, won election to the state assembly and, after a brief hiatus from office, won election to the state senate representing an area around Inglewood. In 2010 Wright was charged with multiple felony counts of perjury and voter fraud, for living in a nice home in Baldwin Hills that was not inside of the state senate district he was elected to represent and that he swore under penalty of perjury he lived in.[249]

The contortions that the political class in the state capitol went through to try and ignore that a member of their elite group was undergoing a felony trial was nothing short of stunning. Wright was convicted by a jury in February of

2014, but was not formally sentenced until September. During that period of time, the senator was permitted to serve as a senator, basically on paid leave—drawing a salary and benefits. A group of Republicans introduced a resolution calling on him to be expelled, which of course never was brought to the floor of the senate. The political support that Wright received from leadership of both political parties postconviction and presentencing sent a strong message that legislators, as a class, feel that they are above the law.

Convicted of many felonies, Wright was sentenced to ninety days in the county jail—and of course forfeited the right to ever again hold an elective office.

Los Angeles Councilman Richard Alarcon

The second prominent politician to go down for falsifying his residency is Richard Alarcon. The Los Angeles Democrat started his career working for Los Angeles Mayor Tom Bradley and parlayed that into election to the Los Angeles City Council, representing part of the San Fernando Valley. He was elected to the California State Senate in the middle of his second council term, and due to term limits the popular Alarcon ran uncontested for a seat in the state assembly. At the time questions of legal residency in the district dogged the assembly campaign, but nothing came of it. However, after serving just over one hundred days of his assembly term, he won election back to the Los Angeles City Council. It was after this election that complaints that Alarcon was living in Sun City, well outside of his council district, led to an investigation, to charges being filed, and ultimately to a jury convicting the councilman and a judge sentencing him to 120 days in county jail.[250]

While the city of Los Angeles dominates Los Angeles County, there are a lot of much smaller cities that are all in the shadow of California's largest city and are part of the metropolitan area. Many of these cities, all in Democratic-dominated areas, have been the subject of relatively recent corruption scandals. I detail the bad and the ugly in Bell, Vernon, South Gate, Rosemead, and Lynwood. While not detailed below, corruption scandals struck Compton, Carson, and Vernon as well, with ex-politicians landing in prison...

City of Bell Corruption Scandal

If there is one city in California, perhaps nationally, that has come to symbolize public corruption and municipal greed, it's the small, working-class city of Bell, south of Los Angeles. It was there that five Democrats on the city council were best supporting actors in a dramatic performance orchestrated by City Manager Robert Rizzo, also a Democrat.

Get ready for these numbers—they will blow you away. Rizzo's total annual compensation at the time the scandal broke was over $1.5 million a year. His deputy city manager's total compensation was over half of that. The chief of police's total comp was closing on a half-million dollars annually. Part-time council members were making a mint as well. It was discovered in the midst of the investigation that Rizzo, his deputy, and some council members had secreted away over $4 million into secret retirement funds.[251]

In 2005, Rizzo pulled off the big scam, having the council place before voters in a special election whether or not Bell should become a charter city. Only a few hundred voters even participated in this low-profile, successful endeavor that then freed Bell of all of the pesky state laws that would have prevented the legal plunder of the city's treasury for the personal gain of the council members, Rizzo, Rizzo's top deputy, and others.

What strikes one is the brazenness of the scheme. While certainly some funds were being moved around secretly, so much of what was being done was in plain daylight, if you knew where to look. Once awareness of the scandal became public, the voters tossed the entire city council. And the new council, with their attorneys, has worked feverishly to try and avoid a bankruptcy and get the city's finances back on the right track.

Once the dust had cleared, Rizzo was sentenced to twelve years in state prison and an additional thirty-three months of federal prison time (to be served concurrently) from a separate conviction for tax evasion. Rizzo pled guilty to sixty-nine criminal counts, thus avoiding the specter of a high-profile public trial. Five former city council members and the former assistant city manager also were convicted of criminal wrongdoing as well. Rizzo was ordered to make restitution in the amount of $8.8 million. He'll knock a dent out of this with the sale of his large home near the ocean in Huntington Beach and his large horse farm (with racing horses) in Washington State.

Three Corrupt Southern California Mayors

Albert Robles, a Democrat, was called "the King of Southgate"—a title that he apparently enjoyed and promulgated. Since his first election to the South Gate City Council (serving as its youngest-ever mayor), Robles ran the roost, dominating city politics for a decade and a half.

In 2004, "the king" was indicted by a federal grand jury on thirty-nine counts of money laundering, bribery, money fraud, and public corruption. The federal prosecutors said that he used his office and influence to funnel money from the city to family and friends—over $20 million from the small budget of the working-class town.[252]

Robles spent the funds on things such as a luxury condo in Baja, Mexico, and a "platinum membership" in a self-help group run by motivational guru Tony Robbins (yeah, the guy that has people walk on hot coals). The king lost his crown and was sentenced to ten years in federal prison.

First elected as mayor of Lynwood in 1986, Paul Richards served as that blue-collar city's mayor seven times before the voters recalled him in October of 2003. The recall took place after the seventeen-year fixture in city government was charged by the feds with public corruption.

It seems that the enterprising Richards, along with his sister and a friend, had set up a private business enterprise and was steering contracts and kickbacks there. Apparently over a half-million dollars had been absconded with before he was caught. Under the scheme he had structured, if he had not been caught, prosecutors said, Richards would have taken in over $6 million.

Ultimately, Richards was convicted on thirty-five counts of fraud, extortion, money laundering, and lying to investigators. He was sentenced to over sixteen years in prison—one of the longest sentences ever handed out in this sort of local public corruption case. Richards appealed his sentence, of course, but his appeal was denied.[253]

Nestled in the San Gabriel Valley east of downtown Los Angeles, the small city of Rosemead become marred with scandal when its former mayor, Democrat John Tran, who had served on the city council from 2005 to 2009, was charged by the FBI with witness tampering, bribery, and extortion. Obviously, the word was out that Tran was willing sell his votes and influence on the city council, which had the FBI wire up a local developer who was pursuing an approval for a mixed-use development project. What was his price? Over four different meetings Tran took cash payments totaling $38,000. He also managed to ask a female developer with a project before the council for sexual favors. Seriously.

Tran tried to get out of his bind by sharing with the Feds the goods on other local corrupt politicians. Ultimately Tran pled guilty to witness tampering and was sentenced to twenty-one months in federal prison as part of a plea deal.[254]

Local government scandals are not unique to Los Angeles County, of course, and two examples of prominent local elected officials who have imploded with self-created scandals that have ended up costing the taxpayers millions of dollars are ex-San Diego Mayor Bob Filner and ex-Santa Clara County Supervisor George Shirakawa Jr.

San Diego's Mayoral Disgrace, Bob Filner

Before his close election as mayor of the city of San Diego in November of 2012, Democrat Bob Filner served as a member of Congress for five terms, and before that as a member of the San Diego City Council for six years. During his time in Congress, there were stories kicking around that alluded to the congressman behaving inappropriately in and around members of his staff. It turns out these rumors foreshadowed a full-scale scandal that a year and a half into Filner's term as mayor would have him resigning from office and pleading guilty to criminal activity.

On July 11, 2013, three longtime allies and supporters of Filner appeared at a press conference, calling for the mayor's resignation based on a number of unspecified but "credible" allegations that he had sexually harassed women.

Rumors had been circulating about inappropriate behavior, and some news sources had been actively looking into it. The press conference led to a now-infamous video apology and statement that Filner was "seeking help."

The next day Filner's chief of staff resigned, and the day after that there was yet another press conference where more details were shared. This is where we started to hear details such as "forcibly kissed," "groped," and more. The lawsuits began, and even Gloria Allred arrived on the scene, representing the mayor's former communications director in a sexual harassment lawsuit. At this point the who's who of politics was calling on Filner to resign—everyone in city politics as well as many leaders in state and national politics, many from Filner's own political party.

In August, two groups started a recall effort, with one hundred thousand signatures of voters being required to place the matter on a special election ballot. It didn't take long for Filner to read the writing on the wall. Filner resigned his office on August 23. On October 15, 2013, Filner pleaded guilty to a felony count of false imprisonment and two battery charges, filed against him by the state attorney general (the local district attorney had recused herself and her office). Filner as part of a plea deal ended up with three months of house arrest, three years of probation, and partial loss of pension benefits.

As a result of this scandal, Democrats lost this long-sought-after office that had long been held by Republicans. San Diego Mayor Kevin Faulconer today is seen as California's most prominent Republican elected official. Also, left holding the bag for huge liability as sexual harassment lawsuits wind through the process? You guessed it—San Diego taxpayers.

Santa Clara County Supervisor George Shirakawa Jr.

George Shirakawa Jr., a Democrat, was a popular and powerful supervisor in densely populated Santa Clara County, where San Jose is the dominant city. While it seemed "sky's the limit" for the upwardly mobile Democrat, everything came crashing down when it was discovered that the Supervisor, apparently due to a gambling addiction, had for years been absconding with public funds and also stealing campaign contributions. In 2013 Shirakawa pleaded guilty to twelve charges, including corruption, gambling with public funds, and duping political donors, whose campaign contributions he siphoned off into a secret slush fund. The former supervisor was ultimately sentenced to a year in jail—and served about half of his sentence before being released.[255]

But wait, there's more. Shirakawa was separately charged in another matter in which the then supervisor sent out a campaign mailer that was designed to help a political ally, but that was written to appear to come from another candidate in the race. This was totally false, and DNA evidence was found that was connected to the fraudulent mailer. On top of his jail sentence for the corruption charges, Shirakawa in April of this year was sentenced to forty-five days of community service for this unrelated crime.

This next former politician…well, there aren't really words to help preface the story of "Mug Shot Mary"—so I will just tell the tale…

Mug Shot Mary Hayashi

In 2011, everything was looking awesome for the charismatic and popular Mary Hayashi, an elected Democratic assemblywoman from the East San Francisco Bay Area. Chairman of a key assembly committee and considered a policy heavyweight, Hayashi was gearing up for a state senate run, in which she was expected to fare well. Her standing in the community was no doubt bolstered by her marriage to respected Superior Court Judge Dennis Hayashi.

Until later in that year, when Hayashi's house of cards came tumbling down. That's when Hayashi was detained by store security at the Union Square Neiman Marcus for putting $2,445 in merchandise into her bag without paying, and walking out of the store. Store security called the San Francisco Police Department, and Hayashi was arrested and ultimately charged by the district attorney's office with felony grand theft. Ultimately the assemblywoman pleaded no contest to a lesser shoplifting charge, was sentenced to a $180 fine and three years probation, and was ordered to stay more than fifty feet away from that Neiman Marcus store.[256] At one point her attorney suggested her actions could have been the result of a benign brain tumor, but when questions were raised about this it was never mentioned again.[257]

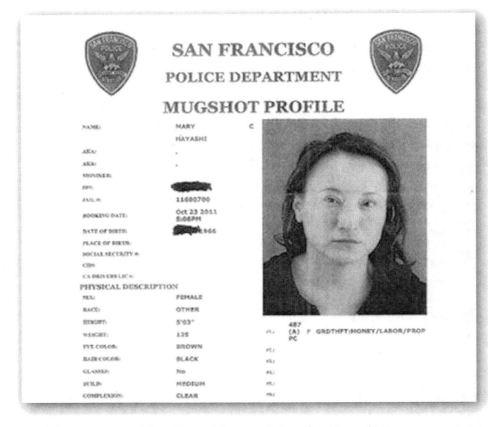

SAN FRANCISCO
POLICE DEPARTMENT
MUGSHOT PROFILE

The entire scandal really sunk her candidacy for Alameda County supervisor in 2012, where she was the embarrassing third-place vote getter. Unfazed, apparently, Hayashi turned around and jumped into a very competitive Democratic primary for an East/South Bay state senate seat. In that campaign her shoplifting arrest and conviction were used mercilessly by her opponent, who even launched a website entitled Mug Shot Mary, featuring her arrest photo, as well as details about the incident. Inconveniently for Hayashi, in the midst of this campaign the video from the Neiman Marcus store surveillance camera surfaced, providing fresh fodder for the news.

Hayashi's political career appears at this point to be all done. It could go without saying, but it won't, that assembly Speaker John Perez was strongly publicly supportive of Hayashi all of the way through. And at least one observer has noted that Hayashi, who did not resign her seat, ended up with a rather light sentence for the felony she was charged with, and even wasn't required to show up in court for all her hearings, by rulings from a fellow partisan liberal, a San Francisco Superior Court Judge who campaigned for his own supposedly highly nonpartisan judicial office as a "Democrat" in mass advertising, an action considered by some legal professionals as unprincipled.[258]

Solutions Easy to Find, Hard to Achieve

They say that absolute power corrupts absolutely. This is the textbook example. While I have highlighted many politicians who either were ethically corrupt, attempting to use their offices for person gain, or who were morally challenged, committing illegal acts while holding public office, it is worthy of note that the list is actually much longer.

As this is a chapter on recent political corruption in California, since the turn of the century, other elected officials who were either criminally charged or resigned in the face of pending or potential charges or scandal are almost too numerous to mention. Some notable former politicians include former insurance commissioner Chuck Quackenbush,[259] former secretary of state Kevin Shelly,[260] former assemblyman Mike Duvall,[261] former Orange County sheriff Michael Carona,[262] former congressman Duke Cunningham,[263] former San Bernardino County tax assessor Bill Postmus,[264] former San Diego mayor Dick Murphy,[265] and former San Diego council members Michael Zucchet and Ralph Inzunza.[266] State senator Ben Hueso[267] and assemblyman Roger Hernandez[268] were both charged with driving under the influence in separate incidents, the latter driving an hour from the capitol, at night, with a female lobbyist in the car. While charges were filed against Hernandez, a jury ultimately found him not guilty.

As of the publication of this book, in addition to the pending trials of Ron and Tom Calderon and Leland Yee (which are rumored to potentially draw in other serving Democratic legislators), the former police chief of the Port of Los Angeles is facing charges of tax evasion and public corruption,[269] former Los Angeles County tax assessor John Noguez is facing grand theft and embezzlement charges,[270] and a host of Los Angeles County sheriff's officials tied to misconduct inside L.A. County jails[271] under former sheriff Lee Baca, including former undersheriff Paul Tanaka,[272] are all under criminal indictment. Baca himself resigned from office before completion of his term and cancelled plans to run for re-election in the wake of the County jails scandal.[273] And the tiny City of Industry, just south of downtown Los Angeles, is now embroiled in a scandal that seems to mirror the pattern of Bell, Southgate, and Vernon.[274]

Some of the bad actors we've covered are clear cases of individually ethically challenged people holding public office, and they are out of office today because of poor decisions that they made. But a disturbingly large number of those profiled committed crimes or are alleged to have committed crimes that clearly show how California's political environment seems to have become one that is almost welcoming or inviting opportunities for corruption.

As you leave this chapter perhaps more cynical about California politics, you might be asking yourself, "What can be done to stop this raft of corruption that strikes at the core of the democratic republic that is America's largest state?"

The solutions are easy to proffer—but are difficult to achieve. The first would be to rejuvenate civic engagement in California—getting average people more engaged in the process of running for office and even participating in the election of people to office. It is the absence of citizen engagement that helps foster an environment where bad behavior can thrive and bad people can get elected.

The other not-so-simple fix is simply to shrink the size and scope of government at every level. So much of what occurs is temptation tied to the immense power held by elected officials to "play God"—granting favor to some and disfavor to others. This kind of big government will always bring forward an unsavory element of office seeker.

As a practical matter, it is likely that corruption is going to become only more institutionalized and more extreme, as government grows even larger and more powerful. So many special interests have a stake now in the Democratic Party, which dominates politics statewide and whose politicians seem to have no problem, and in fact relish in, a system where the government routinely picks winners and losers.

As Louisiana governor and GOP presidential contender Bobby Jindal wrote in *National Review*, "Big government invites corruption and imperils the generosity of the American spirit."[275] Nowhere within America is this the case more so than in California.

About the Author: Jon Fleischman

Jon Fleischman is publisher of the FlashReport.org website on California, a daily aggregator and provider of news and views on California politics and policy. Dubbed the "Matt Drudge of California" by Congressman Darrell Issa, Fleischman regularly appears on television, radio, and in print media to provide analysis and opinion. Fleischman is a former executive director of the California Republican Party.

Thirteen

TRANSPARENCY

By T. J. Fuentes

C alifornia has a public corruption problem, fueled in large part by a lack of transparency in how government, at the state and local level, operates, and a failure to enforce existing transparency laws. The examples are plentiful.

When three state senators were indicted on various felony charges in 2014, the state senate responded by deleting their websites and online archives, effectively blocking journalists from researching the connections and any legislation affected by the corruption.

In September of 2014, Gov. Jerry Brown refused to release details of the state's failed effort to woo automaker Tesla to build a battery factory in California. Tesla decided to build its battery facility in Nevada, but many Californians were rightly left wondering how and why California lost out, and what offers and promises the state had made to Tesla.

Beginning in 2013, the City of Los Angeles waged a vicious legal fight against its own Department of Water and Power (DWP) to force an accounting of two trusts connected to the DWP, which squandered $40 million of taxpayer dollars on bogus training initiatives and conferences over a ten-year period.

And in perhaps the worst ongoing example of a lack of government transparency, the High Speed Rail Authority (HSRA), the entity in charge of the billion-dollar California bullet train, refuses to provide notice to landowners that the train might run through their property and refuses to provide accurate projections of the cost of completion or the fares the train will charge if it is (ever) completed. Further, its own website lists the crucial documents it does not have to provide, including correspondence between the HSRA and the governor's office.

In view of these failings, one would be forgiven for thinking that California lacks for laws requiring openness and transparency in government. The truth is the opposite. Over the last forty years, several laws have been passed requiring transparency in government deliberations and decision making. Yet none has ensured that citizens and journalists are afforded the information and access they require to hold California's leaders accountable. Why?

In part, the laws' futility stems from their age—some were passed over forty years ago, and the problems they were passed to address are no longer relevant. Legislators and government employees have also found ways around the laws (private e-mail accounts), or just stopped enforcing them. Also, those holding government positions have the least interest in enforcing laws that expose government's inner workings, or the deals struck between government employees and those campaign contributors who keep them in office.

Because of California's outdated transparency laws, which were created before the advent of the Internet, advanced electronic communications, and social media, average citizens and journalists are unable to uncover the truth about the government's actions and hold those in power responsible before it's too late. This disconnects citizens from their government and leaders and renders those in authority virtually unaccountable. This is not how government should operate.

As further discussed below, California needs new and updated transparency laws that are tailored to how government operates today, in an era defined by increasingly complex electronic communications. In the age of self-driving cars, drone delivery of goods, and the iPad, we need transparency laws to match. At a minimum, any new laws and regulations should provide citizens ongoing and meaningful access to the most crucial government records relating to contracting, deliberations, decision making, and discipline of government employees. And this access should be provided electronically, for a very minimal fee, if any, within days of a request, not weeks or months.

In spite of California's archaic laws and extant transparency challenges, some creative and resourceful citizens are trying to pull back the veil on government secrecy. Efforts are under way to post local municipal codes and city contracts on the Internet through groups such as the Madison Project. The state's political disclosure records are being digitized and made searchable by groups such as Maplight. Other good government advocates are posting public employee salary data online.

California's culture of corruption continues unabated due to outdated transparency laws and a lack of government transparency. Until the outdated laws are updated, citizens can use technology to open government on their own with projects that disclose government salaries, campaign contributions, and city codes. But citizen initiatives, successful as they might be, are not the complete answer.

By surveying the relevant laws and discussing some egregious examples of government secrecy and scandal, it is possible to understand the imperative for updated laws and what any revised laws should include. In the interim, and in the hope of pushing California's leaders toward greater transparency, citizens and journalists should pursue every option that shines light on the processes and procedures that determine who gets elected, how laws are made, and how leaders are held to account when they violate the public trust.

Brown Act

Since 1953, California has attempted to ensure public access to government meetings and records, and several laws on the books purport to ensure this goal. The most important statutes are set forth below.

Enacted in 1953 in response to concerns about secret deliberations by local government bodies, the Brown Act[276] guarantees the public's right to attend and participate in meetings of city and county commissions, boards, councils, and other public agencies. In passing this bill, named for state assemblyman Ralph M. Brown, the legislature observed:

> The people of this State do not yield their sovereignty to the agencies which serve them. The people, in delegating authority, do not give their public servants the right to decide what is good for the people to know and what is not good for them to know. The people insist on remaining informed so that they may retain control over the instruments they have created.

The language is remarkable for its expression of the balance between the governed and those governing, a balance which has clearly been altered since 1953, and not for the better. Deliberations conducted in secret, away from the sunshine of the public's scrutiny, reflect the antithesis of the Brown Act, and perhaps explain the failures in transparency that so plague the Golden State.

Of course, statutory language is only as good as its enforcement, and several open-government advocates have criticized local governments for either ignoring the Brown Act or construing it in such a manner as to bar citizen participation in government meetings. One possible method of ensuring compliance with the Brown Act, which will be more fully explored below, is greater and immediate electronic access to local government meetings, which could ensure greater accountability.

Bagley-Keene Open Meeting Act

While the Brown Act ensured citizen access to county and city meetings, the Bagley-Keene Open Meeting Act[277] declared that "the meetings of public bodies and the writings of public officials and agencies shall be open to public scrutiny." It was passed to ensure that citizens had access to the meetings of state agencies, boards, and commissions. In other words, it was the Brown Act applied to state agencies.

This law sounds good in theory, but, as discussed below, it has not been adequately enforced, and in some cases the state legislature has blatantly ignored it in pursuit of contentious or unpopular political objectives.

California Public Records Act

Passed by the legislature and signed into law in 1968, this law was premised on the belief that "access to information concerning the conduct of the people's business is a fundamental and necessary right of every person in this state."[278] Section 6253(b) provides, in relevant part,

> Except with respect to public records exempt from disclosure by express provisions of law, each state or local agency, upon a request for a copy of records that reasonably describes an identifiable record or records, shall make the records promptly available to any person upon payment of fees covering direct costs of duplication, or a statutory fee if applicable. Upon request, an exact copy shall be provided unless impracticable to do so.

Section 6253(c) requires that a government agency determine within ten days of a receipt of a request whether the request seeks copies of "disclosable public records," and notify the requesting party of the agency's determination. Further, in "unusual circumstances," an agency head may extend the ten-day period upon written notice to the requesting party.

Thus, unless a requesting party seeks public records that have been exempted from disclosure, the state or local agency fielding the request must respond within ten days and, if the records are "disclosable," make the records promptly available to the requesting party upon payment of a fee. Sounds good in theory, but, as with all government endeavors, the devil is in the details, and, as set forth below, one of the worst devils is the current practice of government agencies charging exorbitant rates and imposing unreasonable waiting periods for production of requested records.

Importantly, the courts and the legislature were not made subject to the Public Records Act. This was rectified, at far as it concerned the legislature, in the Open Records Act.

Legislative Open Records Act

Passed in 1975 and codified at Government Code sections 9070 to 9080, the Legislative Open Records Act (LORA), another Orwellian-named statute, purports to ensure the public's access to legislative records, but in reality ensures that the legislature can keep secret documents and information it does not want released.

The statute reads in part, "The Legislature finds and declares that access to information concerning the conduct of the people's business by the Legislature is a fundamental and necessary right of every citizen in this state."

The state assembly website summarizes the act as follows: "LORA provides for review, reproduction, and access to all records not restricted under its terms and places time constraints on the Legislature's response. Normally the Assembly Rules Committee responds to LORA requests within three days when the Legislature is in session and 10 days when the Legislature is not in session." Notably, requests made under this act are processed by the chief administrative officer and/or the chief counsel of the Assembly Rules Committee, a procedure which enables the legislature to control and effectively limit what records it produces. But as discussed below, a recent judicial decision may provide the basis for further disclosure of legislative records.

In 2001, the legislature enacted section 6253.9 of the California Public Records Act. This amendment to the act requires public agencies to make available in an electronic format an identifiable public record maintained in an electronic format that is not otherwise exempt from disclosure.

Under the California Public Records Act,

"Writing" means any handwriting, typewriting, printing, photostating, photographing, photocopying, transmitting by *electronic mail* or facsimile, and every other means of recording upon any tangible thing any form of communication or representation, including letters, words, pictures, sounds or symbols, or combination thereof, and any record thereby created, regardless of the manner in which the record has been stored. *Cal. Government Code* § 6252(f)

This expansive definition arguably includes e-mails and text messages, but, as noted below, public officials have found ways to skirt this law.

Proposition 59: The Sunshine Amendment

In 2004, California voters overwhelmingly passed Proposition 59, the "Sunshine Amendment," which wrote into the California Constitution language requiring openness in California's executive, judicial, and legislative branches. Proposition 59 provided, in relevant part, "The people have the right of access to information concerning the conduct of the people's business, and, therefore, the meetings of public bodies and the writings of public officials and agencies shall be open to public scrutiny."[279] According to the Reporters Committee for Freedom of the Press, this amendment was important because it required public bodies to make express findings demonstrating the interest purportedly protected and the need for protecting that interest before they adopt new laws, court rules, or other regulations that restrict the right of access. Thus, the adoption of restrictive regulations can no longer be based on "the whim of the agency's governing body but will require actual on-the-record findings demonstrating the need for secrecy and demonstrating how the exemption will achieve that need—findings similar to that required by a court before sealing a court record or closing a court proceeding."

As more fully discussed below, this important amendment was the subject of an important court ruling because of the implications it has for the secrecy of legislative records, and the potential unearthing of heretofore restricted legislative records.

* * *

The above laws form the foundation of the current statutory scheme relating to government openness and transparency. Yet in spite of the legislature's good intentions, or perhaps because of the limitations and exemptions it included in the above statutes, openness and transparency remain elusive goals, as evidenced by the following examples.

In late March of 2014, the state senate took down the websites of state senators Leland Yee of San Francisco, Ron Calderon of Montebello, and Rod Wright of Inglewood, all of whom had been placed on leave after being accused of various criminal offenses. Senator Calderon had been accused of bribery and corruption. Senator Wright was ultimately found guilty of eight felonies related to his living outside his district. Senator Yee was charged with gun trafficking and accepting bribes. The senators' websites had contained important information about their voting histories, legislative work, and current legislative efforts.

In connection with the corruption charges against senators Yee and Calderon, the Bay Area News Group requested documents related to the senators' calendars, including appointment books. Senate officials denied the request on the grounds that the requested records were exempt from production under the Legislative Open Records Act. Faced with this refusal, the media outlets sued the senate.

The media outlets argued that the calendars should be produced under the Legislative Open Records Act and Proposition 59. Attorneys for the legislature argued, predictably, that the senators' records of meetings were exempt from the reach of Proposition 59, and thus the lawsuit should be dismissed.

The judge, Michael Kenny, ruled that the Legislative Open Records Act, as amended by Proposition 59, does not exclude the legislature, and allowed the suit to proceed on its merits. Judge Michael Kenny wrote, "If the intent of Proposition 59 was to exclude legislative proceedings and records from its reach, it could have plainly so stated," Kenny wrote in an April 3, 2015 decision.

While that decision did not require the immediate production of the senators' calendars, it set an important precedent about the reach of the transparency laws that could impact future records requests, for it was the first ruling to hold that legislative records are subject to the state constitution, according to the attorney for the media outlets, Duffy Carolan.

In the summer of 2014, after failing in his attempt to convince automaker Tesla to build a battery factory in California, Gov. Jerry Brown refused to release details of the negotiations between Tesla and the Brown administration, specifically the office of Business and Economic Development. Media outlets had sought, under the California Public Records Act, all records relating to the negotiations, as well as records relating to the state's incentive packages offered to defense contractors Lockheed Martin and Northrop Grumman.

In response the Brown administration stated, "Disclosure of such information would be detrimental to these efforts and would seriously impede California's ability to grow its economy." Whether or not this explanation is true, the problem is obvious: the people of California, despite clear statutory authority, are being denied access to key documents that bear on the state's finances and the efforts by state leaders to negotiate large contracts with important companies. Score another point for secrecy.

In a replay of an episode that plagued Hillary Clinton's early days of her 2016 presidential campaign, several top officials in California confirmed in March of 2015 that they too used personal e-mail accounts to conduct state business. If anything will foil transparency, it is the use of private, personal e-mail for public purposes. Private e-mail accounts are not subject to state open records laws, and, as such, they may be wiped clean with impunity, resulting in the potential destruction of key records citizens are entitled to view and evaluate.

In response to a survey of California's senior elected officials by the Associated Press, it was found that Gov. Jerry Brown, Lt. Gov. Gavin Newsome, and many other top officials used private e-mail accounts for their official business. Governor Brown's office noted that the governor used his private e-mail account to contact his staffers. Superintendent of Public Instruction Tom Torlakson responded that he conducted most of his state business on a private e-mail account.

Given the poor performance of California's public schools and the lack of accountability at the local level, Mr. Torlakson's use of private e-mail for official business raises profound concerns about the public's ability to hold Mr. Torlakson to account and to determine the propriety of the decisions he has made in the course of his public duties. As recommended below, one immediate change that should be made is to require all government employees to conduct *all* government business through government e-mail accounts, and on government devices if possible. Without such requirements, public officials will remain free to communicate without the obligation of retaining or providing their communications.

Orange County's Great Park

The story of the Orange County Great Park is one of the most cautionary tales of government corruption in a generation. After the Pentagon abandoned the 4,700 acre El Toro Marine Air Corps base in 1999, local interests attempted to turn the base into an international airport. After that effort was defeated in 2002, opposing interests prevailed on a plan to turn part of the base property into a park that would rival other large city parks. It would be a "great park."

Conceived in 2002 and still not complete in 2015, the endeavor was, in large part, the pet project of Irvine City Councilman Larry Agran and was expected to cost $1.2 billion. Big promises were made: within three years there would be a golf course, soccer fields, educational facilities, a lake, a garden, a wildlife park, a museum, a cemetery, and a war memorial.

Thirteen years and $220 million later, almost none of that was true. As of June 2015, the park offered only a hot air balloon, a carousel, and sports fields. The explanation for this is simple: an absence of transparency; political patronage masquerading as legitimate contracting; false promises; no accountability, and bloated administrative expenses. The Ralph Brown Act never stood a chance.

For example, from 2008 to 2011, the park managed to consume $56 million in "administrative costs" and to spend $0 on construction costs. Further, the city council spent $46 million on a design for the park that was never utilized. No citizen would stand for such waste if apprised of it and given a vote. A grand jury was even convened to review the park and compared the park's planning and finances to an *Alice in Wonderland* fantasy. Yet the city council dismissed the grand jury's finding and planning proceeded apace.

A 2009 audit raised serious questions about management practices, cost controls, accounting procedures, and the "suspicious movement" of unallocated public funds between the consultants hired to work on the great park. Yet nothing changed.

It took Agran's electoral defeat and the election of a majority of Republican city council members in Irvine to request an honest audit of the program. The two-year audit revealed that Agran awarded his political cronies lucrative "consulting" contracts to advise on public relations for park development and wasted millions of city dollars on a park that failed to live up to every campaign promise.

Specifically, Agran gave a $100,000 per month consulting contract to a political ally of his to do public relations work for a park that existed only on paper. As if that was not wasteful enough, Agran hired a "public information officer" for $112,579 per year. To ensure the park was sufficiently promoted, Agran deposited an additional $80,000 into an earmarked "contingency contract" for the park's budget for fiscal year 2010.

Irvine was able to remove Larry Agran from office, but has not been able to remove the park or extricate itself from the contracts he signed with various parties, including housing developers, who are understandably intent on building the homes they were promised they could build.

The park stands as a stark reminder that the current laws are insufficient to prevent the kinds of waste, fraud, and abuse so exemplified by the great park. Central to any meaningful legal reforms must be a requirement for yearly audits of large projects and mandated reporting to the citizens in free, easily accessible sources. The absence of such reforms will only invite future great parks.

More Government Secrecy

Nowhere are public employee unions stronger in California than in Los Angeles. Perhaps the strongest Los Angeles area union is the International Brotherhood of Electrical Workers (IBEW), which represents the employees of the Department of Water and Power (DWP), the nation's largest municipal water and power agency. Its chief, Brian D'Arcy, is public enemy number one for Los Angeles ratepayers and government transparency.

In 2013, after various media outlets reported that two nonprofit trusts tied to the DWP, the Joint Training Institute and the Joint Safety Institute, had wasted over $40 million of taxpayer funds in the prior ten years with no discernible impact and no accounting for their spending, the city attempted to audit the trusts to account for the lavish and unaccountable spending. While the trusts exist ostensibly to conduct safety and training programs, the DWP was already spending over $115 million per year on these exact same programs.

In 2014, the city issued a subpoena for documents related to the trusts and for testimony by Brian D'Arcy and other trust leaders. Rather than account for their spending, the union sued to quash the subpoenas. A Los Angeles judge ruled for the city and ordered the trusts to produce the requested accounting records within ten days. The union filed an appeal, which put the legal effort on hold.

While the appeal was pending, the parties brokered a compromise in November of 2014 whereby the union agreed to allow the city to inspect five years of records in exchange for dropping its lawsuit, and the union would purportedly forgo its claim that the city had violated the terms of the labor agreement. Predictably, the union did not live up to its word, and in December of 2014, only two weeks into the process, failed to provide the city controller access to the documents. Six months later, the stalemate persisted, and Los Angeles ratepayers were no closer to knowing where $40 million of their money had been spent.

When the legislature passed the Open Meeting Act in 1967, no one was talking about global warming, climate change, a carbon trading exchange, or the imposition of huge fees to combat "global warming." However, if they had been, surely the legislature would have required any meetings on such topics to be open to the public. Fast forward almost fifty years, and things have changed.

In 2012, the legislature passed Senate Bill (SB) 1018, which in Section 12894(b)(2) exempted from the requirements of the Bagley-Keene Open

Meeting act a company called Western Climate Initiative, Inc. (WCI). What is WCI? A *Delaware* corporation established by the *California* Air Resources Board (CARB) to manage the auction of cap and trade credits. Thus, in service of the radical green global warming agenda, specifically the cap and trade program, the legislature exempted from any open meeting requirements an entity directly tied to CARB, which was responsible for imposing billions of dollars in energy taxes on California ratepayers. And the reason behind this was obvious: CARB thought that by incorporating its subsidiary entity in Delaware, it would not be subject to California's open meeting laws. So much for open meeting requirements.

Thus, if the legislature can exempt from compliance with the Open Meeting Act any corporation it deems fit, the Open Meeting Act is rendered a nullity and transparency has been forfeited. One possible solution is to amend the Act to preclude exemptions from the act by any state board, commission, agency, or council that considers and has the power to implement any tax, fee, levy, duty, or fine on any ratepayer.

Administrative Roadblocks to Transparency

Whether roadblocks are created by authorities to discourage those seeking information or are simply a by-product of bureaucracy and tighter budgets, greater costs to fulfill freedom of information requests ultimately interfere with the public's legitimate right to know. Such costs are a growing threat to open and honest government, a cornerstone of Sunshine Week.

"It's incredibly easy for an agency that doesn't want certain records to be exposed to impose fees in the hopes that the requester is dissuaded," said Adam Marshall, a fellow with the Reporters Committee for Freedom of the Press, which sponsors Sunshine Week with the American Society of News Editors. "If the people don't know what's going on, either because they don't have direct access to information or because the media isn't able to provide them with access to information about what their government is doing, it's impossible for the people to exercise any sense of informed self-governance."

Fees can be charged for searching for records, making copies, paying a lawyer to redact certain parts of the information, or hiring technical experts to analyze the data. In most cases, the fees imposed are at the agency's discretion. In some cases, those agencies waive the costs or requesters can appeal them to an administrative board. But in other cases, Marshall said news organizations and private citizens are faced with the "ridiculous choice" of weighing the costs and benefits of being a responsible public steward.

Exhibit A: The California Department of Motor Vehicles (DMV) demanded nearly $20,000 from the Associated Press (AP) to fulfill an open-records request seeking to determine "whether poor people had their driver's licenses suspended at a disproportionate rate." The DMV's justification for the fee: the request would allegedly require 120 hours of special programming at $135 per hour.

In response to this outlandish fee, the AP sought a meeting with the DMV's public information and technology staff. Predictably, the agency never responded. DMV spokesman Artemio Armenta said the agency does not conduct research for the public and is protected by law from doing so. Consider that: an agency funded by citizens and accountable to citizens takes the position that it does not have to answer to citizens' inquiries for information. This violates both the letter and the spirit of the laws discussed above. Further, for requests covered by the state Public Records Act, the DMV charges for copying or the cost of computer programming and document retrieval.

Not to be denied, the AP winnowed down its request and was given a new estimate of $377 for a copy of a statistical report. Ultimately, the AP decided not to pay for the report because it was unlikely to contain a breakdown of license suspensions.

Practical Solutions

Clearly, the laws discussed herein are insufficient to ensure the kind of meaningful transparency needed to police California's out-of-control elected officials and bureaucrats. Many laws were written before the advent of modern technology; others have been interpreted or applied in ways that render them meaningless. In other cases, California's leaders have simply ignored the laws, or found ways to get around them. It is clear that California has come a long way from the promise of the 1953 Ralph Brown Act, which declared,

> The people of this State do not yield their sovereignty to the agencies which serve them. The people, in delegating authority, do not give their public servants the right to decide what is good for the people to know and what is not good for them to know. The people insist on remaining informed so that they may retain control over the instruments they have created.

The question is: What can be done to rein in the government beast and ensure that California's citizens "retain control over the instruments they have created"? The following are offered in the hope of doing just that.

Upgrade transparency and open meeting laws for the twenty-first century: Laws written in 1953 and 1968 are inadequate to meet today's challenges. Thus, new laws are required. These laws should require more advanced notice of scheduled hearings, should afford shorter cutoff times for citizens to participate in hearings, should require legislators or agency employees to actually listen to citizen concerns, and deliberations should be broadcast electronically, for free, over state websites. Further, any revisions should apply equally to the executive, legislative, and judicial branches. Special carve-outs for the legislature should be eliminated.

Require public e-mail addresses: As noted herein, when public officials conduct public business on private devices and with private e-mail accounts, the public is effectively prevented from any meaningful review of the official business. Private e-mail accounts are easily concealed, easily destroyed, and potentially vulnerable to security risks. Moreover, private e-mail addresses prevent accountability. Thus, the public should demand that all elected leaders, legislators, and all heads of state agencies, councils, and commissions conduct official business with official e-mail accounts. Periodic audits should be conducted to ensure compliance with these rules, and severe fines and penalties should be assessed against those who fail to comply.

End paper copy fees: In the digital age, there is no good reason for state agencies to require exorbitant fees to copy records. To facilitate expedient production of paper records, state offices and agencies should simply add to each employee's job description the occasional requirement of providing copies of documents on which he or she has worked. Moving forward, the state should transition to electronic delivery of requested records and should provide this service without fees to citizens. While it will always require some investment of time to procure requested records, the fees associated with producing the records are a great impediment to accountability, and should thus be eliminated as much as possible.

Impose penalties when government loses or obstructs public records requests: Under the current public records regime, there are no meaningful penalties on a state or local government office that fails to provide records timely and appropriately requested by citizens or the media. This needs to change. Integral to any productive reforms will be two measures: creating a legal presumption in favor of providing the requested records; and clearly setting forth penalties for a state or local agency's failure to timely provide requested records. In addition, if a citizen or media outlet is initially refused documents and subsequently prevails in procuring documents, the state or local agency should reimburse the requesting party $250 plus any costs borne by the requesting party in the pursuit of the records.

Criminal penalties for officials that delay or destroy records: In tandem with the prior recommendation, any revision to the state's transparency laws should enhance and widen the reach of Government Code section 6200, which sets forth criminal penalties for public officers who destroy "in whole or any part of the record, map, book, paper, or proceeding." Unless and until all state officials, both elected and appointed, face stiffer sanctions for the destruction of state records, they will continue to do so with impunity.

Make Public Disclosure Searchable

MapLight, a nonpartisan research organization that tracks money's influence on politics, recently announced the launch of a search tool that allows journalists and citizens to easily search the California secretary of state's newly released bulk data to find campaign contributions to candidate and ballot committees dating back to 2001. More functionalities will be added in the coming weeks. If this program proves successful, it should be adopted by the state and made available to the public at no costs.

<u>Publicizing public employee pay</u>: Recently, the California Public Policy Center launched a database, transparentcalifornia.com, which publishes public employee names, base salary, overtime pay, and total pay and benefits. This is a good step in the right direction, but the database should be expanded and maintained by the state, with free and continually updated records of all public employee positions and salaries. While many public employees' job duties may never truly be known, understanding their salaries is a good beginning to holding them accountable to those who pay their salary.

California's transparency problem did not develop overnight, and is likely to get worse. As the baby-boomer generation of California public employees begins to retire with the most lucrative pensions ever awarded, those retiring and those in power protecting the retirees will have every incentive to hide from the public view the full value of the pensions and the manner in which they are calculated. Consider these two statistics.

In 1999, there were 16,071 retirements of public employees, and the average retirement benefit was only $20,532 per year, according the California Public Employee Retirement System. By 2012, there were nearly twice as many retirements, 33,330, and the average benefit had nearly doubled, $36,468. Even more alarming, in 2012 alone, more than 14,000 California public employees were projected to receive retirement benefits exceeding $100,000 per year. In other words, they stood to be paid $100,000 per year to do nothing. This is simply unsustainable.

Worse yet, these rising pensions are driving cities and counties into bankruptcy. Recent bankruptcies in Stockton, San Bernardino, and Vallejo have resulted, in part, from public employee pension obligations that have vastly outpaced tax receipts and the rate of inflation.

As the *Los Angeles Times* has reported, this problem is not confined to outlying or small areas of California. In Los Angeles, as of 2013, the Fire and

Police Pension System was $3 billion in the hole for its pension obligations. The California Public Employees' Retirement System was $57 billion short. And the state teachers' pension fund came in last: it reported a $70 billion shortfall. These figures will only rise as more public employees retire with unsustainable pension costs.

While this information has finally been made public because of State Treasurer John Chiang's efforts to post the information online at ByTheNumbers.sco.ca.gov, this is a pyrrhic victory for transparency, like being handed an invoice for car repairs the day an accident happened: it's nice to know the damage, but it would be more helpful to know when the accident is going to happen so it can be prevented.

The ultimate goal of government transparency is for the citizens and journalists to be able to know what is going to happen, to participate in the process, and not to just be apprised of the mess after the mess has been made. Unfortunately, for too long in California, that is just the scenario that has played out, as those in power have made every effort to prevent California's taxpayers from knowing who is pulling the strings and calling the shots.

Unless and until commonsense reforms are made to California's transparency laws, California will continue to fall short of the vision set forth in the 1953 Ralph Brown Act, and Californians will yield their sovereignty to the agencies that serve them, give their public servants the right to decide what is good for the people to know and what is not good for them to know, and cede control over the instruments they have created.

About the Author: Thomas A. Fuentes Jr.

Thomas A. ("T. J.") Fuentes Jr. is an elected member of the Republican Party of Orange County Central Committee, where he serves in a leadership role as the assistant treasurer. He is the son of the late Tom Fuentes, former chairman of the Republican Party of Orange County. T. J. received his bachelor's degree from UC Irvine. T. J. and his wife, Tish, reside in Newport Beach with their young daughter, Addison.

Fourteen

WHY I WON'T GIVE UP ON CALIFORNIA

By James V. Lacy

"*This is the height of ridicule! How can you possibly stay in California with this kind of nonsense?!*" an incensed Stuart Varney, Fox Business News Channel's most popular anchor, bellowed at me on air, sitting erect behind his news desk in New York City. Varney was outraged that California officials had confirmed their intention to spend $33 million of taxpayer funds just to move eight hundred wild seabirds and their nests—at an incredible $40,000 per bird—from a moribund section of the Oakland Bay Bridge, itself scheduled for demolition.[280]

Staring directly at him into the teleprompter, I responded to Varney's challenge. "Now come on," I exclaimed. "I am a native of California and I was born in Oakland near this bridge...and I am never going to leave. *I am never going to give up.*" And then I blurted out, "Angela Merkel didn't give up on East Germany and she became chancellor!" and I chuckled. And Stuart, who himself at one time lived and broadcasted from San Francisco, had to laugh, too.

Though I had been inside Varney's busy New York studio at Fox headquarters at 1211 Avenue of Americas many times before to discuss California's unending problems and my first book, *Taxifornia, Liberals' Laboratory to Bankrupt America*, on this particular day I was glad that I wasn't sitting right next to him. The segment was being produced remotely with me on a satellite link, and I was sheltered in the relative safety of Fox's more bucolic West Los Angeles news bureau on the other side of the continent. But Stuart was genuinely angry about the ever-increasing, foolhardy public waste in the state. And frankly so was I. As a lifelong Californian who shares Varney's opinions and emotions about the many things wrong with California's government and the need for reform, I was nevertheless at my most vulnerable point. If California is such a bad place, why the heck do *you* still live there?

When I wrote the original *Taxifornia*, published in 2014 by Post Hill Press, my intention was to highlight in detail the troubling policies of the liberal Democrats and their public employee union allies who actually run the state, with their extreme environmentalist cronies, and expose the negative consequences of their policies, lay the blame on them for those consequences, and attempt to persuade my reader, logically, about the urgent need for reform. I did the job with over eight hundred footnotes. And it seemed to me to be a pretty straightforward proposition; an easy connection of the dots and a call to action that if you want a better California, you need to stop empowering the current ruling clique leading the state to more poverty, local government bankruptcies, and general economic calamity.

After all, as I wrote, liberal Democrats, who are in total control of every statewide office and both houses of the state legislature, have imposed on Californians the highest state income tax in the nation, the highest state sales tax, among the highest gasoline taxes, and a higher corporate business tax than most other states. Yet in doing so, the poverty rate in the state has risen dramatically and become the highest in the nation during the same period. More Californians are now on welfare per capita than in any other state. Unemployment and underemployment remain alarmingly high in many regions of California, as much as 20 percent or even more unemployed in one northern California county. Therefore, the illogic of liberal Democratic policies and their ruinous economic results over the years seemed rather obvious. And there was more to say about how these liberals have hurt the state: in our education system, we pay and reward our teachers at the highest salaries in the nation, yet on student achievement tests, our young people consistently score near the bottom of the barrel nationally. Environmental regulations are outdated and so burdensome that businesses and jobs are fleeing the state, new businesses routinely chose to not locate in California, and *CEO* magazine has annually declared the state to be the most "business unfriendly" in the nation for eleven years running. So I wrote *Taxifornia* to root out these facts, lay them out clearly for all to see, with an expectation that on having those facts, the book would contribute to the dialogue to make California better by rejecting liberal policies and inspiring reforms.

Many responded positively to my message. But after the book went into circulation, and I started speaking out on current events programs such as *Varney & Company*, the feedback I received wasn't always the reform-minded, "now let's change things" spirit I had hoped for. In fact, what I got back from more than a few commenters was that my facts were persuasive, but that California was in such bad shape that it was an utterly hopeless cause, and that I should simply forget about trying to reform it and just leave the liberals in control!

"California has reached critical mass. There's no saving it!" wrote one of *Taxifornia*'s Facebook friends. "California is toast!," "So glad to be out of CA," and "God I hate California!" wrote others.

But one Facebook comment on *Taxifornia* in particular stood out:

I have come to the conclusion that the people of this state want to continue to feed the leviathan until it just consumes them. So, I plan to fill out my ballot accordingly. Give them what they want. If you like your oligarchy, you can keep your oligarchy. If you like your big government wasteful spending, you can keep your big government wasteful spending. If you like your failing schools, you can keep your failing schools. I hate this state and have no problem voting for every single progressive candidate or measure so I can drive a stake through it just before making my exit. Let the Progressive Fundamentalists just have their Socialist utopia. I am leaving for saner territory.

However true these commenter's words, this was not exactly the reader response I was aiming for. In writing my book, I wanted to make the case to fix California and motivate readers to take action and not just give up!

California has immense problems, but it is surely not the only state in the country with troubles. Yet it seems that California is almost always the leading example of such problems. For example, while Detroit's municipal bankruptcy was the largest in the nation, caused by massive overspending, too much borrowing, and too expensive public employee union salaries and benefits, it had been preceded by Stockton's bankruptcy filing, then the largest in the nation. Wisconsin has had similar problems to California of high unemployment, deterioration of the manufacturing base, capital flight, and public employee union pension funding issues, accrued during a long period of liberal Democratic domination in state power, but its political system proved healthy enough more recently to balance itself out with the election of GOP Governor Scott Walker and GOP majorities in the state legislature who have been able to implement reforms that California's leaders wouldn't dream of. Other jurisdictions have had rough patches too because of the generally poor economic conditions nationwide.

And historically there have been even worse situations, if one can conceive of that, than California's current plight. My friend the late M. Stanton Evans had his office in the District of Columbia. Stan was a Yale graduate and as a young man the editor of the *Indianapolis News*. He later authored in 1969 *The Future of Conservatism*, predicting the rise of Ronald Reagan and modern conservatism. For a time, the district was presided over by the notorious Mayor Marion Barry, who mismanaged an already deteriorating city into further shambles and was convicted of using cocaine while in office. Nothing worked right in the District of Columbia under Barry's corrupt administration. Potholed streets got worse, crime was rampant, unemployment seemed permanent and endemic, schools were in chaos, and the court system and the water, police, and fire departments were all broken and unreliable. Stan observed it all and used to quip that the District of Columbia government under Barry was "similar to the Soviet Union's, only without the amenities."

California is surely not Marion Barry's DC, at least not quite as to the extent of the corruption. But plenty of people do indeed think the state is moving in the overall tragic direction of a major breakdown, and I suspect Stuart Varney could be one of them. Yet as bad as the taxes, as sorry as the business environment, as detestable as the growing poverty, or as incongruous and irrational as some of the environmental policies seem, I have never felt like just giving up on California.

There are a lot of good reasons to live in California. In fact, 70 percent of voters say they would rather live in California than any other state, citing so-called "quality of life" reasons such as the great weather and beaches, the state's coastal location, a diverse atmosphere, and a laid-back pace of life.[281]

But despite the liberal lock on political control, voters also are unhappy with their state in many ways. They think there is too much congestion and traffic; they believe that the cost of living and cost of owning a home are too high, that taxes are too high, and that the business climate is bad.[282]

And the fact is, according to voter attitudes, California is really not as liberal as the politicians it continues to elect. A March 2015 poll conducted by the Public Policy Institute of California (PPIC), a respected bipartisan organization, found *an eye-popping plurality of 35 percent of Californians consider themselves to be "conservative"* while 34 percent consider themselves to be "liberal," and 30 percent identify themselves as "middle of the road."[283] Looked at another way, a huge majority of 65 percent of Californians identify themselves as center-right!

Moreover, in May of 2015, PPIC found that a majority, by 52 percent to 40 percent of Californians believe the state is moving in the wrong direction.[284] Fifty-two percent of likely voters in California disapprove of the way that the California Legislature is handling its job, and only 30 percent approve.[285] Fifty-seven percent of likely voters think that state government wastes "a lot" of money, and only 6 percent think state government doesn't waste very much.[286]

The truth is that respected public opinion polls conducted by multiple organizations such as PPIC, USC/*Los Angeles Times*, and the Field Organization reveal a markedly more politically diverse, moderate, and even conservative outlook of the populace of California than reflected by the cast of characters the state almost routinely elects to office. Actual voter sentiment on many issues is in some cases startlingly different from the actions of the people's elected leaders. *It is these opinions of Californians themselves that give hope for the state.* Just as the personal views of the East German people themselves were not reflected by their own communist government before those citizens tore down the Berlin Wall, it is these voter sentiments in California that serve as the reason for me not giving up on the state.

Other important findings in the March 2015 PPIC poll demonstrate a real divide between voter sentiment and the policies California's elected leaders in control seek to impose. While Sacramento politicians still introduce new tax increase measures by the dozen, 62 percent of voters think the tax burden is already near the top or above average compared to other states; 57 percent think they are paying more taxes than they should be; 78 percent think that the state and local tax system should be changed, and of that 47 percent favor *major* changes; 81 percent oppose raising the state gasoline tax; and 74 percent oppose increasing vehicle registration fees.[287] A Field poll confirms PPIC's findings and shows again that 76 percent of Californians think the gasoline tax is too high, while just 4 percent think the state's gas taxes are lower than those in other states.[288] Yet Democratic state legislators in Sacramento continue to propose more and more taxes.

Though voters accepted Gov. Jerry Brown's arguments in November 2012 to "temporarily" raise taxes to record levels, 56 percent of Californians today either oppose the taxes or are against making them permanent.[289] Voters may have accepted Brown's arguments in 2012 that state income taxes and sales taxes should be "temporarily" raised to the highest levels in the nation to keep California schools open, and responded to rhetoric and promises about "doing it for the kids" by voting for Proposition 30, but they nevertheless really don't like the taxes they voted for and cannot be counted on to continue them.

And a few years after the election, we now have learned that voters were persuaded by millions of dollars of public employee union political spending and a "false narrative." Today even neutral observers agree that the case made in the campaign for the Proposition 30 tax hikes was a lie. Their campaigning was terrific, and they were able to control the public narrative on it, but liberal Democrats essentially hoodwinked voters on what Proposition 30 was really about, and got away with it, in more or less the same manner as Barack Obama lied to America about his health care proposal. Obama's false promises that "you can keep your plan, you can keep you doctor" was much akin to Brown's urgent plea about how new taxes were needed "so the school year will not be cut." Yet just a few years after passage of the Proposition 30 tax hike, we have learned that the new tax revenues really weren't needed and haven't been used as promised. *Sacramento Bee* columnist Dan Walters, who notes state tax revenues are in 2015 sharply increased beyond even Brown's budget estimates, has questioned whether the tax increases were really needed at all, and observed:

> The question, really, was whether Proposition 30's sales and income tax increase was needed in the immediate future, especially in light of the union-backed campaign that told voters it was vital for the schools. The school pitch was always somewhat bogus, since education was already guaranteed a major chunk of state revenues. Clearly, Brown et al. chose education as the focal point of the campaign simply because it is, by far, the most popular category of state spending. They would never have told voters to raise taxes to give more money to prisons or welfare.[290]

Just as Obama would not have been able to get his health care proposal enacted by Congress if people knew the truth (that they would be at risk of losing their plans or choices in doctors) so too did the liberal Democrats understand that they could not pass a tax hike in California by telling voters the truth about how they intended to use most of the money. So claiming it was needed to stop school shutdown days became the campaign mantra. This false "do it for the kids" theme is repeated again and again by the politicians in control of the state to win votes of caring Californians, but it is simply a big con to win elections.

The con works when liberal Democrats and their special interest allies control the public debate. Yet when the liberals lose control of the debate and voters can see the facts for themselves, their deceptions generally fail at the ballot box. The historic big property tax cut of 1978, Proposition 13, which reduced the state's property tax rates by almost two thirds, is perhaps the best example of what voters in the state once did when they perceived that their taxes were both too high and unfair, voting then in droves to lower taxes. Times have surely changed in California since 1978, but what is most interesting is that even almost four decades after Proposition 13 passed, and after years of liberals trying to lay blame for many of the state's problems on this tax cut measure, a large majority of voters continue to support this tax cut. In fact, 58 percent of Californians today still believe the Proposition 13 tax cut has been good for the state.[291]

The contrast today in voter attitudes and the philosophies of the people Californians elect could not be starker than in the case of voter sentiment in favor of the Keystone XL pipeline. The pipeline is favored by congressional Republicans but opposed by environmentalists and President Obama, and by both of California's liberal US senators, Barbara Boxer and Diane Feinstein, who voted against it. While the majority of Californians approve of the job Obama, Boxer, and Feinstein are doing, 54 percent favor building the pipeline.[292]

The conflict between California voters' attitudes and the politicians they elect is further evidenced by a recent USC/*Los Angeles Times* poll that asked voters—in a question that did not specifically name Feinstein or Boxer—whether the state would be better off if California's two US senators, who have served for twenty-two years, continued to run for reelection or if new candidates should become senators. Nearly 60 percent of voters said the state would be better off with new candidates, as opposed to 29 percent who said California would be better off if the long-serving senators continued to run. And 48 percent of voters said they felt "strongly" that the state would be better off with new candidates, according to the poll.[293]

Californians vote repeatedly for education funding and for lawmakers who support the California Teachers' Association (CTA), which is the largest lobbying group in the state, having spent over $500 million to influence elections and legislation since 2000. CTA strongly supports California's law allowing teacher tenure and strong job security after only a little more than a year on the job. Yet according to another recent poll, 73 percent of Californians said teachers shouldn't be given tenure at all, or that it should not be granted until a teacher has been on the job for at least four to ten years, another poll showed.[294]

On the economy, when asked to choose between two statements describing the business climate, 50 percent of Californians said that "state rules and regulations are getting in the way of business creation and growth," while just 41 percent of Californians said the state provides "opportunity for entrepreneurship and promotes innovation," according to another poll. In commenting on the poll results, David Kanevsky, vice president of Republican polling firm American Viewpoint, said: "California voters still want to believe in California—they haven't completely soured on it—but they no longer have the sense of optimism or attractiveness that earlier generations saw. If Californians thought the economic and business climate was as good as the meteorological climate, they would be a lot more satisfied about how things are going in the state."[295]

Why do Californians, then, keep electing politicians who don't really reflect their sentiments? The problem is political spending and the failure of many voters to both vote and also to associate California's problems with the policies of the liberal Democrats in control.

Californians are sadly among the worst voters in the nation. As I wrote in an article for FlashReport.org, in the November 2014 midterm congressional election, our largest state in the nation also had practically the lowest voter participation of any state in the country. Hardly more than 42 percent of California's registered voters bothered to mail in their ballots in the conveniently provided preaddressed envelopes, or even show up at the polls.[296] This dismal voter participation was even worse than voter disinterest in one of the state's other previous bad showings in 2002, when just over 50 percent of participants elected Gray Davis, the Democrat, over the GOP's Bill Simon. In neighboring Oregon, voter participation in the November 2014 election at 69.5 percent was more than half again by percentage the level of participation of California voters in the same election.[297]

Why is California voter participation so low? Some pundits have offered that the 2014 election year was not a presidential election, when voter interest would be higher, and that popular Gov. Jerry Brown, who was on the ballot, was destined to cruise to a big victory over feeble Republican opponent Neel Kashkari anyway, thus lessening voter interest. Democrats have a big political registration edge in the state, control every statewide elective office, and have near two-thirds control of both houses of the state legislature. And even with low voter turnout, the state bucked the national trend in which the GOP picked up seats in Congress, and Californians who did vote actually expanded the number of Democratic congressional seats in Washington, DC, from California.

Yet a recent Public Policy Institute of California (PPIC) poll reveals that more Californians, by 46 percent to 45 percent, think their state is headed in the wrong direction than the right direction.[298]

One reason for low voter turnout, and even for failures of the GOP to have made more gains in California in the November 2014 election, could be a failure to give voters a really good reason to turn out and feel their vote will be counted and make a difference. There are, after all, plenty of GOP and middle-of-the-road, independent voters in the state, as the same PPIC poll says 65 percent of California voters are center/Right, with conservatives, at 35 percent, having the plurality. An earnest young political consultant might conclude these voters just need to be contacted and given a good reason to get fired up to change the results of many elections in the state.

Though Republican Party registration in California, currently at 28 percent of the state's voters and still slipping,[299] is much less than Democratic Party registration at 44 percent and is only slightly above registration of independent voters at 21 percent, GOP voters have historically had a better record of turning out to vote, and actually represent about 32 percent of so-called likely voters, according to the Public Policy Institute of California.[300] In an environment where voter turnout is generally apathetic and low, invigorated GOP voters who turn in their ballots in higher numbers can make a big difference in elections. This affect can be seen in nonparty demographics of voting as well. For example, while non-Hispanic adult white voters make up 44 percent of the state's population, they represent 62 percent of the state's likely voters, according to the Public Policy Institute of California.[301] Latinos comprise 34 percent of the adult population but, according to the same study, represent just 17 percent of voters.

One election where better voter turnout would have resulted in a Republican victory rather than a loss was the election in the Fifty-Second Congressional District in conservative San Diego County. Just four years ago this seat was represented in Congress by Republican Brian Bilbray. But a Democrat won the seat in 2012 and the Republican challenger in 2014 was Carl DeMaio, a former member of the San Diego city council who had lost a close race for mayor of San Diego. Unfortunately, DeMaio's campaign became embroiled in a sexual harassment scandal, some key aspects of which were found to have been manufactured against him. Scott Peters, the incumbent Democrat who was thought to be vulnerable in the GOP sweep in other states, ended up winning the election with 51.6 percent, to DeMaio's 48.4 percent.

Yet a key factor in DeMaio's loss was low voter turnout. At 49 percent, if DeMaio's campaign could have brought out the same level of base voter participation as even the lopsided victory of fellow Republican, Majority Leader Kevin McCarthy of Bakersfield (about 56 percent), if the campaign had not seen the scandal in the press, and had the campaign redirected resources to inspire more baseline "core" Republicans to do their public duty and come out to vote in larger numbers, the result could have been quite different, a GOP victory.

Top 18 California Special Interest Groups
Campaign Spending and Lobbying Spending: 2000–2015[302]

Special Interest Group	Total Spent
California Teachers' Association	$312,410,475
CA State Council of Service Employees	$165,010,578
Pharmaceutical Research & Manufacturers Assoc.	$108,959,753
Chevron Corporation	$96,641,257
Phillip Morris USA	$91,346,013
Morongo Band of Mission Indians	$86,732,560
Pechanga Band of Luiseno Indians	$75,273,781
Pacific Gas and Electric Company	$74,810,605
AT&T, Inc.	$74,076,232
California Association of Realtors	$63,716,641

California Hospital Association	$55,082,392
CA Correctional Peace Officers Assoc.	$51,635,454
Western States Petroleum Assoc.	$51,509,508
California Chamber of Commerce	$51,497,512
Agua Caliente Band of Cahuilla Indians	$51,458,142
Southern California Edison	$51,227,727
CA School Employees Association	$49,347,917.60
Aera Energy LLC	$36,451,062.10

Even with comparatively lower registrations in California for Republicans than Democrats, the GOP has great opportunity to win elections in the state and bring reform in the current dismal low-voter-turnout environment. A few victories could help Republicans grow in numbers. Voters are truly unhappy with the direction liberal Democratic leaders are taking the state, and if the GOP can seize on ideas, candidates, strategies and tactics that really motivate conservative and middle-of-the-road voters to return their millions of empty ballots, they can win.

Yet the biggest obstacle to reform in California and at the polls is the massive amount of special interest money poured into elections and lobbying by the state's dominant public employee unions' political committees, in comparison to Republican or business interests, small or large. It is this overwhelming financial advantage that allows liberal Democrats to dominate the political messaging during elections and get away with essentially lying to the voters about the need for higher taxes and what they really intend to use the new money for, as in the unnecessary Proposition 30 tax hike and campaign.

Little has changed since I first detailed the political spending by special interest groups in my first book, *Taxifornia*. An updated review of spending shows the same liberal special interests at the top of the list. Since 2000, the California Teachers' Association has spent a combined $312 million on campaigns and lobbying. As disheartening as it may be to see the state's dwindling business community and conservatives outspent by hundreds of millions of dollars, we must press forward in presenting the philosophy of limited government. I firmly believe that politics is cyclical and that if more voters can come to understand that the problems of the state must logically be blamed on those in control—the liberal Democratic Left, and not a property tax cut initiative that voters adopted over thirty-five years ago (Proposition 13)—things can start to turn around for the better.

If California is to be saved—and I firmly believe it is worth fighting for— then we must not shy away from debates on issues currently dominated by the powerful liberal elites in control. Issues such as income inequality and poverty are traditionally viewed as issues controlled by liberal thinking. Is there any question that with a quarter of California living in poverty, liberalism has failed the public? There is no disputing that California has been a petri dish for liberal experimentation. Conservatives and middle-of-the-road voters, who truly dominate the state, must come to understand these fully exposed failures that have hurt and not helped our poor and working classes, and have harmed and diminished our state's middle class.

Indeed, even with limited resources, better ideas will prevail. Even under the terrible circumstances of a murderous, dreary, totalitarian communist German Democratic Republic, a young chemistry student named Angela Merkel did not give up. And she is indeed the leader of a united and free country today.

I hope that the ideas presented by the earnest and dedicated authors in this book will help bring forward a renaissance in our political thinking in the state of California, and help set the stage for a time in which moderate and conservative advocates and politicians will proudly take on the ruling class in California.

Acknowledgments

*T*axifornia 2016 would not have been possible without the essential editorial assistance I received from John Hrabe. John was a very good partner in helping me select topics and authors, refining the contributions, and keeping the project moving forward. I am delighted to have the opportunity to work with this fine young journalist and look forward to reading his own book someday in future. And, of course, immense thanks are due to every one of the authors who contributed so generously to this work.

My friend and business partner Floyd Brown inspired the title and provided excellent insights into the "business side" of producing this publication, and I thank him so much as well for his substantive contribution to this work. I also want to acknowledge the able assistance of my great friend Darin Henry, who helped with designing the cover of the book, as well as Thomas A. Fuentes Jr.

The line-editing of this book by CreateSpace at Amazon was superb.

Fox Business News Channel has offered me the opportunity to appear and discuss California issues almost monthly since March 2014, and I am grateful for these opportunities to contribute to the public debate.

I love California, and while I have had a lot of critical commentary on its public policies over the last few years, those policies would never cause me to leave the state. As I have said, I want to inspire reforms to fix the state, and not have my points used as reasons to just pick up and leave. I hope *Taxifornia 2016* will help inspire reform, not retreat! So to all those who join me in a vision for reform of our great state and who might also see a better tomorrow, despite the drawbacks of the day, thank you!

About the Editor

James V. Lacy is a frequent guest on Fox Business News Channel's *Varney & Company* and is author of *Taxifornia: Liberals' Laboratory to Bankrupt America*, a Politico.com best seller. An attorney, Jim was recognized by the American Association of Political Consultants with their "Pollie Award" for his work in election campaigns. Jim's law firm, Wewer and Lacy, LLP, represents advocacy organizations, PACs, and initiative committees. Jim also owns, with his wife, Janice, Landslide Communications, Inc., which is the largest publisher of election slate mail in California, producing fourteen million pieces of mail in the 2014 election cycle. Landslide also conducts polling and other publishing.

Jim holds degrees from USC and Pepperdine Law School, and is admitted to practice law in California, the District of Columbia, and the US Supreme Court. He served as chief counsel for technology at the US Department of Commerce in Washington, DC, from 1989 to 1991 during the first Bush administration, and as general counsel to the US Consumer Product Safety Commission (1987–89) during the Reagan administration. He was a delegate from California to the Republican National Convention in 1976, pledged to Ronald Reagan, and was as an aide to Howard Jarvis, the author of California's historic Proposition 13 tax cut initiative. Jim served as national chairman of Young Americans for Freedom, helped preserve the "Reagan Ranch" in Santa Barbara, and is a member of the board of the American Conservative Union. He has been chairman of the planning commission and a member of the Dana Point City Council and has served on the Board of Visitors of Pepperdine University School of Law in Malibu.

Endnotes

Introduction

1. Dan Walters, "California is nation's top tax collector," *Sacramento Bee*, April 16, 2015, http://www.sacbee.com/news/politics-government/capitol-alert/article18676590.html.

2. James V. Lacy, *Taxifornia: Liberals' Laboratory to Bankrupt America*, Post Hill Press, 2014.

3. Jim Miller, "State income tax revenue blows past Jerry Brown's estimates," *Sacramento Bee*, May 1, 2015, http://www.sacbee.com/news/politics-government/capitol-alert/article20047671.html.

4. Dan Walters, "California sales tax rates going higher," *Sacramento Bee*, March 31, 2015, http://www.sacbee.com/news/politics-government/capitol-alert/article17014328.html.

5. California Legislative Digest, Legislative Language, "AB-464 Transactions and use taxes: maximum combined rate" (2015–2016). *See* http://www.lao.ca.gov/.

6. *Orange County Register*, editorial, June 24, 2015, "California, Once Again, Ranks 50th," http://www.ocregister.com/articles/state-668192-california-business.html.

Chapter 1

7. Victor Davis Hanson, "Lawmakers Gone Wild," *City Journal*, Spring, 2014, http://www.city-journal.org/2014/24_2_california-legislature.html.

8. Tom Gray and Robert Scardamalia, "The Great California Exodus: A Closer Look," *Manhattan Institute for Policy Research*, No. 71,

September, 2012, http://www.manhattan-institute.org/html/cr_71.htm#. VcDzurc4IUc.

9. http://joelkotkin.com/content/001006-progressives-war-suburbia.

10. CBS Sacramento, "Report: California's Actual Debt At Least $848B; Could Pass $1,1T, http://sacramento.cbslocal.com/2013/05/01/ report-californias-actual-debt-set-at-848b-could-pass-1-1t/.

11. http://www.limitstogrowth.org/articles/2014/10/18/census-california-has-highest-poverty-rate/.

12. http://transparentcalifornia.com/.

13. Brian Calle, "Lifeguarding in OC is totally lucrative; some make over $200K," Orange County Register, August 21, 2013, http://www. ocregister.com/orangepunch/lifeguards-490717-beach-newport.html.

14. Steven Malanga, "The Pension Fund That Ate California," *City Journal*, Winter, 2013, http://www.city-journal.org/2013/23_1_calpers.html.

15. http://www.reuters.com/article/2015/01/14/california-villalobos-idUSL1N0UT2RA20150114.

16. http://pension360.org/calpers-board-member-facing-stiffer-penalty-after-latest-failure-to-file-campaign-documents/.

17. Allysia Finley, "Slaking California's Thirst – If Politics Allow," Wall Street Journal, May 15, 2015, http://www.wsj.com/articles/slaking-californias-thirstif-politics-allows-1431729692.

Chapter 2

18. Dan Walters, "How much is California really spending?," *Sacramento Bee*, July 19, 2015, http://www.sacbee.com/news/politics-government/dan-walters/article27869797.html.

19. Tax Foundation, Annual State-Local Tax Burdens Rankings, April 1, 2014, http://taxfoundation.org/blog/release-annual-state-local-tax-burdens-rankings.

20. Dan Walters, "California is nation's top tax collector," *Sacramento Bee*, April 16, 2015, http://www.sacbee.com/news/politics-government/capitol-alert/article18676590.html.

21. Kathleen Pender, "California Sees a Tax Revenue Surge," *San Francisco Chronicle*, April 20, 2015, http://www.sfchronicle.com/72hour-sale-event/article/California-sees-a-tax-revenue-surge-6212272.php.

22. Daniel DiSalvo, "California's Public Unions Have Too Much Clout and Compensation," *Los Angeles Times*, February 27, 2015, http://www.latimes.com/opinion/op-ed/la-oe-0301-disalvo-public-unions-20150301-story.html.

23. Ballotpedia, The Text of California Proposition 30 (November 2012), http://ballotpedia.org/Text_of_California_Proposition_30_%28November_2012%29.

24. Diana Lambert, "Torlakson: Prop 30 Tax Increases Should Be Extended," *Sacramento Bee*, January 9, 2014, http://blogs.sacbee.com/capitolalertlatest/2014/01/torlakson-proposition-30-tax-increases-should-be-extended.html.

25. "Time to Consider Extending Prop 30 Taxes, Mark Leno Says," by John Wildermuth, *San Francisco Chronicle*, May 3, 2014, http://www. sfgate.com/education/article/Time-to-consider-extending-Prop-30-taxes-Mark-5449768.php.

26. "Yoga Happy," Tax Talk at the Budget Press Conference, *Fox and Hounds Daily*, January 12, 2015, http://www.foxandhoundsdaily.com/2015/01/ yoga-happy-tax-talk-budget-press-conference/.

27. PPIC statewide survey, "Californians and Their Government," January 2015, http://www.ppic.org/main/publication.asp?i=1125.

28. "Brown's Popularity Key to Prop 30's Future," *Fox and Hounds Daily*, January 29, 2015, http://www.foxandhoundsdaily.com/2015/01/ browns-popularity-key-prop-30s-future/.

29. Michael B. Marios and James Nash, "Brown Reaches Deal with Union on Tax Increase Compromise," *Bloomberg Business*, March 14, 2012, Brown Reaches Deal with Union on Tax Increase Compromise," *Bloomberg Business*, March 14, 2012.

30. "Budgeting with Revenues Growing Means California Must Confront Its Past," Standard & Poor's Capital IQ Global Credit Portal, Gabriel J. Petek, CFA, primary credit analyst, January 28, 2015.

31. "An Analysis of the Split Roll Property Tax Issues and Impacts," Pepperdine University, School of Public Policy, Davenport Institute, March 2012, http://publicpolicy.pepperdine.edu/davenport-institute/content/research/ archived-reports/split-roll.pdf.

32. "Unintended Consequences, Proposition 13, and the Future of the Golden State," documentary film proposal, http://www.imdb.com/title/ tt4366154/.

33. Evolve website, http://www.evolve-ca.org/.

34. PPIC statewide survey, "Californians and Their Government," January 2015, http://www.ppic.org/main/publication.asp?i=1125.

35. Split Roll Property Tax Policy Brief, California Taxpayers Association, February 2013, http://www.caltax.org/SplitRollPolicyBrief.pdf.

36. Bradley Olson, "Steyer Pushes Oil Tax to Pay Dividends to Californians," *Bloomberg Business*, April 9, 2014, http://www.bloomberg.com/news/articles/2014-04-09/steyer-pushes-fracking-tax-to-pay-californians.

37. Catherine Reheis-Boyd, "Think California Is Too Generous with Oil Companies? Think Again," *Los Angeles Times*, December 24, 2013, http://articles.latimes.com/2013/dec/24/news/la-ol-oil-severance-tax-blowback-20131224.

38. "Energizing California: Mapping Chevron's Economic Impact on the Golden State," Milken Institute, March 1, 2009, http://www.milkeninstitute.org/publications/view/382.

39. Patrick Gleason, "A Laffer Curve for Smokes, Another Tax-Hike Dream Falls to Ashes: Higher Cigarette Levies Reduce Revenue and Increase Smuggling," *Wall Street Journal*, April 12, 2015, http://www.wsj.com/articles/a-laffer-curve-for-smokes-1428875897.

40. "Cigarette Taxes and Cigarette Smuggling," 2013, The Tax Foundation, February 6, 2015, http://taxfoundation.org/article/cigarette-taxes-and-cigarette-smuggling-state-2013-0.

41. PPIC Blog, "The Importance of California's Tax Ranking," by Mark Baldassare, April 7, 2015, http://www.ppic.org/main/blog_detail.asp?i=1738.

42. David Doerr, speech to California Taxpayers Association conference, Sacramento, California, March 24, 2015.

43. George Skelton, "A Smart California Tax Bill Points the Way to Needed Reform," *Los Angeles Times*, December 17, 2014, http://www.latimes.com/local/politics/la-me-cap-hertzberg-20141218-column.html.

44. California Commission on Tax Policy in the New Economy, http://www.library.ca.gov/crb/catax/.

45. Commission on the 21st Century Economy, http://www.cotce.ca.gov/.

46. Allysia Finley, "California's Revenue Roller Coaster," *Wall Street Journal*, December 5, 2015, http://www.wsj.com/articles/political-diary-californias-revenue-roller-coaster-1417811566.

47. Dan Walters, "Jerry Brown Should Push for Tax Reform," *Sacramento Bee*, February 23, 2015, http://www.sacbee.com/news/politics-government/capitol-alert/article11037803.html.

48. "There's No Time Like April to Talk about Tax Reform," *Sacramento Bee* editorial, April 12, 2015, http://www.sacbee.com/opinion/editorials/article18320900.html.

49. Board of Equalization, "Estimate of Potential Revenue to Be Derived from Taxation of Currently Nontaxable Services," April 14, 2015, http://www.boe.ca.gov/legdiv/pdf/ServicesRevEstimate.pdf.

50. George Runner press release, "Revenue Report 'Dangerous in the Wrong Hands,' *Says Tax Reform Must Be Revenue Neutral, Eliminate Other Taxes," April 14, 2015, http://www.boe.ca.gov/runner/newsreleases/Runner_TaxOnService_Response.htm.*

51. http://sd18.senate.ca.gov/news/1122015-sen-bob-hertzberg-pushes-plan-modernize-california%E2%80%99s-tax-structure-promote-upward.

Chapter 3

52. Chip Johnson, "Oakland crime issue goes far deeper than racial profiling," *San Francisco Chronicle*, March 28, 2014, http://www.sfgate.com/bayarea/johnson/article/Oakland-crime-issue-goes-far-deeper-than-racial-5355633.php.

53. Henry Lee, "Oakland homicide victims' families demand action," *San Francisco Chronicle*, August 27, 2013, http://www.sfgate.com/crime/article/Oakland-homicide-victims-families-demand-action-4765716.php.

54. http://www.nbcbayarea.com/news/local/FBI-Oakland-Dangerous-City-282469281.html.

55. http://www.cityrating.com/crime-statistics/california/oakland.html.

56. http://urbanstrategies.org/programs/csj/documents/2006HomicideReport.pdf.

57. http://www.cdcr.ca.gov/realignment/

58. http://ballotpedia.org/California_Proposition_47,_Reduced_Penalties_for_Some_Crimes_Initiative_%282014%29.

59. Sandra Hutchins, Sheriff, Sacramento County, interview by the author, April 13, 2015

60. Donny Youngblood, Sheriff, Kern County, interview by the author, April 22, 2015.

61. Sandra Hutchins, Sheriff, Orange County, interview by the author, April 28, 2015.

62. Nick Warner, Partner, Warner & Pank, Governmental Relations and Legislative Advocacy, Sacramento, CA, interview by the author, April 28, 2015.

63. Anne Marie Schubert, District Attorney, Sacramento County, interview by the author, April 16, 2015.

64. Paige St. John, "New York foundations bankrolled Proposition 47," *Los Angeles Times*, February 2, 2015, http://www.latimes.com/local/political/la-me-ff-new-york-foundations-bankrolled-prop-47-20150202-story.html.

65. http://www.kcra.com/news/sacramento-sheriff-warns-of-prop-47-public-safety-impact/29569986.

66. http://www.kcra.com/news/wrong-way-driver-on-highway-99-crashes-into-big-rig/34478510.

67. http://www.kcra.com/news/inmates-released-under-prop-47-where-are-they-now/31833734.

68. Joan Petersilia, PhD., "Voices from the Field: How California Stakeholders View Public Safety Realignment," Stanford Law School, Stanford Criminal Justice Center, Nov. 2013, Vol. 2., http://www.law.stanford.edu/sites/default/files/child-page/183091/doc/slspublic/Petersilia%20VOICES%20no%20es%20Final%20022814.pdf.

Chapter 4

69. Alejandro Lazo, "Gov. Brown Unveils Budget Plan Reflecting California's Financial Comeback," *Wall Street Journal*, May 14, 2015, http://www.wsj.com/articles/gov-brown-unveils-budget-plan-reflecting-californias-financial-comeback-1431632528.

70. Dan Walters, "Census Bureau: California Still Has Highest US Poverty Rate," *Sacramento Bee*, October 16, 2014, http://www.sacbee.com/news/politics-government/capitol-alert/article2916749.html.

71. Chris Kirkham, "Wages Shrink for State's Middle-Income Workers," *Los Angeles Times*, July 2, 2015, http://www.latimes.com/business/la-fi-wage-stagnation-20150702-story.html.

72. PPIC Survey, "Californians and Their Government," March 2015, http://www.ppic.org/main/publication.asp?i=1143.

73. Beth Willon, "Bay Area Income Gap Now More Than $250,000 between Top and Bottom," KQED, June 29, 2015, http://ww2.kqed.org/news/2015/06/29/bay-area-income-gap-now-more-than-250000-between-top-and-bottom.

74. Staff report, *Oakland Tribune*, "Bay Area News Group Photographer Robbed in West Oakland," February 19, 2014, http://www.contracostatimes.com/news/ci_25173247/bay-area-news-group-photographer-robbed-west-oakland.

75. Darwin BondGraham, "Throwing More Money at Police," May 29, 2013, *East Bay Express*, http://www.eastbayexpress.com/oakland/throwing-more-money-at-police/Content?oid=3560590.

76. David Mills, "The Highest Paid Employees at Oakland City Hall," Berkeley Patch, June 25, 2013, http://patch.com/california/berkeley/the-highest-paid-employees-at-berkeley-city-hall.

77. Mike Rosenberg and Daniel J. Willis, "BART Workers' Paychecks Already Outpace Their Peers," *San Jose Mercury News*, July 27, 2013, http://www.mercurynews.com/bart/ci_23742276/bart-workers-paychecks-already-outpace-their-peers.

78. Ibid.

79. Ibid.

80. Ibid.

81. Mike Rosenberg and Rick Hurd, "Major BART Unions Approve Contract That Ended Strike," *San Jose Mercury News*, November 2, 2013, http://www.mercurynews.com/bart/ci_24435384/bart-union-members-now-voting-contract-that-ended.

82. Denis Cuff, "Bill to Ban BART Strikes Is Introduced by Republican Lawmaker," *Contra Costa Times*, February 24, 2015, http://www.contracostatimes.com/breaking-news/ci_27591534/bill-ban-bart-strikes-is-introduced-by-republican.

83. "San Francisco Firefighter Makes $221,000 in OT Due to Understaffing," April 25, 2013, Associated Press and Fox News at http://www.foxnews.com/us/2013/04/25/san-francisco-fire-lieutenant-makes-221000-in-ot-due-to-understaffing/.

84. John Cote, "SF Fire Dept. Dominates List of Highest-Paid City Workers," *San Francisco Chronicle*, December 21, 2013, http://www.sfgate.com/bayarea/article/S-F-Fire-Dept-dominates-list-of-highest-paid-5085237.php.

85. William Avila, "Clerk Typist Among LA's Top-Paid City Employees," NBC 4 News, October 29, 2013, http://www.nbclosangeles.com/news/local/Clerk-Typist-Among-LAs-Top-Paid-City-Employees-229731131.html.

86. Ibid.

87. Chris Palmeri and Rodney Yap, "LA Pilots Steer for $374,000 a Year While Long Beach Profits," *Bloomberg News*, December 1, 2011, http://www.bloomberg.com/news/articles/2011-12-01/los-angeles-port-pilots-steer-for-374-000-a-year-while-long-beach-profits.

88. Ashe Schow, "Democrat's Latest Approach to Income Inequality: Some People 'Are Just Too Rich,' " *Washington Examiner*, March 10, 2014.

89. Press release, Sen. Dianne Feinstein, February 20, 2014, "Feinstein Statement on Gap Minimum Wage Announcement," http://www.feinstein.senate.gov/public/index.cfm/press-releases?ID=be9e6c8b-0f2f-4da9-b3b9-b0ca263d51e5.

90. *Christian Science Monitor*, "Who Are the 10 Richest Members of Congress?" October 25, 2012, http://www.csmonitor.com/Business/2012/1025/Who-are-the-10-richest-members-of-Congress/Rep.-Jim-Renacci-R-Ohio.

91. Michelle Murphy, "Feinstein, Pelosi Among Richest in Congress," *San Francisco Chronicle*, October 5, 2012, http://www.sfgate.com/politics/article/Feinstein-Pelosi-among-richest-in-Congress-3924070.php.

92. Richard Johnson, "Senator's Husband Stands to Profit Big from Government Deal," *New York Post*, January 16, 2015, http://nation.foxnews.com/2015/01/18/senator-s-husband-stands-profit-big-government-deal.

<u>Chapter 5</u>

93. Office of the Governor, "Twelve Point Pension Reform Plan, October 27, 2011, http://gov.ca.gov/docs/Twelve_Point_Pension_Reform_10.27.11.pdf; *also see* http://calpensions.com/2014/06/18/calstrs-gets-5-billion-increase-over-seven-years/.

94. http://toped.svefoundation.org/2010/10/25/cta-outspends-acsa-in-superintendent-race/.

95. Beth Barrett, "Mark Berndt's $40,000 Payoff," *LA Weekly*, February 16, 2012, http://www.laweekly.com/news/mark-berndts-40-000-payoff-2173991, also see Hillel Aron, "IFail: Why John Deasy's Risky IPad Gambit Crashed and Burned at LAUSD," *LA Weekly*, August 27, 2014, http://www.laweekly.com/news/ifail-why-john-deasys-risky-ipad-gambit-crashed-and-burned-at-lausd-5032831.

96. Alejandro Sandoval, "Student Progress Ignored: An examination of California school districts' compliance with the Stull Act." *EdVoice Institute*, January 2015, http://edvoice.org/sites/default/files/STUDENT%20PROGRESS%20IGNORED.pdf.

97. Legislative Analyst's Office, "Analysis of School District Reserves, January 21, 2015, http://www.lao.ca.gov/reports/2015/edu/district-reserves/district-reserves-012115.aspx; *also see* https://www.csba.org/Advocacy/LegislativeAdvocacy/RepealReserveCapSB858AB146.aspx.

98. http://edsource.org/publications/local-control-funding-formula-guide.

99. Legislative Analyst's Office, "Implementation of LCFF and LCAPS, January 21, 2015, http://www.lao.ca.gov/handouts/education/2015/LCFF-LCAP-Implementation-012115.pdf.

100. Jennifer Medina, "Judge Rejects Teacher Tenure for California," New York Times, June 10, 2014, http://www.nytimes.com/2014/06/11/us/california-teacher-tenure-laws-ruled-unconstitutional.html?_r=1.

101. Lance Izumi with Alicia Chang, "Not So Good As You Think, Why Middle-Class Parents in Texas Should Be Concerned about Their Local

Public schools," *Pacific Research Institute*, October, 2014, http://www.pacificresearch.org/fileadmin/documents/Studies/PDFs/2013-2015/NAGAYT_Texas_Final_Web.pdf.

Chapter 6

102. Mark Cuban, "The Coming Meltdown." http://blogmaverick.com/2012/05/13/the-coming-meltdown-in-college-education-why-the-economy-wont-get-better-any-time-soon/.

103. New York Federal Reserve, April 16, 2015, "Just Released: Press Briefing on Student Loan Borrowing and Repayment Trends, 2015," http://libertystreeteconomics.newyorkfed.org/2015/04/just-released-press-briefing-on-student-loan-borrowing-and-repayment-trends-2015.html#.Vb-lh7c4IUc.

104. Ibid.

105. Liberty Street Economics, New York Federal Reserve, February 20, 2015, "Payback Time? Measuring Progress on Student Debt Repayment," http://libertystreeteconomics.newyorkfed.org/2015/02/payback_time_measuring_progress_on_student_debt_repayment.html#.Vb-k57c4IUc.

106. Beth Akers, Brookings Institution, June 19, 2014, "The Typical Household with Student Loan Debt," http://www.brookings.edu/research/papers/2014/06/19-typical-student-loan-debt-akers.

107. *Former students* is a more accurate term than *graduates*, as many borrowers failed to graduate.

108. Liberty Street Economics, New York Federal Reserve, February 20, 2015, "Payback Time? Measuring Progress on Student Debt Repayment," http://libertystreeteconomics.newyorkfed.org/2015/02/

payback_time_measuring_progress_on_student_debt_repayment. html#.Vb-k57c4IUc.

109. Ibid.

110. Mark Cuban, "The Coming Meltdown." http://blogmaverick.com/ 2012/05/13/the-coming-meltdown-in-college-education-why-the-economy-wont-get-better-any-time-soon/.

111. New York Federal Reserve, press release, "Household Debt Continues Upward Climb While Student Loan Delinquencies Worsen," February 17, 2015, http://www.newyorkfed.org/newsevents/news/research/2015/ rp150217.html.

112. Kathleen Pender, "Average SF Rent Hits Shocking New High: $3,458," *San Francisco Chronicle*, April 29, 2015, http://www.sfchronicle. com/business/networth/article/Average-S-F-rent-hits-shocking-new-high-3-458-6232039.php.

113. Pete Carey, "Bay Area Apartment Rents at Record High," *San Jose Mercury News*, October 16, 2014, http://www.mercurynews.com/ business/ci_26733312/bay-area-apartment-rents-at-record-high.

114. 114 Erin Carlyle, "San Francisco Tops *Forbes*'s 2015 List of Worst Cities For Renters," *Forbes*, April 16, 2015, http://www.forbes.com/ sites/erincarlyle/2015/04/16/san-francisco-tops-forbes-2015-list-of-worst-cities-for-renters/.

115. Ibid.

116. George Avalos, "Bay Area, Powered by South Bay, Produces Strongest Job Gains Since Dot-Com Era," *San Jose Mercury News*, September 19,

2014, http://www.mercurynews.com/business/ci_26566790/bay-area-powered-by-south-bay-produces-strongest.

117. Susannah Snider, "Take 4 Steps to Understand Student Loan Interest Rates," *US News and World Report*, March 25, 2015, http://www.usnews.com/education/best-colleges/paying-for-college/articles/2015/03/25/take-4-steps-to-understand-student-loan-interest-rates.

118. Ibid.

119. Lee Siegel, "Why I Defaulted on My Student Loans," *New York Times,* June 6, 2015, http://www.nytimes.com/2015/06/07/opinion/sunday/why-i-defaulted-on-my-student-loans.html?_r=0.

120. John W. Schoen, "Student Loan Debt Piles Up to $1.16 Trillion: NY Fed," by CNBC, February 17, 2015, http://www.cnbc.com/2015/02/17/student-loan-debt-piles-up-to-116-trillion-ny-fed.html.

121. CNN Money Calculator, accessed June 15, 2015, http://money.cnn.com/tools/.

122. Jeffrey Sprashott, "Congratulations, Class of 2015. You're the Most Indebted Ever (For Now)," *Wall Street Journal*, May 8, 2015, http://blogs.wsj.com/economics/2015/05/08/congratulations-class-of-2015-youre-the-most-indebted-ever-for-now/.

123. Mark Cuban, "The Coming Meltdown." http://blogmaverick.com/2012/05/13/the-coming-meltdown-in-college-education-why-the-economy-wont-get-better-any-time-soon/.

124. Beau Yarbrough, "15 California Community Colleges to Offer Four-Year Degrees," *San Bernardino Sun*, January 20, 2015,

http://www.sbsun.com/social-affairs/20150120/crafton-hills-among-15-california-community-colleges-to-offer-four-year-degrees.

125. Larry Gordon, "State Audit Details Mismanagement at Compton Community College," *Los Angeles Times*, March 13, 2007, http://articles.latimes.com/2007/mar/13/local/me-compton13.

126. Andrea Koskey, " 'Deja Vu All Over Again' at CCSF," *San Francisco Examiner,* August 19, 2013, http://archives.sfexaminer.com/sanfrancisco/deja-vu-all-over-again-at-ccsf/Content?oid=2551005.

127. Nanette Asimov, "City College Near Bankruptcy, Audit Says," *San Francisco Chronicle*, September 20, 2012, http://www.sfgate.com/education/article/City-College-near-bankruptcy-audit-says-3875651.php.

128. Fiscal Crisis and Management Assistance Team, September 14, 2012, California Community Colleges Chancellor's Office. http://www.ccsf.edu/BOT/Special%20Meeting%20Notices/2012/Sept_2012/Sep18/FCMAT%209_14_2012.pdf.

129. Nanette Asimov, "CCSF Chancellor Steps Down, Interim Named," *San Francisco Chronicle*, June 5, 2015, http://www.sfgate.com/education/article/CCSF-chancellor-steps-down-interim-named-6309744.php.

130. Fiscal Crisis and Management Assistance Team, September 14, 2012, California Community Colleges Chancellor's Office, http://www.ccsf.edu/BOT/Special%20Meeting%20Notices/2012/Sept_2012/Sep18/FCMAT%209_14_2012.pdf.

131. "Why Even Top Tier Students Should Consider Community Colleges," *PBS Newshour*, October 6, 2014, http://www.pbs.org/newshour/updates/revenge-community-college/.

132. Rob Jenkins, "What Graduate Students Want to Know about Community Colleges, Part 2," *Chronicle of Higher Education*, May 20, 2012, http://chronicle.com/article/What-Graduate-Students-Want-to/131903/.

133. "Stop the Snobbery! Why You're Wrong about Community Colleges and Don't Even Know It," *In the Library*, Kim Leeder.

134. "Schwarzenegger Faces Boos, Turned Backs at Santa Monica College," *Malibu Times*, June 15, 2005, http://www.malibutimes.com/news/article_346084be-e034-5fb2-a335-4cbf85212384.html.

135. Delta College press release, "A Morning with Dolores Huerta," September 22, 2010, "Delta College Cultural Awareness Programs." https://www.deltacollege.edu/dept/publicinfo/prel/2010/DoloresHuerta.html.

136. "George Lucas—Director—Modesto Junior College," California Community Colleges, http://californiacommunitycolleges.cccco.edu/Newsroom/NotableAlumni/GeorgeLucas.aspx.

137. "What Chabot College Did for Me," May 8, 2015, Medium.com.

138. "Key Facts about California Community Colleges," California Community Colleges, http://californiacommunitycolleges.cccco.edu/PolicyInAction/KeyFacts.aspx.

139. "Crazy Smart: When a Rocker Designs a Mars Lander," NPR News, August 3, 2012, http://www.npr.org/2012/08/03/157597270/crazy-smart-when-a-rocker-designs-a-mars-lander.

140. "Adam Steltzner—NASA Jet Propulsion Labs Lead Engineer—College of Marin," California Community Colleges, http://californiacommunitycolleges.cccco.edu/Newsroom/NotableAlumni/AdamSteltzner.aspx.

Chapter 7

141. Kevin Fagan, "BART Workers' Pay Plus Benefits among Top in US," *San Francisco Chronicle*, August 14, 2013, http://www.sfgate.com/bayarea/article/BART-workers-pay-plus-benefits-among-top-in-U-S-4723315.php.

142. Ronald Reagan, news conference, August 12, 1986, http://www.reagan.utexas.edu/archives/speeches/1986/081286d.htm.

143. http://www.fresnobee.com/2015/04/20/4486957_eminent-domain-becoming-more-frequent.html?rh=1.

144. http://www.fresnobee.com/2015/04/20/4486957/eminent-domain-becoming-more-frequent.html.

145. http://touch.latimes.com/#section/-1/article/p2p-83504064/.

146. 1http://news.bbc.co.uk/2/shared/spl/hi/uk/05/london_blasts/what_happened/html/.

147. http://www.fresnobee.com/2015/01/06/4316901_ground-officially-broken-in-fresno.html?rh=1.

148. http://www.fresnobee.com/2015/04/10/4471838_state-authorizes-condemnation.html?rh=1.

149. http://californiahighspeedrailscam.com/top-40-donors-to-main-campaign-committee-to-convince-california-voters-to-borrow-10-billion-to-start-building-high-speed-rail-proposition-1a-november-2008/.

150. http://cal-access.ss.ca.gov/Campaign/Committees/Detail.aspx?id=1305068&session=2007.

151. http://www.sec.gov/cgi-bin/browse-edgar?action=getcompany&CIK=0000847243&type=&dateb=&owner=include&start=200&count=100.

152. http://www.berkeleydailyplanet.com/issue/2007-03-09/article/26520. http://articles.latimes.com/2010/jul/14/business/la-fi-hiltzik-column-20100714.

153. http://www.breitbart.com/california/2015/04/21/democrats-vote-down-bill-to-stop-high-speed-rail-eminent-domain-suits/.

154. http://leginfo.legislature.ca.gov/faces/billHistoryClient.xhtml.

155. http://www.bakersfieldcalifornian.com/business/local/x2127194258/USGS-finds-land-sinking-rapidly-in-Central-Valley.

156. http://www.lao.ca.gov/ballot/2008/1A_11_2008.aspx.

157. http://californiahighspeedrailscam.com/how-much-will-this-california-high-speed-rail-cost-people-are-making-up-numbers/.

158. http://www.hsr.ca.gov/docs/about/legislative_affairs/SB1029_ProjectUpdate_FINAL_111414.pdf.

159. http://gao.gov/assets/660/650608.pdf.

160. http://www.gao.gov/assets/660/653401.pdf.

161. http://www.breitbart.com/california/2014/06/08/chinese-company-at-heart-of-bay-bridge-s-problems/.

162. http://media.sacbee.com/static/sinclair/sinclair.jquery/baybridge/index.html.

163. http://www.dot.ca.gov/hq/paffairs/news/pressrel/15pr017.htm.

164. http://www.sfgate.com/bayarea/article/Tests-of-Bay-Bridge-rods-find-more-widespread-6135790.php#photo-4449253.

165. http://www.sfgate.com/bayarea/article/Tests-of-Bay-Bridge-rods-find-more-widespread-6135790.php#photo-4449253.

166. http://www.bart.gov/sites/default/files/docs/FY16   PBM   FINAL 03.31.15.pdf.

167. http://www.contracostatimes.com/daniel-borenstein/ci_27929716/daniel-borenstein-bart-looking-2016-voters-property-tax.

168. http://www.nbcbayarea.com/news/local/BART-Unions-Sue-Board-Over-Illegal-Labor-Contract-Negotiations-234250331.html.

169. http://www.leginfo.ca.gov/pub/15-16/bill/asm/ab_0501-0550/ab_528_bill_20150223_introduced.html.

170. http://www.nbcbayarea.com/news/local/Assemblywoman-Introduces-No-Strike-BART-Clause-302756771.html.

171. http://www.bayareacouncil.org/press-releases/bay-area-council-poll-shows-resounding-opposition-to-bart-strike/.

172. http://wn.ktvu.com/story/28203497/new-bill-would-make-it-illegal-for-bart-workers-to-strike.

173. http://www.kcra.com/news/barts-embarcadero-closed-due-to-protest/30756994.

174. Carla Marinucci, "Public Sentiment Solidly against BART Strike," *San Francisco Chronicle*, August 15, 2009, http://www.sfgate.com/politics/article/Public-sentiment-solidly-against-BART-strike-3222226.php.

175. http://touch.latimes.com/#section/-1/article/p2p-82560840/.

176. http://ens.lacity.org/ladot/taxicabreports/ladottaxicabreports 242493506_02132015.pdf.

177. http://ens.lacity.org/ladot/taxicabreports/ladottaxicabreports 242493624_02192015.pdf.

178. http://touch.latimes.com/#section/-1/article/p2p-82237859/.

179. http://www.sfgate.com/bayarea/article/DMV-says-UberX-Lyft-drivers-need-commercial-6035318.php.

180. http://www.forbes.com/sites/jaymcgregor/2014/08/26/uber-trials-fast-food-delivery-service-uberfresh/.

181. http://www.greatamericanstations.com/Stations/ANA.

182. http://www.ocregister.com/articles/city-658476-artic-revenue.html.

183. http://www.mercurynews.com/portlet/article/html/imageDisplay.jsp?contentItemRelationshipId=6503946.

184. http://articles.latimes.com/2011/jan/13/local/la-me-artic-transit-station-20110113.

185. http://voiceofoc.org/2015/02/glitter-of-new-transit-center-hasnt-translated-into-ridership-gold/.

Chapter 8

186. Paul Wenger, "It's Time for an Honest Discussion about Water," *Sacramento Bee*, April 18, 2015. Republished at "Keep California Farming," at http://keepcaliforniafarming.org/california-water-crisis/politics/its-time-for-an-honest-discussion-about-water/.

187. Tony C. Drebus, "Food Prices Surge as Drought Exacts a High Toll on Crops," *Wall Street Journal*, March 18, 2014, http://www.wsj.com/articles/SB10001424052702303287804579445311778530606.

188. www.water.ca.gov - History of the California State Water Project.

189. http://www.fws.gov/sfbaydelta/cvp-swp/cvp-swp.cfm.

190. California Energy Commission, "California's Water-Energy Relationship," November 2005, http://www.energy.ca.gov/2005publications/CEC-700-2005-011/CEC-700-2005-011-SF.PDF.

191. University of California, Tulare County Cooperative Extension Publication IG6-96, http://cetulare.ucanr.edu/files/82040.pdf.

192. California Energy Commission, "California's Water-Energy Relationship," November 2005, http://www.energy.ca.gov/2005publications/CEC-700-2005-011/CEC-700-2005-011-SF.PDF.

193. http://www.arb.ca.gov/cc/ab32/ab32.htm.

194. Alejandro Lazo, "California Gov. Brown Orders Major Cut in Greenhouse Gas Emissions," *Wall Street Journal*, April 29, 2015, http://www.wsj.com/articles/california-gov-brown-orders-major-cut-in-greenhouse-gas-emissions-1430324905.

195. http://www.cpuc.ca.gov/NR/rdonlyres/1865C207-FEB5-43CF-99EB-A212B78467F6/0/33PercentRPSImplementationAnalysisInterimReport.pdf.

196. Karl Marx, "A Contribution to the Critique of Political Economy," contained in *The Collected Works of Karl Marx and Frederick Engels: Volume 29*, p. 270.

197. "Policy Statement," Orange County Taxpayers Association, www.octax.org.

198. *Capistrano Taxpayers Association, Inc., v. City of San Juan Capistrano*, Super. Ct. No. 30-2012-00594579.

199. Jonathan Ferziger, "Netanyahu Offers to Help Brown Manage California Drought," *Bloomberg Business*, March 5, 2015, http://www.bloomberg.com/news/articles/2014-03-05/netanyahu-offers-to-help-brown-manage-california-drought.

200. Teri Sforza, "Imported Water Prices: Up 96 Percent Since 2006," *Orange County Register*, April 15, 2012, http://www.ocregister.com/taxdollars/strong-478683-water-mwd.html.

201. Brooke Edwards Staggs, "Agencies line up for desalinated water from planned plant," *Orange County Register*, Jan. 21, 2013, http://www.ocregister.com/articles/water-408745-poseidon-district.html.

202. http://www.lockheedmartin.com/content/dam/lockheed/data/ms2/documents/Perforene-datasheet.pdf.

203. Independent Energy Producers Association comment letter dated February 5, 2015, addressed to California Energy Commission Dockets Office, http://iepa.com/documents/CEC_--_IEP_Comments_on_Draft_2015_IEPR_Scoping_Order__--_FILED_2-5-15.pdf.

<u>Chapter 9</u>

204. http://calpensions.com/2015/05/26/san-bernardino-exit-plan-cuts-some-pension-costs/.

205. http://www.mercedsunstar.com/news/state/article3278651.html.

206. Ibid.

207. http://www.city-journal.org/2013/23_1_calpers.html.

208. http://www.utsandiego.com/uniontrib/20070529/news_mz1ed29middl.html.

209. http://www.sfgate.com/politics/article/At-tribute-for-women-Schwarzenegger-angers-2665978.php.

210. http://www.labornotes.org/2006/02/california-nurses-lead-fight-against-arnold-schwarzeneggers-anti-union-ballot-measures.

211. http://www.lao.ca.gov/reports/2011/stadm/pension_proposal/pension_proposal_110811.pdf.

212. Ibid.

213. http://www.lhc.ca.gov/studies/204/Executive%20Summary204.pdf.

214. http://www.city-journal.org/2013/23_1_calpers.html.

215. http://www.businesswire.com/news/home/20150612005949/en/Fitch-Rates-135MM-San-Francisco-CA-COPs#.VYsqaGA0OJU.

216. Ibid.

217. http://www.manhattan-institute.org/html/cr_98.htm#.VYvgOmA0OJU.

218. Ibid.

219. Ibid.

220. Ibid.

221. http://www.city-journal.org/2012/cjc0530sg.html.

222. Ibid.

Chapter 10

223. A Portrait of Race and Ethnicity in California," Public Policy Institute of California, http://www.ppic.org/content/pubs/report/R_201BRR.pdf.

224. According to California Department of Finance data analyzed by the Lucile Packard Foundation for Children's Health, http://www.kidsdata.org/topic/31/births-race/table.

225. "Hispanic Voters in the 2014 Election," Pew Research Center, http://www.pewhispanic.org/2014/11/07/hispanic-voters-in-the-2014-election.

226. "Behind the Numbers Survey," Asian American Justice Center, http://www.advancingequality.org/sites/aajc/files/Behind_the_Numbers-2012_AAPI_Post-Election_Survey_Results.pdf.

227. "Voting in the 1994 General Election," California Opinion Index, Field Poll Online, January 1995, http://www.field.com/fieldpollonline/subscribers/COI-94-95-Jan-Election.pdf.

228. The term as used in "Anti-Immigrant Politics and Lessons for the GOP from California," published by Latino Decisions at http://www.latinodecisions.com/blog/2013/09/20/anti-immigrant-politics-and-lessons-for-the-gop-from-california/.

229. Matt A. Barreto and Ricardo Rameriz, "Anti-Immigrant Politics and Lessons for the GOP from California, Latino Decisions, http://www.latinodecisions.com/blog/2013/09/20/anti-immigrant-politics-and-lessons-for-the-gop-from-california/.

230. John Pitkin and Dowell Myers, "Generational Projections of the California Population by Nativity and Year of Immigrant Arrival" for USC's PopDynamics Research Group, http://www.usc.edu/schools/price/futures/.

231. "The Aerospace Industry in Southern California, Los Angeles County Economic Development Corporation. August 2012, http://laedc.org/reports/AerospaceinSoCal_0812.pdf.

232. http://www.joelkotkin.com/content/00834-los-angeles-will-city-future-make-it-there.

233. "Economic Tale of Two Regions: Los Angeles vs. Bay Area, California Center for Jobs and the Economy, http://www.centerforjobs.org/economic-tale-of-two-regions-los-angeles-county-vs-bay-area/.

234. Victoria Colliver, "Hospitals new No. 1 industry in S.F., report shows," *San Francisco Chronicle*, September 7, 2011, http://www.sfgate.com/bayarea/article/Hospitals-new-No-1-industry-in-S-F-report-shows-2310717.php.

235. "Economic Tale of Two Regions: Los Angeles vs. Bay Area, California Center for Jobs and the Economy, http://www.centerforjobs.org/economic-tale-of-two-regions-los-angeles-county-vs-bay-area/.

236. NALEO Education Fund's "National Directory of Latino Elected Officials," http://www.naleo.org/downloads/2014_National_Directory_of_Latino_Elected_Officials.pdf.

<u>Chapter 11</u>

237. Karen de Sá, "Sponsored Bills in Sacramento: Outsiders Have Hijacked State Legislature," *San Jose Mercury,* July 11, 2010, http://www.mercurynews.com/california/ci_15489181.

238. San Jose State University Department of Economics, "Arthur Samish: A Political Boss of California," http://www.sjsu.edu/faculty/watkins/samish.htm.

239. Election returns, California Secretary of State, 2014, http://www.ss.ca.gov/elections/prior-elections/statewide-election-results/.

240. CBS Sacramento, "Jerry Brown Spent Less Than Neel Kashkari on Campaign for California Governor," January 30, 2015, http://sacramento.cbslocal.com/2015/01/30/jerry-brown-spent-less-than-neel-kashkari-on-campaign-for-california-governor/.

241. The Initiative and Referendum Institute of the University of Southern California, http://www.iandrinstitute.org/California.htm.

242. CBS SF Bay Area, "San Jose Mayor Abandons Pension Reform Measure for 2014 Ballot," March 14, 2014, francisco.cbslocal.com/2014/03/14/san-jose-mayor-abandons-pension-reform-measure-for-2014-ballot/.

243. Ibid.

244. State of California Department of Justice, Office of the Attorney General, March 26, 2013, http://oag.ca.gov/news/press-releases/attorney-general-kamala-d-harris-issues-statement-prop-8-arguments.

245. Huffington Post, June 26, 2013, http://www.huffingtonpost.com/2013/06/26/supreme-court-doma-decision_n_3454811.html.

Chapter 12

246. Scott Glover, "California Sen. Ronald S. Calderon, Brother Charged in FBI Probe," *Los Angeles Times*, February 21, 2014, http://articles.latimes.com/2014/feb/21/local/la-me-0222-calderon-20140222.

247. Times staffer, "A Guide to Leland Yee Corruption Scandal: From 'Shrimp Boy' to Guns," *Los Angeles Times*, March 28, 2015, http://www.latimes.com/local/lanow/la-me-ln-a-guide-to-leland-yee-corruption-scandal-shrimp-boy-to-guns-20140328-story.html#page=1.

248. Associated Press, "Ex-State Sen. Leland Yee Pleads Guilty to Racketeering in Corruption Case," *New York Times*, July 1, 2015, http://www.nytimes.com/aponline/2015/07/01/us/ap-us-san-francisco-chinatown-crime.html?_r=0.

249. Jean Murl, "State Sen. Roderick Wright Sentenced for Perjury, Voter Fraud," *Los Angeles Times*, September 12, 2014, http://www.latimes.com/local/politics/la-me-pol-rod-wright-20140913-story.html.

250. Soumya Karlamangla, "Guilty verdicts another blow to Alarcon family," Los Angeles Times, July 23, 2014, http://www.latimes.com/local/cityhall/la-me-alarcon-trial-20140724-story.html.

251. Jeff Gotlieb, "Bell's Rizzo Sentenced to 12 Years in Prison," *Los Angeles Times*, April 16, 2014, http://www.latimes.com/local/la-me-0417-rizzo-prison-20140417-story.html#page=1.

252. Hector Bacerra, "Robles sentenced to 10 years," Los Angeles Times, November 29, 2006, http://articles.latimes.com/2006/nov/29/local/me-robles29.

253. Jean Guccione, "Former Mayor Gets 16 Years in Scam," *Los Angeles Times*, March 21, 2016, http://articles.latimes.com/2006/mar/21/local/me-lynwood21.

254. Richard Winton, "Ex-Rosemead Mayor Tran Gets 21 Months for Witness Tampering," *Los Angeles Times*, July 21, 2014, https://search.yahoo.com/yhs/search?p=Ex-Rosemead+Mayor+Tran+Gets+21+Months+for+Witness+Tampering&ei=UTF-8&hspart=mozilla&hsimp=yhs-001.

255. Staff writer, "Ex-Supe George Shirakawa Released After Serving 7 Months," NBCBayArea.com, May 27, 2014, http://www.nbcbayarea.com/news/local/George-Shirakawa-Released-From-Jail-After-Serving-7-Months-of-1-Year-Term-259663301.html.

256. Laura Anthony, "Video from Hayashi's Shoplifting Case Made Public," ABC7news.com, May 21, 2014, http://abc7news.com/politics/video-from-hayashis-shoplifting-case-made-public/72501/.

257. John Wildermuth, "Mary Hayashi's Campaign Foe Puts Shoplifting Case Front and Center," *San Francisco Chronicle*, April 30, 2014, http://blog.sfgate.com/nov05election/2014/04/30/mary-hayashis-campaign-foe-puts-shoplifting-case-front-and-center/.

258. http://www.capoliticalreview.com/blog/will-judge-sandoval-further-delay-democrat-assemblywomans-shoplifting-trial/.

259. http://articles.latimes.com/2000/jun/29/news/mn-46157.

260. http://www.sfgate.com/politics/article/SHELLEY-QUITS-Secretary-of-state-says-2701049.php.

261. http://www.ocregister.com/articles/sacramento-217559-gop-sex.html.

262. Christine Hanley, "Scolding and a stiff sentence for Carona," *Los Angeles Times,* April 28, 2009, http://www.latimes.com/news/la-me-carona28-2009apr28-story.html.

263. George E. Condon, Jr., "Disgraced Congressman Randy "Duke" Cunningham is a Free Man Again," *National Journal,* July 10, 2016, http://www.nationaljournal.com/congress/disgraced-congressman-randy-duke-cunningham-is-a-free-man-again-20140710.

264. http://www.inlandnewstoday.com/story.php?s=18435.

265. http://www.webcitation.org/6QPl8P3IS.

266. http://articles.latimes.com/2005/jul/20/local/me-sandiego20.

267. http://www.eastcountymagazine.org/state-senator-ben-hueso.

268. http://www.sgvtribune.com/general-news/20120426/assemblyman-roger-hernandez-legally-drunk-when-arrested-for-dui.

269. http://www.dailybreeze.com/government-and-politics/20150430/port-of-los-angeles-police-chief-indicted-on-tax-evasion-corruption-charges.

270. http://losangeles.cbslocal.com/2013/10/28/new-embezzlement-grand-theft-charges-announced-against-noguez/.

271. http://www.latimes.com/local/lanow/la-me-ln-sheriff-indicted-jail-misconduct-20131209-story.html#page=1.

272. http://www.scpr.org/news/2015/05/14/51683/feds-indict-former-undersheriff-paul-tanaka-in-la/.

273. http://www.nbclosangeles.com/news/local/Sheriff-Baca-Expected-Announce-Retirement-Sources-239003811.html.

274. https://soundcloud.com/randy-economy-show/may-2-2015-city-of-industry-scandal-globechat.

275. Gov. Bobby Jindal, "American Rights, American Responsibilities," *National Review*, November 17, 2010.

Chapter 13

276. Cal. Gov. Code §§ 54950 et sec.

277. Cal. Gov. Code §§ 11120 et sec.

278. Cal. Gov. Code §§ 6250 et sec.

279. Cal. Const., Art. 1, § 3(b).

Chapter 14

280. *Varney & Company*, Fox Business News Channel, November 12, 2014.

281. PPIC statewide survey, March 2015, http://www.ppic.org/main/publication.asp?i=1143.

282. Ibid.

283. Ibid.

284. http://www.ppic.org/content/pubs/survey/S_515MBS.pdf.

285. Ibid.

286. Ibid.

287. Ibid.

288. http://field.com/fieldpollonline/subscribers/Rls2502.pdf.

289. Ibid.

290. Dan Walters, "Perhaps Brown's Tax Hike Wasn't Needed After All," *Sacramento Bee*, January 20, 2014, http://www.sacbee.com/news/politics-government/dan-walters/article2589145.html.

291. Wyatt Buchanan, "Poll Finds Support for Prop 13 change," *San Francisco Chronicle*, May 29, 2013, http://www.sfgate.com/news/article/Poll-finds-support-for-Prop-13-change-4559564.php.

292. http://www.ppic.org/main/publication.asp?i=1143.

293. USC Dornsife/*Los Angeles Times* poll, November 7, 2014, http://www.latimes.com/local/politics/la-me-pol-poll-boxer-feinstein-20141108-story.html.

294. USC Dornsife/*Los Angeles Times* poll, April 11, 2015, http://dornsife.usc.edu/usc-dornsife-la-times-poll-teachers-april-2015/.

295. USC Dornsife/*Los Angeles Times* press release, March 1, 2015, "What's the California Dream?", http://www.latimes.com/local/politics/la-me-pol-poll-california-dream-20150301-story.html#page=1.

296. Christopher Cadelago, "California's Record-Low Voter Turnout Stirs Anxieties," December 1, 2014, *Sacramento Bee*, http://www.sacbee.com/news/politics-government/election/article4237488.html.

297. "Oregon Voter Turnout Reaches 69.5 Percent," *Oregonian*, November 5, 2014, http://www.oregonlive.com/politics/index.ssf/2014/11/oregon_ballot_turnout_as_of_no.html.

298. PPIC statewide survey, March 2015, http://www.ppic.org/main/publication.asp?i=1143.

299. "Republican Voter Registration Continues to Erode in California," March 31, 2015, *Sacramento Bee*, http://www.sacbee.com/news/politics-government/capitol-alert/article17032118.html.

300. PPIC survey, "Just the Facts," http://www.ppic.org/main/publication_show.asp?i=255.

301. Ibid.

302. Data compiled by Alexander Tomescu from "Big Money Talks—California's Billion Dollar Club," California Fair Political Practices Commission, March 2010, http://www.fppc.ca.gov/reports/Report38104.pdf; and California Secretary of State Campaign Finance website: http://cal-access.sos.ca.gov/Campaign/ Spending from 2000 through June 30, 2015.

FOR MORE INFORMATION:

Visit James V. Lacy's author page at Amazon:
www.Amazon.com/author/james.lacy

Visit *Taxifornia*'s Facebook page at:
https://www.facebook.com/taxifornia.book

Visit and subscribe to the daily e-mail newsletter at
California Political Review at:
www.capoliticalreview.com

CPSIA information can be obtained at www.ICGtesting.com
Printed in the USA
LVOW08s2252291215

468355LV00014B/527/P